WRITING & GRAMMAR 12 for Christian Schools™

second edition

TEACHER'S EDITION

Maisie E. Douglas
Judith W. Lanier
Elizabeth Rose
Kimberly Y. Stegall

BJU PRESS
GREENVILLE, SOUTH CAROLINA

NOTE: The fact that materials produced by other publishers may be referred to in this volume does not constitute an endorsement by BJU Press of the content or theological position of materials produced by such publishers. The position of BJU Press, and of Bob Jones University, is well known. Any references and ancillary materials are listed as an aid to the student or the teacher and in an attempt to maintain the accepted academic standards of the publishing industry.

Writing and Grammar 12 for Christian Schools™ Teacher's Edition, Book 2
Second Edition

Coordinating Writers
Maisie E. Douglas
Judith W. Lanier, M.A.
Elizabeth Rose, M.Ed., M.A.
Kimberly Y. Stegall, M.Ed.

Contributing Writers
Seth W. Carper
June W. Cates
Elizabeth R. Cole, M.S.
Glenda H. Guthrie
Grace Collins Hargis, Ph.D.
Rachel A. Maes
Rachel S. Matzko, M.A.
Rebecca A. Osborne, M.Ed.
Sarah Abigail Stahl

Consultants
Will Gray
Grace Collins Hargis, Ph.D.
Chairman of the Departments of Linguistics and English Education, Bob Jones University
Bryan Smith, Ph.D.

Project Managers
Kathryn E. Martin
Denijer Peña

Editor
Elizabeth M. Morgan

Compositor
Kelley Moore

Cover Designer
Duane Nichols

Designers
Christy K. Bruckner
US Color

Photo Acquisition
Brenda Hansen

Illustrators
Matthew Bjerk
Aaron Dickey
Johanna Ehnis
Cory Godbey
Preston Gravely Jr.
Dyke Habegger
John Roberts

Cover Photo
PhotoDisc/Getty Images

Produced in cooperation with the Bob Jones University Division of English Language and Literature of the College of Arts and Science and the School of Education.

ISBN 1-57924-897-7 (set)
ISBN 1-57924-902-7 (Book 2)

15 14 13 12 11 10 9 8 7 6 5 4 3 2 1

TABLE OF CONTENTS

TO THE TEACHER

The reproducible blackline masters in this volume supplement Book 1 of the Teacher's Edition for *WRITING AND GRAMMAR 12 for Christian Schools,* Second Edition. Each blackline master serves a specific purpose. Since every teaching situation is different, these blackline masters are provided to help you adapt your teaching to your students' needs. Refer to Book 1 for more specific instructions about how and when to use these tools.

Pretests

Pretests are diagnostic tools for Chapters 2–13. Evaluating your students' skill levels prior to teaching will allow you to tailor your lessons to the needs of your students.

Teaching Helps

Teaching Helps accompany specific grammar, usage, and reference lessons. Some are designed to be used as overhead transparencies; some are designed to be used as student worksheets.

ESL Helps

ESL Helps accompany specific grammar and usage lessons. These materials give ESL students (those who speak English as a second language) extra help and practice with difficult concepts.

Concept Reinforcements

Concept Reinforcements accompany specific grammar and usage lessons. These worksheets provide students with extra review of certain skills taught in the student worktext. Each set of fifteen questions is divided into three sections, with each group of five questions being more challenging than the previous group.

Writing Worksheets

Writing Worksheets accompany specific writing assignments in the student worktext. These worksheets guide students through the steps of the writing process.

Writing Rubrics

Writing Rubrics accompany each specific writing assignment in the student worktext. The rubrics inform the students of your expectations and give you a method for evaluating each student's work fairly yet quickly. The grids allow objective and balanced scoring, and the space at the bottom that begins with the prompt "Overall, this writing . . ." provides room for personalized instruction. Each rubric can be used by students as a revision checklist or by you as an evaluation tool. (See "To the Teacher: Grading Student Writing" on p. xi of Book 1 for further help.)

Name ____________________

Chapter 2 Pretest: Parts of Speech

I. Nouns

Underline each noun.

1. Have you ever visited the Grand Teton National Park?
2. This park includes land that Congress designated in 1929 as well as land that John D. Rockefeller Jr. donated in 1950.
3. The Grand Teton, the highest mountain in the Teton Range, reaches an elevation of 13,770 feet.
4. The Snake River meanders through the valley on the eastern side of the Teton Range.
5. Several species of wildflowers, such as Indian paintbrush, and wildlife, including marmots, inhabit the park.

II. Pronouns

Underline each pronoun and label it personal *(per)*, indefinite *(ind)*, demonstrative *(dem)*, relative *(rel)*, indefinite relative *(ind rel)*, interrogative *(int)*, reflexive *(ref)*, or reciprocal *(rec)*.

6. Anyone visiting the Tetons in the summer can choose from a variety of activities to amuse himself.
7. Hiking, mountaineering, fishing, and whitewater rafting—these are only a few of the activities that might interest a tourist.
8. Outdoor enthusiasts may hire professionals to guide them on climbing and rafting trips, or they may venture into the wilderness by themselves.
9. Groups rafting on the Snake River often amuse themselves by having water fights with each other.
10. Whatever you choose to do will be a blast! Who wants to visit the park with me?

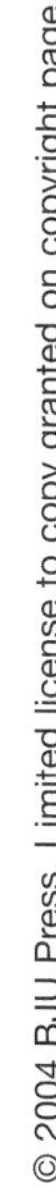

III. Verbs

Underline the main verb of each clause once; underline each auxiliary twice.

11. When the Grand Teton National Park has closed for the winter, the nearby town of Jackson Hole becomes a hub of activity.
12. Jackson is known for its world-famous downhill ski resorts.
13. Those who want to stay warm might try shopping at the Jackson square or visiting a museum.
14. Every tourist should take a sleigh ride through the National Elk Refuge, where thousands of elk congregate for food and shelter.
15. Don't miss the breathtaking view of the sunset behind the Tetons.

IV. Adjectives and Adverbs

Underline each adjective once and each adverb twice.

16. Paul Petzoldt made the first ascent of the Grand Teton when he was only a sixteen-year-old youth.
17. Having a natural inclination for dealing with people, Petzoldt soon began skillfully and safely guiding hikers in the Tetons.
18. Petzoldt deftly traversed the Matterhorn twice in one day and took part in the first American expedition to K2.
19. When a New Tribes Mission plane crashed on Mount Moran in the Tetons, Petzoldt led a recovery team to search for survivors.
20. Petzoldt's most significant accomplishment was founding the National Outdoor Leadership School.

V. Prepositions

Underline each preposition once and the object of each preposition twice.

21. Having gray-green leaves, sagebrush grows abundantly in the Teton valley.
22. Except for aspen and cottonwood trees, most trees inside the Grand Teton National Park are conifers.
23. Only hardy flowers and a few dwarfed shrubs grow above the timberline on the peaks.
24. Lupine, Colorado columbine, and Indian paintbrush brightly carpet meadows with purple, white, and red flowers.
25. Unfortunately, flower picking is not permitted within the park.

VI. Conjunctions and Interjections

Underline each conjunction once. Then label each conjunction as coordinating *(coord)*, correlative *(corr)*, or subordinating *(sub)*. Underline each interjection twice.

26. Both the Tetons and Yellowstone display beautiful scenery.
27. Please, do not feed the bears or other wildlife.
28. In the spring, you may see a bull elk in velvet if you're lucky.
29. Hey, check out herds of bison while you're in the area.
30. Because they range in high alpine meadows, bighorn sheep are difficult to spot.

Name ______________________________

Chapter 3 Pretest: Sentences

I. Identifying Types of Sentences

Identify each sentence as *declarative, interrogative, imperative,* or *exclamatory.* Insert the appropriate end punctuation for each sentence.

_______________ 1. Discover the fascinating and beautiful lighthouses of America

_______________ 2. Did you see the incredible sunset at the Pemaquid Point lighthouse in Maine

_______________ 3. In 1978 a ferocious blizzard destroyed much of the Boon Island lighthouse, forcing the lightkeepers to take refuge in the lantern room for two days

_______________ 4. Curtis Island lighthouse, named after Cyrus H. Curtis, the founder and publisher of the *Ladies' Home Journal*, is located near Camden, Maine

_______________ 5. Before mesh wiring reinforced the dome, migrating birds often crashed into the lantern of Old Barney in Barnaget, New Jersey

_______________ 6. Why is the Cape Hatteras lighthouse considered a symbol of lighthouses

_______________ 7. Standing 205 feet high, the Hatteras tower warns ships of the treacherous waters caused by the joining of the Labrador Current and the Gulf Stream

_______________ 8. Did the famous pirate Blackbeard make his home in Ocracoke, North Carolina, near the future site of a lighthouse

_______________ 9. Notice the octagonal tower of the Sand Island lighthouse on Lake Superior

_______________ 10. The Rock of Ages, the brightest of all lighthouses, shines on Lake Superior with a 700,000 candlepower light

II. Finding Subjects and Predicates

Underline the simple subject once and the simple predicate twice. If the subject of the sentence is understood, write *you* in the blank.

_______ 11. One lightkeeper lost his mind while tending the isolated Stannard Rock lighthouse fifty miles off the coast of Michigan.

_______ 12. Beauty and tranquility characterize the sunset view of Heceta Head lighthouse in Oregon.

_______ 13. Watch the red-and-white flashing lens in the Umpqua River lighthouse.

_______ 14. What historical event prompted the construction of the Alcatraz lighthouse?

_______ 15. Low-lying fog along the California coast made some early lighthouses ineffective.

_______ 16. Check out the Golden Gate Bridge from the Point Bonita lighthouse.

_______ 17. Augustin Fresnel invented a unique lens for lighthouses in 1822.

_______ 18. Fresnel lenses are white, red, or green glass.

_______ 19. Why would the center of Fresnel lenses be shaped like a magnifying glass?

_______ 20. This beehive-shaped lens can be up to twelve feet tall.

III. Analyzing Sentence Patterns

Label the sentence patterns *S-InV, S-TrV-DO, S-TrV-IO-DO, S-LV-PN, S-LV-PA, S-TrV-DO-OC,* or *S-be-Advl.* If the adverbial is a prepositional phrase, underline it.

21. Lighthouses in New Brunswick, Canada, are often square with red-and-white vertical stripes.

22. Slangkop lighthouse guides ships around the hidden reefs and dangerous rocks in South Africa.

23. Automated lighting systems, in lighthouses such as Hangklip, make lightkeepers unnecessary.

24. Vasily Ilchenko is a lightkeeper on the Egershelde Peninsula in Russia.

25. *Almagrundet* is one of several Swedish lightships.

26. Some lightkeepers' quarters, converted into youth hostels, provide travelers a place to stay.

27. Fastnet lighthouse off the coast of Ireland features an annual yacht race.

28. Australia's Cape Wickham lighthouse is on King Island.

29. Restoration efforts by the Australian government saved the octagonal South Channel Pile Light from decay.

30. Gabo Island's red granite tower stands firm.

Name ______________________________

Chapter 4 Pretest: Phrases

I. Prepositional Phrases

Place parentheses around each prepositional phrase. Draw an arrow from each prepositional phrase to the word it modifies.

1. On clear nights with brightly shining stars you can identify constellations.
2. The Big Dipper in the Northern Hemisphere and the Southern Cross in the Southern Hemisphere are the easiest constellations to find.
3. By beginning at the Big Dipper, you can find other constellations more easily.
4. Dubhe and Merak, two stars in the cup of the dipper, point to the North Star.
5. Boötes is located across the sky in line with the handle of the Big Dipper.

II. Appositive Phrases

Underline each appositive or appositive phrase. Draw an arrow from each appositive or appositive phrase to the word it renames.

6. Leo, a constellation visible in both hemispheres, includes the star Regulus.
7. *Cor Leonis*, another name for Regulus, means "Heart of the Lion."
8. Positioned in the mane of Leo, the double star Algeiba is yellow-orange in color.
9. Denebola, the star representing the lion's tail, is a white double star about 1.5 times the diameter of the Sun.
10. According to ancient mythology, the Nemean Lion (memorialized as the constellation Leo) presented a formidable foe to Hercules, the immortal son of Zeus.

III. Verbal Phrases

Identify each italicized verbal phrase as noun *(N)*, adjective *(Adj)*, or adverb *(Adv)*.

_______ 11. *Defeating the Nemean Lion after a month-long battle,* Hercules wore the lion's impenetrable hide as a protective cloak.

_______ 12. *Knowing the mythical stories* serves as a useful tool for remembering the location of and details about the individual constellations.

_______ 13. The Nemean Lion, Cancer, and Draco are just a few constellations *to associate* with the Hercules myth.

_______ 14. The goddess Hera placed the crab, *crushed by Hercules's heel,* in the stars as the constellation Cancer.

_______ 15. *To memorialize him,* Hera turned the dragon Ladon into the constellation Draco.

IV. Verbal Phrases

Underline each verbal or verbal phrase. Above each verbal or verbal phrase, label it as a gerund *(G)*, a participle *(P)*, or an infinitive *(I)*.

16. Locating the constellations requires obtaining some knowledge of Greek myths.

17. One myth to know concerns the famed hunter Orion.

18. Accompanied by his dogs Canis Major and Canis Minor, Orion moves across the sky hunting Lepis, the hare, and Taurus, the bull.

19. According to Greek mythology, Scorpius, having killed Orion, was placed on the opposite side of the sky from Orion by the gods to prevent his hurting Orion again.

20. Various names attached to the constellation mean "hunter," "giant," "mighty one," and "fool."

21. The Bible word translated *Orion* is also translated *fool* to refer to one who rejects God.

22. Knowing Jewish tradition provides an alternate story of Orion from that of the Greek myth.

23. Nimrod, an acknowledged hunter (Gen.10:9), supposedly called this constellation by his own name.

24. Amos exhorts the Israelites to seek Him who made Orion (5:8).

25. To illustrate God's omnipotence, Job cites God's creation of Orion and other heavenly bodies (Job 9:9).

Name ______________________

Chapter 5 Pretest: Clauses

I. Identifying Independent and Dependent Clauses

Identify each italicized clause as independent *(IC)* or dependent *(DC)*.

_______ 1. In 1943, *as a naval engineer conducted experiments to develop an antivibration device,* the Slinky was invented.

_______ 2. Since its debut at the Gimbels Department Store in Philadelphia, *the Slinky has become famous for its ability to "walk."*

_______ 3. Using simple materials and the scientific method, *the Slinky demonstrates how forces are transmitted by waves and other physics principles.*

_______ 4. *Though it is an enjoyable toy,* the Slinky has one problem: its propensity to tangle.

_______ 5. Have you ever noticed *that a badly tangled Slinky is almost impossible to fix?*

II. Adjective Clauses

Place parentheses around each adjective clause. Write the word it modifies in the blank. Underline each relative pronoun once; underline each relative adverb twice.

_______________ 6. Recent research has been conducted concerning the use of springs in prosthetic limbs, which are normally extremely hard to use.

_______________ 7. The incorporation of advanced design springs in prosthetics is the reason that wearers will expend less effort when using their artificial limbs.

_______________ 8. Prosthesis wearers, who have many adjustments to make when learning to use artificial limbs, will greatly enjoy the advanced technology.

_______________ 9. The same technology is used in many things that we operate on a daily basis, such as cars.

_______________ 10. For instance, the hood of the car usually has a spring at its hinge, where it can assist us as we lift the hood.

III. Adverb Clauses

Place parentheses around each adverb clause. In the blank write the word or words it modifies. Underline each subordinating conjunction.

_______________ 11. Whereas springs function well for a variety of purposes, they are frequently used in conjunction with shock absorbers.

_______________ 12. Car and wagon rides were very bouncy before shock absorbers were invented.

_______________ 13. Since spring suspensions and shock absorbers have been refined greatly, cars now drive with virtually no vibration.

_______________ 14. While many bikes have shocks, suspension systems in cars are much more elaborate than those of bikes.

_______________ 15. Someday airplanes may have shock absorbers so that turbulence will cause less trauma for passengers.

IV. Noun Clauses

Place parentheses around each noun clause. Identify the functions of each noun clause as subject *(S)*, predicate noun *(PN)*, direct object *(DO)*, indirect object *(IO)*, object of the preposition *(OP)*, or appositive *(App)*. Underline each subordinating conjunction, indefinite relative pronoun, or indefinite relative adverb.

______ 16. Every day we use springs in almost whatever we do.

______ 17. Some mechanical and electrical devices require that springs as small as 0.08 mm in diameter provide precise movements.

______ 18. The fact that the technology for such small springs was not developed until the end of the twentieth century is amazing.

______ 19. How this technology works is still a mystery to most people.

______ 20. The coil shape, as well as the elasticity, is what makes the spring a very useful invention.

V. Avoiding Sentence Errors

Identify each group of words as a sentence *(S)*, a fragment *(F)*, a comma splice *(CS)*, or a fused sentence *(FS)*.

______ 21. Three basic types of springs.

______ 22. There are compression springs, torsion springs, and tension springs.

______ 23. The compression spring is designed to be compressed it resists or aids circular movement, depending on the desired direction of motion.

______ 24. The torsion spring twists against a force in a circular motion, productive circular movement results.

______ 25. Pulling two objects or components toward each other, the tension spring holds the objects in place, sometimes the tension moves them together.

Name ______________________

Chapter 6 Pretest: Agreement

I. Subject-Verb Agreement

Underline the subject(s) in each sentence. Then underline the correct verb from the choices in parentheses.

1. Building violins or other stringed instruments *(is, are)* a work of art.
2. Few *(understands, understand)* the time and painstaking work involved in the process.
3. Maple or sycamore *(is, are)* used for the back, ribs, and neck of a violin.
4. Both the spruce for the belly of the violin and the maple *(needs, need)* to air-dry for eight to ten years.
5. The acoustics of each instrument *(depends, depend)* on its intricate, mathematical design and precise construction.
6. Violin makers through the years *(has, have)* used hide glue because it, unlike common wood glue, will come apart when necessary.
7. Gouges, scrapers, and planers *(is, are)* used to carve the wood.
8. Aesthetically beautiful as well as functional, the inlaid ebony purfling around the edge of a violin *(requires, require)* great patience and practice.
9. When mixed and applied correctly, the two-layered varnish *(beautifies, beautify)* the wood but does not stifle its resonance.
10. Precision in all aspects of construction *(affects, affect)* the sound of each violin.

II. Pronoun-Antecedent Agreement

Underline the correct pronoun from the choices in parentheses.

11. Peter Paul Prier, a violin maker and restorer, opened *(his, their)* violin making school in 1972.
12. Though he uses a tough curriculum including physics, sculpture, and music history, Prier encourages *(his, its)* students to persevere.
13. Each beginning student faces discouragement as *(he, they)* makes mistakes and ruins months of work.
14. If a violin's wood is not carefully chosen and prepared, *(he, it)* will crack under the tension of the strings.
15. As a violin maker files away at a piece of maple, blond-colored shavings pile up on *(its, their)* surface.

16. Neither the students nor Prier forget to set aside one day each year to rest from *(his, their)* work and ski in the Wasatch Mountains near the school.

17. After months of hard work, the students who don't give up see *(his, their)* instruments finished and ready to be sold.

18. Many of the school's graduates have now started *(his, their)* own schools.

19. The Violin Making School of America and *(its, their)* graduates are serving the needs of musicians in America and around the world.

20. As a result of *(its, their)* high quality of workmanship, the school has produced and sold over a thousand instruments, including violins, violas, cellos, and basses.

III. Agreement Overview

Identify each error in the sentences below as a subject-verb agreement error *(SV)* or a pronoun-antecedent agreement error *(PA)*. If the sentence is correct, write *C*.

______ 21. The famed quartet prepare for a concert in honor of the great violin maker Stradivarius.

______ 22. Antonio Stradivarius and Andrea Guarneri, also a famous violin maker, made his homes in Cremona, Italy.

______ 23. Actually, Stradivarius and Andrea Guarneri apprenticed themselves to Nicolo Amati.

______ 24. Everybody recognize these three as the masters of violin making.

______ 25. Stradivarius's artistry in decorating instruments are obvious in his intricate purfling designs.

______ 26. Some violinists prefer to use the instruments of Joseph Guarnerius del Gesu, grandson of Andrea Guarneri, because of its variant design and beautiful sound.

______ 27. The identification labels inside violins sometimes give people false hope that they own an original Stradivarius violin.

______ 28. Many violins bear the Stradivarius label to acknowledge that its model was a Stradivarius.

______ 29. The 1701 "Servais" cello, a true Stradivarius, bears the name of his owner Adrien Francois Servais, who lived in the nineteenth century.

______ 30. In April 2002 someone stole the beautiful 1714 Stradivarius "Le Maurien" in New York City!

Name ______________________

Chapter 7 Pretest: Verb Use

I. Simple and Perfect Tenses

Underline each complete verb. Then identify it as *present, past, future, present perfect, past perfect,* or *future perfect.*

______________ 1. Have you read Gracia Burnham's book *In the Presence of My Enemies*?

______________ 2. Gracia and her husband Martin had served as missionaries in the Philippines for fifteen years.

______________ 3. May 27, 2001, marked an irrevocable change in the Burnhams' lives.

______________ 4. The Abu Sayyaf, who kidnapped the Burnhams, claims to be part of Osama bin Laden's terrorist group al-Qaeda.

______________ 5. Gracia will always remember the lessons God taught her during her captivity.

II. Progressive Tenses

Underline each progressive verb. Then identify it as *present progressive, past progressive, future progressive, present perfect progressive, past perfect progressive,* or *future perfect progressive.*

______________________ 6. Martin had been flying supplies to missionaries in the Philippines, and Gracia had been teaching their children.

______________________ 7. Martin and Gracia were vacationing in Dos Palmos Resort to celebrate their eighteenth wedding anniversary.

______________________ 8. The Abu Sayyaf had been using any means necessary to accomplish their goal of instituting a Muslim state in the southern Philippine Islands.

______________________ 9. Reflecting on the Burnham's story, I have been seeing that God does not always do what we think He ought to do but what He knows is best.

______________________ 10. Christians years from now will be learning from the Burnhams' experiences.

III. Tense Sequence and Consistency

Underline each verb written in incorrect tense. Write the correct verb. If the sentence is already correct, write *C* in the blank.

______________ 11. During their time of captivity, God provides food—even a Mcdonald's hamburger—for the Burnhams.

______________ 12. Could you have been eating a live minnow straight out of a stream as Gracia did?

____________ 13. The Abu Sayyaf abduct the Burnhams so quickly that Gracia did not have time to grab her Bible.

____________ 14. Gracia's niece will have sent the Burnhams two letters crammed with Bible verses, but only one letter reached them.

____________ 15. Despite her dangerous and difficult situation, Gracia came to enjoy the fellowship with God that resulted from complete dependence on Him.

IV. Voice

Underline the complete verb in each independent clause. Then identify it as either *active* or *passive*.

____________ 16. Gracia was faced with her own rebelliousness and lack of faith in God's guidance.

____________ 17. God loves and guides His people in difficult times as well as in good times.

____________ 18. Martin demonstrated his desire to see souls saved by witnessing to his captors and serving them in every way possible.

____________ 19. Already familiar with the gospel message, the Abu Sayyaf members rejected the Burnhams' witness.

____________ 20. The Burnhams' captors have been forgiven by Gracia.

V. Mood

Identify the mood of the italicized verb as *indicative, imperative,* or *subjunctive.*

____________ 21. God *answered* many specific prayers for the Burnhams.

____________ 22. If it *had been* God's will, the Abu Sayyaf would have released them.

____________ 23. During the seventeenth gun battle between the Philippine military and the Abu Sayyaf, a bullet *hit* Martin in the chest.

____________ 24. God desires that Christians *be* willing to trust Him in all circumstances.

____________ 25. *Read* Gracia's book to learn more about the struggles and triumphs that God allowed her to face.

Name ____________________

Chapter 8 Pretest: Pronoun Use

I. Pronoun Case: Personal Pronouns

Underline each personal pronoun and identify it as subjective *(S)*, objective *(O)*, possessive *(P)*, or independent possessive *(IP)*.

______ 1. Adventurous men and women throughout the years have sought to establish their names in history for exploratory firsts.

______ 2. Robert Edwin Peary chose Matt Henson to accompany him to the North Pole.

______ 3. He designed a special ship, the *Roosevelt*, that would break through the ice of the Arctic.

______ 4. Henson, the first black explorer of the Arctic, and Peary's wife, the first white woman to winter in the Arctic, wrote books of their experiences.

______ 5. Peary and Henson finally reached the North Pole in 1909, but theirs was not the first claim.

II. Pronoun Case: Appositives and Comparisons

Underline the correct pronoun from the choices in parentheses.

6. Though Dr. Fredrick Cook argued that he had reached the North Pole a year before Peary and Henson, Cook's account is less believable than *(theirs, him)*.
7. The northern coast of Ellesmere Island was also explored by the team led by Peary—Henson, Dr. Dedrick, some Eskimos, and *(he, him)*.
8. On his fourth expedition Peary reached a personal record of 84° 17' N, but Fridtjof Nansen had reached a point farther north than *(he, him)* three years earlier.
9. *(We, us)* Americans can take pride in the accomplishments of Peary.
10. Several of the men who aided Peary accomplished the same goal as *(he, him)*—reaching the North Pole.

III. Pronoun Case: "Subjects" and Objects of Verbals and *Who* vs. *Whom*

Underline the correct noun or pronoun from the choices in parentheses.

11. *(His, Him)* losing his toes to frostbite did not deter Peary from his goal.
12. Because George Borup would soon return with supplies, Peary wanted *(he, him)* to bring more fuel.
13. Ross Marvin was the man *(who, whom)* Peary had deliver the message to Borup.
14. Seeing *(they, them)* return with the fuel relieved Peary.
15. *(Who, Whom)* knows what would have happened if Peary's supplies had not been restocked.

IV. Courtesy Order and Reflexive and Intensive Pronouns

Underline the correct pronoun(s) from the choices in parentheses.

16. Reaching the Pole, even the team's dogs enjoyed (*themselves*, *them*) with a special meal provided by Peary.
17. Peary double-checked (*him*, *himself*) by crisscrossing the area of the North Pole and by taking multiple measurements.
18. Between (*me and you*, *you and me*), Peary's account of his expedition and the claims of his witnesses are much more convincing than the unfounded claims of Cook.
19. The monument on Peary's grave, which has a star representing the North Pole, came from a suggestion that Peary (*himself*, *hisself*) made to his wife.
20. During the class trip to Washington, D.C., with Mr. Lloyd, did (*you and he*, *he and you*) take a picture with the monument in the background?

V. Pronoun Shift

Underline each incorrect pronoun. In the blank write a correct pronoun. If the sentence is already correct, write *C* in the blank.

_______________ 21. Each of the explorers has their own memories of the expedition.

_______________ 22. Not only should we honor Peary, but you should also remember the sacrifices his wife Josephine made.

_______________ 23. Anyone who will accompany their husband into a freezing world and bear a child there deserves acknowledgment.

_______________ 24. Just before Peary retired from the navy in 1911, Congress promoted him to the rank of rear admiral and gave its full recognition of his reaching the North Pole first.

_______________ 25. Peary is just one of many explorers who have earned his place in history.

Name ____________________

Chapter 9 Pretest: Pronoun Reference

I. Ambiguous and Remote Reference

Underline each pronoun that refers to an ambiguous or remote antecedent. Then rewrite the problem sentence correctly, replacing the unclear pronoun with the intended antecedent.

1. Booker T. Washington attended a school founded by General Samuel Armstrong because he had an insatiable desire to learn and improve himself.

 ____

 ____

 ____

2. Hampton Institute's head teacher Mary F. Mackie presented Washington with an unusual entrance examination. It had a classroom that needed to be cleaned, and Mackie told him to sweep it.

 ____

 ____

 ____

3. Because Washington saw that Mackie was just like his previous employer Mrs. Ruffner, a woman who insisted on absolute cleanliness, he knew how she wanted the classroom to be cleaned.

 ____

 ____

 ____

4. Not only did he move all the furniture and sweep the floor three times, but he also dusted it inside and out four times so that not a speck of dust remained.

 ____

 ____

 ____

5. Mackie's inspection lived up to Washington's expectations. She checked the corners of the closets and the railing on the wall for dust but found it immaculate. He passed the test, so she admitted him to the school.

 ____

 ____

 ____

II. Reference to an Implied Noun or to a Noun that is a Modifier

Underline each pronoun once and each antecedent twice. If there is no antecedent or if the antecedent is a modifier, supply an appropriate antecedent in the blank.

_______________ 6. Washington struggled to get an education because they didn't offer educational opportunities to emancipated slaves after the Civil War.

_______________ 7. Washington's mother somehow acquired a spelling book that included the alphabet for him.

_______________ 8. At their own expense, blacks in Washington's community opened a school for the children. But it did not help Washington because he had to work.

_______________ 9. Sometimes the only night-school teacher Washington could find lived in a different town, and he had to walk several miles to and from school after working all day.

_______________ 10. One day while working in a dark coal mine, Washington overheard two men talking about the Hampton Institute, where poor but hardworking blacks could receive an education. This became Washington's one passion.

III. Indefinite Reference of Personal Pronouns

Rewrite each sentence to correct any unclear or informal pronoun reference. If the sentence is already correct, write *C* in the blank.

11. Before Washington left home to attend Hampton Institute, it was apparent to him that no one expected him to succeed in his endeavor.

____

____

12. Washington set out for the school to prove to himself and others that you can achieve great things through hard work and determination.

____

____

13. During his trip to the school, Washington learned that they didn't like to provide room and board to a person of his race regardless of whether he had money or not.

____

____

Name ______________________________

Chapter 9 Pretest: Pronoun Reference (continued)

14. Washington sought a place to sleep under an elevated portion of the board sidewalk where no one could see him.

    ____

    ____

15. It was well worth the long, difficult journey when Washington saw the three-storied brick school buildings.

    ____

    ____

IV. Reference to a Broad Idea

Identify each sentence as clear *(C)* or unclear *(U)*. If the meaning is unclear, underline the pronoun causing the indefinite or broad reference.

______ 16. Washington thought that getting an education meant a life of ease without hard labor, but he learned that this was a misconception.

______ 17. The unselfish giving of the teachers at the Institute impressed Washington greatly. It taught him that happiness comes from serving others.

______ 18. Miss Natalie Lord taught Washington the importance and relevance of the Bible. This appreciation for the Bible remained with him throughout his life.

______ 19. Observing Mary Mackie clean windows and floors taught Washington an important lesson: a good education and high social standing does not exempt a person from hard work.

______ 20. After Washington graduated from Hampton, he returned home to begin his lifelong mission of educating other members of the black community, which is a noble goal.

Name ____________________

Chapter 10 Pretest: Adjective and Adverb Use

I. Identification and Comparison of Modifiers

Underline each adjective, including the correct choice from the adjectives in parentheses. Double underline each adverb that modifies a noun.

1. The *(more common, most common)* species of sea turtle is the loggerhead with its exceptionally large head.
2. Because loggerhead turtles are only a threatened species and not an endangered species, they are *(more numerous, most numerous)* than the other species of sea turtles.
3. Having a reddish-brown carapace (upper shell) and a dull brown plastron (lower shell), these *(large, larger)* turtles can weigh up to 350 pounds.
4. A primarily carnivorous animal, the loggerhead uses its *(strong, stronger)* jaw muscles to eat shellfish, including horseshoe crabs, clams, and mussels.
5. Of the two favorite nesting areas for loggerheads today, Masirah Island in the Middle East and the southeastern coast of the United States, Masirah Island has *(more, the most)* nests—about thirty thousand.

Underline each adverb. Double underline each noun that modifies a verb.

6. In Lewis Carroll's story, the Mock Turtle sighs deeply and sings Alice a song about turtle soup.
7. According to some people, green sea turtles taste curiously good in turtle soup.
8. If you've never had green turtle soup, you've also probably never had a steak from a green sea turtle's calipee.
9. The single pair of scales in front of the eyes of the green sea turtle easily distinguishes it from other turtles that have two pairs of scales.
10. Compared to green sea turtles in the Atlantic Ocean, those in the Pacific Ocean many times appear quite black and small.

II. Problems with Modifiers

Underline each incorrect adjective or adverb and write an appropriate correction in the blank. If the sentence is already correct, write C in the blank.

________________ 11. Moving slowly but steadily up the beach, a female leatherback turtle plans to lay her eggs in a very deep hole.

________________ 12. The turtle digs somewhat quickly in her very unique way.

_______________ 13. She is not making no snow angel design, though she moves her front flippers in a wing-like manner as she digs.

_______________ 14. Measuring up to 8 feet long and weighing up to 1,300 pounds, leatherbacks grow to be more bigger than all the other sea turtles.

_______________ 15. Having small bones under their skin, leatherbacks possess a most unique leathery skin rather than a hard shell that other turtles have.

III. Placement of Modifiers

Underline each misplaced or dangling modifier. Then rewrite each sentence, making the modifiers clear and correct. If the sentence is already correct, write *C* in the blank.

16. Breaking free from their buried nest and scurrying toward the ocean, birds love to eat the newly hatched turtles.

____

____

17. Fishermen who unknowingly use nets to catch fish also trap and drown turtles in their nets.

____

____

18. All arriving on the same day, hundreds of Kemp's ridleys' nests line the beach near Rancho Nuevo, Mexico.

____

____

19. Even flies, laying their eggs in Kemp's ridleys' nests, pose a threat to the turtle population as the maggots feed on the unhatched eggs.

____

____

20. Many conservationists hope to especially protect the remaining sea turtles and to encourage the growth of their population.

____

____

Name ____________________

Chapter 11 Pretest: Capitalization

I. Personal Names, Religions, Nationalities, and Proper Adjectives

Underline each word containing a capitalization error.

1. History recognizes many great Visual Artists, including rembrandt, claude monet, leonardo da vinci, and pierre-auguste renoir.
2. The spanish Pablo Picasso painted in several different styles, such as Cubism and Expressionism.
3. Originally producing sad, dark paintings, vincent van gogh incorporated more color and happiness into his later Works after viewing colorful japanese paintings.
4. The florentine family de Medici patronized the Masterful artist Michelangelo Buonarroti. Michelangelo most often depicted christian subjects in his art, but on one occasion he produced a larger-than-life sculpture of the pagan god bacchus.
5. You can see rembrandt's painting *The Music Party* at the rijksmuseum in Amsterdam.

II. Place Names, Transportation, and Astronomy Terms

Underline each word containing a capitalization error.

6. Astronomical art—the Bayeux Tapestry of A.D. 1073, for example—dates back to early sightings of halley's comet.
7. Giotto, an artist of florence, accurately depicts all the parts of halley's comet in his painting *The Adoration of the Magi*.
8. In 1986 the European space agency launched the spacecraft *giotto* to photograph the nucleus of halley's comet and the Comet grigg-skjellerup.
9. Thomas Rowlandson of england caricatured the drastic reactions of people viewing Comets.
10. While most modern astronomical art utilizes photography and digital art, artist Steven Florides uses gouache to depict a large crater on mimas, one of saturn's moons, in his painting *The Eye of Mimas*.

III. Businesses and Organizations, Cultural and Historical Terms

Underline each word containing a capitalization error.

11. Staying current on art trends is possible through organizations such as the national assembly of state art agencies (nasaa).
12. Modern artists, such as Sculptor Karen McCoy, the head artist for a project commemorating the lewis and clark expedition, contribute to the development of historical and cultural sites.

13. Recording New Hampshire rural life during the depression, artists Nathaniel Burwash and Herbert Waters were celebrated in an art exhibition of the department of cultural resources from march to june of 2003.

14. The crowning achievement of sculptor Gutzon Borglum is mount rushmore, which memorializes four American presidents.

15. Students attending the university of missouri-columbia have the option of taking serigraphy classes.

IV. Titles, First Words, and Single Letters

Underline each word containing a capitalization error.

16. A taut piece of fabric (Early serigraphers used silk), paint, and a squeegee are necessary to produce a serigraph.

17. "I have printed only one serigraph," my friend Debbie remarked, "Not several. Serigraphy is just one type of printing that I learned in advanced printmaking."

18. With six different screens, Debbie printed a beautiful serigraph called *autumn leaves*.

19. In *cowboy coffee* G. Harvey, a prominent American artist, combines the processes of serigraph and lithograph to produce a beautiful print of brilliant color and subtle shading.

20. To find out more about serigraphy and other forms of printmaking, read *the bevelled edge* magazine.

Name ______________________

Chapter 12 Pretest: Punctuation

I. End Marks and Other Uses of the Period

Insert any missing periods or decimal points, question marks, or exclamation points.

1. Wow Alaska is a huge state

2. Did you know that Alaska is 2.3 times the size of Texas and one-fifth the size of all the other states combined

3. The tour guide asked me if I knew that William H Seward negotiated America's purchase of Alaska from Russia for only 72 million dollars in AD 1867

4. At 9:30 AM we will visit the Anchorage Museum of History and Art on 121 W Seventh Ave

5. Help me This king salmon must weigh at least 50 lb

II. Commas: In a Series and After Introductory Elements

Insert any missing commas. If the sentence is already correct, write *C* in the blank.

_______ 6. While we're still in the Kenai Peninsula area I'd also like to try some sea kayaking bear watching and hiking.

_______ 7. On one hike a magnificent bald eagle flew out of a tree in front of me, and I snapped a quick picture of him.

_______ 8. Cracking and rumbling loudly the Holgate Glacier in Kenai Fjords National Park calves into the bay.

_______ 9. I paddle my sea kayak in Aialik Bay seal families float by on icebergs and whales swim in the distance.

_______ 10. Finally my tour of Kenai has ended and I head to the interior of Alaska.

III. Commas: To Separate

Insert any missing commas.

11. The Alaska Range home of Denali and Mt. Foraker is located two hours north of Fairbanks.

12. Denali not Mt. McKinley is the original name of the highest mountain in North America.

13. Climbing either of these mountains involves potential dangers; therefore each climber must pre-register with the Denali National Park rangers and pay a fee to offset the costs of rescue efforts.

14. You've heard that Denali rises 20,320 feet above sea level haven't you?

15. Rachel you would enjoy the photography opportunities as well as many other activities at the Denali National Park and Preserve.

IV. Commas: In Letters, Quotations, Dates, Addresses, and in Special Constructions

Insert any missing commas.

16. February 26 1917 marked the beginning of Denali National Park and Preserve.

17. While visiting the park and Fairbanks Alaska I observed some strange lights in the night sky and asked what they were.

18. "The Aurora Borealis and Australis are caused by the interaction of solar flares with the earth's magnetosphere" explained scientist Jerry Scott "and are most active in the fall, winter, and spring."

19. The Aurora Borealis creates a beautiful light show in the north; the Aurora Australis in the south.

20. For more information about the Aurora Borealis, write to the Nome Convention and Visitors Bureau P.O. Box 240 Nome Alaska 99762.

V. Incorrect Commas

Circle any incorrect commas. If the sentence is already correct, write *C* in the blank.

______ 21. Amanda McFarland, and Isabelle Barnette are two women who contributed to Alaskan history.

______ 22. Having mushed a dog sled over the Alaska Range, Isabelle Barnette and her husband established a trading post and named it Fairbanks.

______ 23. For her brave work among Alaskan girls, Amanda McFarland earned the name, "Alaska's Courageous Missionary."

Name ______________________________

Chapter 12 Pretest: Punctuation (continued)

______ 24. Alaska's first female pilot, Marvel Crosson, died in August, 1929, when her plane's engine failed and her parachute opened too late.

______ 25. Natasha Shelikof, wife of a Russian ruler, was the first white woman to live in Alaska, and, the native Alaskan women learned about manners and cleanliness from her.

VI. Semicolons and Colons

Insert any missing semicolons or colons. If the sentence is already correct, write *C* in the blank.

______ 26. Before leaving Alaska, I want to ride the famous White Pass railway that I have read about in *Alaska/Yukon Railroads An Illustrated History*.

______ 27. The White Pass Summit Excursion includes a three-thousand-foot rise in only twenty miles, several bridges, and even two tunnels; be prepared for some great sights.

______ 28. The White Pass and Yukon Route also offers other options the Lake Bennett Steam Adventure runs to the end of the Chilkoot Trail a rail trip of just over an hour runs from Skagway, Alaska, to Fraser, British Columbia and Chilkoot Trail hikers can catch a ride back to Skagway after their thirty-three-mile hike.

______ 29. Dear Mr. Danielson

Thank you for the wonderful tour I received on the White Pass and Yukon Route your employees were pleasant and the scenery was spectacular!

______ 30. Psalm 24 1 comes to mind as I think about all the wonders of Alaska "The earth is the LORD's, and the fulness thereof; the world, and they that dwell therein."

Name ____________________

Chapter 13 Pretest: More Punctuation

I. Quotation Marks

Insert any missing quotation marks. If the sentence is already correct, write *C* in the blank.

_____ 1. "Do you remember who wrote The fog comes / on little cat feet? asked Merideth.

_____ 2. "Let's see, replied Drew, "I think it was Carl Sandburg. My teacher said that he lived and worked in Chicago for many years."

_____ 3. "Sandburg's poem Chicago exemplifies his view of the hardworking man as the strength of America," Merideth observed.

_____ 4. "Doesn't Sandburg personify the city as the 'Hog Butcher, Tool Maker, Stacker of Wheat, Player with Railroads / and Freight Handler to the Nation'?"

_____ 5. Yes, answered Merideth, "he is often called the laureate of industrial America for this type of imagery."

II. Ellipses and Brackets

Read the paragraph below. Write the letter of the quotation that is properly punctuated.

Carl Sandburg worked hard at whatever job he could find. He also rode the rails as a hobo. During this time Sandburg observed the life and hardship of the average American struggling to succeed. When he attended Lombard College, several teachers reinforce his developing socialistic ideology, which is very prominent in his poetry.

_____ 6. A. Between the years 1892 and 1897, Sandburg "rode the rails as a hobo . . . [He] observed the life and hardship of the average American."
B. Between the years 1892 and 1897, Sandburg "rode the rails as a hobo. . . . [He] observed the life and hardship of the average American."
C. Between the years 1892 and 1897, Sandburg rode the rails as a hobo. . . . He observed the life and hardship of the average American."

_____ 7. A. "When he attended Lombard College, several teachers reinforce [*sic*] his developing socialistic ideology."
B. "When he attended Lombard College, several teachers reinforced his developing socialistic ideology."
C. "When he attended Lombard College, several teachers reinforce [sic] his developing socialistic ideology."

_____ 8. A. "Carl Sandburg [an American poet] worked hard at whatever job he could find."
B. "Carl Sandburg, an American poet, worked hard at whatever job he could find."
C. "Carl Sandburg (an American poet) worked hard at whatever job he could find."

Chapter 13 Pretest: More Punctuation (continued)

Read the poem below. Write the letter of the quotation that is properly punctuated.

The poet in a golden clime was born,
    With golden stars above;
Dowered with the hate of hate, the scorn of scorn,
    The love of love.

He saw through life and death, through good and ill,
    He saw through his own soul.

From "The Poet" by Alfred, Lord Tennyson

_______ 9. A. Sandburg, “dowered with the hate of hate, … saw through life and death.”
B. Sandburg, “dowered with the hate of hate, ... saw through life and death.”
C. Sandburg, “dowered with the hate of hate, . . . saw through life and death.”

_______ 10. A. The student recited, “‘The poet in a … um … golden clime … was born.’”
B. The student recited, “‘The poet in a, um, golden clime, was born.’”
C. The student recited, “‘The poet in a . . . um . . . golden clime . . . was born.’”

III. Underlining for Italics

Underline any words that should be italicized.

11. When the bombing of the battleship USS Maine began the Spanish-American War, Sandburg signed on with the army to fight for the freedom of Cuba.

12. During much of his life, Sandburg supported the Socialist Party and wrote articles in several socialist newspapers, especially the International Socialist Review.

13. Professor Philip Green Wright published Sandburg's first collection of poems, In Reckless Ecstasy. The publishing of six of his poems in Poetry: A Magazine of Verse gained him recognition in the literary world.

14. In “Jabberers” Sandburg's use of the word jabber implies the significance, and insignificance, of the individual's language to distinguish him from the language of the world around him.

15. Sandburg's personality, interests, and down-to-earth manner made him a persona grata to all classes of American society.

Name ___________________________________

Chapter 13 Pretest: More Punctuation (continued)

IV. Apostrophe and Hyphen

Insert any missing apostrophes and hyphens. Underline any words that contain unnecessary apostrophes or hyphens.

16. As an older man Sandburg collaborated with his brother in law Edward Steichen, a well known painter and photographer, to produce a 503 picture book entitled *The Family of Man*.

17. This book, promoting Sandburgs humanistic view of a global community, sold more than fifty million copies by the mid 1990's.

18. Sandburg also produced several volume's of childrens storybooks during the years 1922–30.

19. Sandburgs multivolume biography of President Lincoln won him the Pulitzer Prize.

20. Lillian Sandburgs passion, goat-raising, led Sandburg to buy Connemara, a 245 acre farm in Flat Rock, North Carolina.

V. Dashes and Parentheses

Insert any missing dashes or parentheses.

21. The Carl Sandburg National Historic Site have you visited there? includes Connemara, a few goats, and hiking trails.

22. The top of Big Glassy Mountain a gentle 1.3 m hike from the house provides a spectacular view of the valley below.

23. A tour of the house, a hike up Big Glassy Mountain, and a visit to the goat barn these will give you a better understanding of the poet and his writings.

24. Park regulations require that pet owners 1 keep pets on leashes at all times, 2 not leave pets unattended, and 3 refrain from taking pets into any buildings or near the goats.

25. Though hailed as a great American poet, Carl Sandburg held and proclaimed a philosophy contradictory to the Bible belief in the goodness of man.

Name ____________________

Teaching Help 1: The Five-Paragraph Essay

Read the following essay and be prepared to answer questions about its structure and development. Underline the thesis statement, the topic sentence of each supporting paragraph, and the thesis restatement.

At the close of the school day each afternoon, many high-school students head home to relax. For other students, however, the day's activity is far from over as they race across athletic fields, dive into swimming pools, and practice gym relays. For some of these students, the choice to play sports in high school may have been a difficult one, especially as athletic commitments invariably involve much valuable time. However, the benefits of high-school athletics far outweigh the obvious time drawbacks.

First, high-school athletes learn discipline in their use of time. When whole evenings of potential study time are not available, students must carefully allocate several hours for study. Further, having time constraints on an evening's study time encourages students to devote quality, not mere quantity, time to school projects. A busy schedule makes student athletes plan ahead and study in advance or on alternate nights of the week. Time-pressed athletes know that when athletic practice ends, serious studying must begin.

Second, high-school athletes gain valuable social skills through team interaction. Consider the social benefit in learning to get along with others of different backgrounds and abilities. Student athletes learn a healthy tolerance for others and an understanding of their own gifts and limitations. Team sports, such as volleyball, basketball, and football, teach the importance of individuals working together to accomplish tasks: In order to score points all the players must work together. Such a lesson learned early will equip these students to be team players in other organizations, such as the church or workplace. Individual sports like track and swimming also foster teamwork because athletes must work toward collective goals like winning the next meet or gaining the regional championship. In all athletic groups, supportive friendships with coaches and teammates foster development of dedication and teamwork.

Third, high-school athletes set a healthy lifestyle with immediate and future rewards. Students who discipline themselves to stay in shape are stronger and healthier than their nonexercising peers, enjoying greater coordination and physical stamina as well as valuable mental alacrity. Students who exercise need not become dependent on artificial sugars and caffeinated beverages that give them second-rate alertness. Further, the well-being enjoyed by high-school athletes encourages them to continue making healthful fitness choices in the future, and as a result, they experience a better quality of life.

As high-school classes are dismissed each day, students make important decisions regarding their quality of life. For some students, the level of commitment involved in playing on an athletic team may seem too high a price to pay. However, the cost of remaining inactive in organized sports looms still higher in terms of a student's lack of disciplined time use, his loss of valuable social lessons, and his need of a healthy lifestyle. High-school students should take full advantage of the benefits available through athletics.

Name ______________________________

Teaching Help 2A: Some Adverb Meanings

Meanings	Adverbs	Examples
Manner (including extent and number)	slowly, well, somehow; very, completely, almost, quite, even; once, twice	After crossing the finish line, Karlee stretches **carefully.**
Place (including direction and order)	here, below, outside, somewhere, everywhere, nowhere; down, northward; first, second	Many runners stretch **here** beside the track.
Time (including frequency)	now, later, sometimes, never; often, usually, seldom, sometimes	They know that if they **always** stretch, they will be less susceptible to injury.
Result and Logical Conclusion	therefore, accordingly, consequently, hence, thus	Karlee stretches **accordingly** after each training session and race.
Cause	why	**Why** should she increase her chances for injury by neglecting to stretch?
Negation	not	Karlee will **not** risk injury!

Name ______________________________

Teaching Help 2B: Idiomatic Use of Prepositions

Many verbs and adjectives, and even some nouns, must be followed by particular prepositions. Most of these combinations we know from long observation. Sometimes others can be found in the illustrations given in a dictionary entry. The reference list below includes many of the prepositional combinations that can be problems.

accuse (someone) of

adhere to

agree on (a plan)
agree to (a proposal)
agree with (someone)

alarmed at

angry at (something)
angry with (someone) (*Informal:* mad at)

between (one) and (another)

capable of

compare to (something of a different sort)
compare with (something similar)

comply with (a requirement)

concur in (an opinion)
concur with (someone)

conform to

consist of

consistent with

contend for (a principle)
contend with (someone)

convince (someone) of (a need or a truth)

die by (violence)
die of *or* from (a disease)
die to (self, worldly pleasures)

differ from (something)
differ with (someone) about *or* over (something)

different from (something)

disapprove of

equal to

familiar to (someone)
familiar with (something)

find fault with

ignorant of

impatient at (the delay)
impatient for (success)
impatient with (someone)

in search of

independent of

indifferent to

infer from (evidence)

inferior to

influence of (one thing) on (another)

married to

oblivious of *or* to

part from (someone)
part with (something)

persuade to (do something)

prefer (this) to (that)

preferable to

prior to

refrain from

required of (someone)

responsible for (something)
responsible to (someone)

result from (a cause)
result in (an effect)
a result of (a cause)

rewarded by (someone)
rewarded for (an action)
rewarded with (a good result)

similar to

succeed in

superior to

wait at (a place)
wait for (someone)
wait on (a customer)

Name ____________________

Teaching Help 3: Sentence Patterns

Label the sentence patterns *S-InV, S-LV-PN, S-LV-PA, S-TrV-DO, S-TrV-IO-DO, S-TrV-DO-OC,* or *S-be-Advl.* If the adverbial is a prepositional phrase, underline it.

1. The Metropolitan Opera House is on the corner of West Sixty-second and Sixty-seventh Streets and Columbus and Amsterdam Avenues.
2. For its opening season in 1883, the Metropolitan Opera paid soprano Marcella Sembrich $1,455 for each of fifty-eight performances.
3. The audience of Henry Abby's benefit concert thought Sembrich an accomplished musician.
4. There were relatively cheap seats in the Family Circle level of the opera house.
5. After the financial loss of its first year, the Metropolitan Opera became a German opera company instead of an Italian one.
6. Cheaper seats, more affordable salaries for the performers, and appeal to the large German-speaking population in New York combined for financial and artistic success in the Metropolitan's second season.
7. As the new manager, Edmund C. Stanton made Anton Seidl conductor and music director in 1885.
8. George Bernard Shaw regarded the Metropolitan's 1884 production of the opera *Hamlet*, which was very different from Shakespeare's play, as being foolish.
9. While performing in San Francisco, the Metropolitan Opera company was devastated by the 1906 earthquake.
10. Struggling with the task of managing the Metropolitan Opera, Heinrich Conried offered Gustav Mahler the position of conductor in 1907.

Name ______________________________

Teaching Help 4A: Absolute Phrases

Identify each introductory element as an *absolute phrase* or a *clause*.

________________ 1. Chinese brush calligraphy differing from western calligraphy, artists elaborate on traditional characters to express their creativity.

________________ 2. Because they symbolize good luck and prosperity, a Huishan craftsman molds "Da A Fu" figurines of a plump boy holding a green fish.

________________ 3. Artists having written poems and painted pictures on fans, the elite of China valued fans for their beauty and the relief they provided from the heat.

________________ 4. The Chinese considering poetry and painting to be complementary art forms, the best Chinese artists are also poets who include characters and seals in their pictures.

________________ 5. When the Chinese began to cut beautifully colored paper to depict everyday objects and events, they created an art form unique to their culture.

Write a sentence containing an absolute phrase.

6. The dragon symbolizes the emperor. Chinese architects use artful statues to represent power and prestige in royal palaces.

____

____

7. Because the Gu Gong palace was the imperial home of the Quin emperors, strict rules governed who could open the ornately carved gates and when they were to be opened.

____

____

8. The Summer Palace is located on the Fine Jade Isle in Kun Ming Hu Lake. Quin emperors enjoyed this elaborate vacation home.

____

____

9. While emperors live and vacation in elaborate palaces, the common people of Northwest China live more simply in caves lined with brick or slate.

____

____

10. The herdsmen of Northern China live a nomadic life. Yurts (portable homes made of animal hide) are common.

____

____

Name ____________________

Teaching Help 4B: Present Participles vs. Progressive Verbs

Underline each present participial phrase once and each progressive verb twice.

1. Do you see that girl climbing high on El Capitan in Yosemite?
2. Lynn is moving effortlessly through a series of reaches and steps toward the top.
3. Deciding on her next move, Lynn confidently executes her plan to reach the next handhold.
4. Photographers hanging from elaborate rope systems snap photos of her graceful movements.
5. Notice how she is controlling her momentum so that her feet don't slip off the miniscule ledges.
6. Ascending the route in record time is one goal propelling Lynn upward.
7. She is using her gear—rope, harness, and carabiners—for safety purposes, not to aid her ascent.
8. Noticing the beauty of the granite, Lynn is enjoying the aesthetics of her climb.
9. The watching crowd cheers her on toward her goal.
10. Reaching the apex, Lynn celebrates her accomplishment!

Name ______________________________

Teaching Help 4C: Verbal and Nonverbal Phrases

Label the sentence patterns in each of the following sentences. Identify the italicized phrase as prepositional *(Prep)*, appositive *(App)*, participial *(Part)*, gerund *(Ger)*, or infinitive *(Inf)*. Then identify the function of the phrase as noun *(N)*, adjective *(Adj)*, or adverb *(Adv)*.

______ ______ 1. *Decorating a home with antique furniture* preserves historical objects from damage.

______ ______ 2. Some collectors travel abroad *to search for valuable objects.*

______ ______ 3. Other people visit antique shops or flea markets *to find hidden treasures.*

______ ______ 4. *During the summer,* we asked an appraiser to value our collection.

______ ______ 5. He stated that our grandfather clock, *retaining its original chimes,* sounded beautiful.

______ ______ 6. The pendulum, *a fascinating device,* has kept precise time for many years.

______ ______ 7. This heirloom fits well *in our hallway.*

______ ______ 8. The 1820s walnut bookcase, *filled with antique books*, came from my great-grandfather's library.

______ ______ 9. The appraiser considered my marble table, *a gift from my grandparents,* the most valuable in our collection.

______ ______ 10. *Saying which of our antiques is my favorite* is too difficult; I love all of them.

Name ____________________

Teaching Help 5A: Subordinating Conjunctions and Prepositions

Identify each italicized word (except titles of works) as either a subordinating conjunction *(SC)* or as a preposition *(P)*. Underline the subject of each dependent clause once and the predicate of each dependent clause twice.

_____ 1. *Before* Jane Austen was twenty-five years old, she had written *Pride and Prejudice,* a novel published in 1813.

_____ 2. The heroine, Elizabeth Bennet, forms a poor opinion of Darcy *before* understanding his character.

_____ 3. Despite Elizabeth's lower social rank, Darcy falls in love with her *because of* her quick wit and charming personality.

_____ 4. Elizabeth grows even more contemptuous of Darcy *when* Lieutenant Wickham accuses Darcy of denying Wickham his inheritance.

_____ 5. Elizabeth refuses to accept Darcy's offer of marriage *because* he has convinced his good friend Mr. Bingley not to marry her sister Jane.

_____ 6. *Upon* seeing Pemberley, Darcy's large estate, Elizabeth contemplates living in such a home.

_____ 7. Darcy saves Elizabeth and her family from disgrace *as* her youngest sister has eloped with Wickham.

_____ 8. Unexpectedly, Lady Catherine de Bourgh, Darcy's controlling aunt, arrives accusing Elizabeth *of* tricking Darcy into loving her and demands that Elizabeth promise not to marry Darcy.

_____ 9. Elizabeth, however, has come to love Darcy *since* his kindness to her family during Lydia's elopement and therefore refuses to make any such promise to Lady Catherine.

_____ 10. Darcy and Elizabeth marry in a double wedding with Jane and Bingley *after* Darcy confesses his error of discouraging Bingley from pursuing Jane.

Name______________________________

Teaching Help 5B: *That* as a Relative Pronoun and a Subordinating Conjunction

Identify each italicized *that* as a relative pronoun *(RP)* or a subordinating conjunction *(SC)*. Identify the grammatical function of each relative pronoun within the dependent clause as subject *(S)*, direct object *(DO)*, or object of the preposition *(OP)*.

______ ______ 1. In one of her novels, Jane Austen portrays Emma, the title character, as a young lady *that* possesses both material wealth and loving friends but is immature in her reasoning and treatment of others.

______ ______ 2. Emma hopes *that* she might arrange a marriage between Harriet Smith, a young lady of low social standing, and Mr. Elton, the village vicar.

______ ______ 3. *That* Emma could place him on the same social level as Harriet greatly offends Mr. Elton.

______ ______ 4. The marriage proposal *that* Mr. Elton makes to Emma is as unwelcome to her as the thought of marrying Harriet is to him.

______ ______ 5. Mr. Knightley, appalled *that* Emma would flippantly play with Harriet's emotions, rebukes her for attempting to make matches.

______ ______ 6. Frank Churchill proves to be a new acquaintance *that* Emma can entertain herself with.

______ ______ 7. By flirting with Emma, Frank succeeds at hiding the love *that* he possesses for Jane Fairfax.

______ ______ 8. The death of his aunt provides Frank the freedom *that* he needs to marry Jane.

______ ______ 9. When Harriet tells Emma of her love for Mr. Knightley, Emma finally realizes *that* she loves him herself and cannot bear the thought of anyone else marrying him.

______ ______ 10. Through all her blunders Emma gains a mature perspective *that* resembles Mr. Knightley's clear judgment.

Name____________________

Teaching Help 6A: Agreement Rules

Write the correct answer in the blank. Then circle each answer in the word-search box.

__________ 1. _?_, including periods of time, are considered singular and require singular verbs.

__________ 2. The true subject, not an _?_ phrase, will agree with the verb.

__________ 3. Compound antecedents joined by *and* or *both—and* require a plural _?_.

__________ 4. Identify the verb with the true subject of an _?_ sentence.

__________ 5. Names of _?_ and organizations that exist in plural form require plural verbs.

__________ 6. Do not use a _?_ personal pronoun to refer to a singular indefinite pronoun.

__________ 7. A singular collective noun may require a plural verb if the meaning of the sentence emphasizes the _?_ in the group rather than the group as a whole.

__________ 8. A relative pronoun has the same number as its _?_.

__________ 9. Each verb must agree with its subject in _?_ and number.

__________ 10. An indefinite pronoun can be singular or plural depending on the _?_ phrase that modifies it.

__________ 11. The _?_ of an individual work of art, music, or literature is always singular.

__________ 12. For compound subjects joined by *or, either—or,* or *neither—nor,* the subject _?_ the first verb determines the form of the verb.

__________ 13. When the predicate noun differs in number from the subject, the verb agrees with the _?_.

__________ 14. When determining whether a collective noun needs a singular or plural pronoun, analyze the sentence for its _?_.

__________ 15. When a word ending in *ics* refers to a field of study, use a _?_ verb.

Teaching Help 6A: Agreement Rules (continued)

I A T I T L S D E C E T N A
S N S L A M O U N T S V E M
I E T S A E I H P R O N B O
N A J E R G O N S E A F Q U
D E T R E V N I D R M L G N
I S I Y F X N U P A O N N P
V I T N S G W L O E I G O L
I N L S U T J M B N Y L S U
D G E L B E K E E L O Y R R
U U A P J E R V U A L R E A
A R L V E S R T Q H N A P L
L U N O C E R J B U S I E C
S R A N T E C E D E N T N O
I E W N A E T Y P D F H I G
M S I V N R A S M A E T D N

Name________________________________

Teaching Help 6B: Agreement Review

In the blank write the correct form of the verb or pronoun as indicated in the parentheses. Then use your answers to complete the crossword puzzle.

ACROSS

________________ 1. The history surrounding Lewis and Clark's adventures *(fascinate)* Americans today.

________________ 2. The Lewis and Clark Trail Heritage Foundation *(attempt)* to protect and preserve the historic trail for the enjoyment and education of the public.

________________ 3. Woolly mammoths, Peruvian llamas, and Welsh-speaking Indians *(be)* all myths about the West that Americans believed in 1803.

________________ 4. Both Meriwether Lewis and William Clark *(be)* captains in the army and shared command during the expedition.

________________ 5. Knowing that the logistics of such a trip *(require)* extensive preparation, Lewis spent months buying supplies and studying science and navigation.

________________ 6. The Corps of Discovery commissioned by President Thomas Jefferson made *(personal pronoun)* way across the continent in search of the Northwest Passage.

________________ 7. Almost nobody *(realize)* that Lewis took a Newfoundland dog named Seaman on the expedition.

________________ 8. "A Summary View of Rivers and Creeks," Lewis's first report sent to President Jefferson, *(record)* details of the Missouri River water system.

________________ 9. Lewis and Clark spent much of *(personal pronoun)* time surveying, mapping, and studying flora and fauna.

________________ 10. Hired by Lewis to be an interpreter, Toussaint Charbonneau brought with him his Indian wife Sacagawea and *(personal pronoun)* fifty-five-day-old son.

DOWN

________________ 1. At the end of a long line of interpreters, Sacagawea was the one who *(auxiliary)* translate from Hidatsa into Shoshone.

________________ 2. One hundred lashes *(be)* the punishment for Private John Newman's mutinous actions at the beginning of the expedition.

________________ 3. Hauling their boats on wheels made from cottonwood, the explorers *(travel)* eighteen miles in five days to avoid waterfalls near modern day Great Falls, Montana.

________________ 4. Lewis painted *(personal pronoun)* face with red dye as a sign of peace to the Shoshone women that he first encountered.

________________ 5. Neither the Nez Perce nor the Shoshone tribes *(be)* hostile toward the explorers.

________________ 6. Crossing the Bitterroot Mountains on the Lolo Trail *(present)* many hazards to the explorers.

________________ 7. No one *(want)* to remember who shot Lewis in the leg: Pierre Cruzatte accidentally hit Lewis while hunting elk.

________________ 8. Appendicitis *(be)* recorded to be the cause of Sgt. Charles Floyd's death, the only death during the expedition.

________________ 9. Though nobody *(believe)* John Colter's description of an area of geysers and boiling mud pits, many people today know of Yellowstone National Park.

________________ 10. Each American should make it a point to learn about *(personal pronoun)* heritage.

Name ____________________

Teaching Help 7A: Consistency and Sequence of Tenses

Underline each verb in incorrect tense. Then rewrite the paragraph correcting the incorrect verbs.

Last week we study about James Fenimore Cooper in literature class. Miss Rhinier, our teacher, reads part of *Deerslayer* to us, and then we discuss the character Natty Bumppo. Natty, who was an orphan of white settlers, lived with the Delaware Indians. In *Deerslayer* he sets out on a mission to prove himself a man. Though already an accomplished hunter, Natty had never killed another human. He believed that taking scalps was wrong for a white man and that a white man must keep his word. Natty kills a Huron named Le Loup Cervier who wanted Natty's canoe. Because Natty refused to fight unfairly and because of his surprisingly accurate aim, the dying Indian names him Hawkeye. No longer just a good hunter, Natty was now a warrior.

Name ____________________

Teaching Help 7B: Using Active and Passive Sentences

Underline each passive verb once and each retained object or subjective complement twice. Then rewrite the paragraph in active voice, keeping passive voice only when necessary.

During a witty exchange, my friend Lynnelle was told a humorous quotation by her English professor: "If in his study he hath so much care / To hang all old strange things, let his wife beware." Lynnelle decided to find the source of this couplet. Searching the Internet, she found that it had been penned by John Donne to describe an antique collector. As a result of her study, Lynnelle became fascinated by Donne's religious poems. She was challenged by the poem "The Cross," which states, "Since Christ embraced the cross itself, dare I / His image, th' image of His cross, deny?" Lynnelle presented her study to the class and reported that Donne is considered a great metaphysical poet by critics. The class was given an appreciation of Donne and his writing through Lynnelle's presentation.

Name ____________________

Teaching Help 8: Pronouns with Verbals

Write the missing word from each rule in the blank.

________ 1. The "subject" of a gerund is in the ? case.

________ 2. If a pronoun is followed and modified by a participial phrase, not a gerund phrase, the case of the pronoun is determined by its ? within the sentence.

________ 3. The "subject" of an infinitive is in the ? case.

________ 4. A noun or pronoun that follows an infinitive and acts as its object is in the ? case.

________ 5. A pronoun that follows a linking verb infinitive must be in the ? case as the earlier word that it is renaming.

Write the correct pronoun in the blank.

________ 6. Andrew Campbell's curiosity led to ? discovering the Luray Caverns in 1878.

________ 7. After his initial discovery Campbell approached several friends and asked ? to accompany him on an exploratory trip into the cavern.

________ 8. Benton Stebbins photographed ? sliding down a rope into the cavern below for the first time.

________ 9. These early explorers realized that if anyone was going to develop the caverns for public use, it would have to be ?.

________ 10. The cave's features are so captivating that vacationers flock to see ?.

Name ______________________

Teaching Help 9A: Clear Pronoun Reference

Underline the five ambiguous or remote pronoun references. Then rewrite the paragraph, correcting the unclear references.

In a game of cricket, the offensive player attempts to knock over his opponent's wicket with an overhand throw, and the defensive player bats the ball away from the wicket. It is a favorite game among the English and the countries colonized by the English. Robert, who is from England, and Ashish, who is from India, drove to the field to play cricket. He grabbed a bat, ball, and wicket out of the car. While Robert practiced bowling techniques, Ashish practiced various batting techniques. He played cricket professionally in India. They allow the batter to hit the ball in any direction. Eventually the men participated in a close game of cricket. When they finished playing, Ashish told Robert that he had played well.

Name ______________________

Teaching Help 9B: Pronoun Reference

Identify each sentence as *clear (C)* or *unclear (U)*. Underline each pronoun causing unclear reference.

_____ 1. They say that most college students change their major several times during their college careers.

_____ 2. A college's course catalog often provides valuable information concerning its majors.

_____ 3. Many college-bound people think you ought to know what to major in right away, but sometimes waiting a year or two is advisable.

_____ 4. Colleges and universities may offer hundreds of majors to choose from, which can be daunting.

_____ 5. A student's interest in a particular subject can help the student to decide if he would like to pursue it as his major.

_____ 6. Most colleges have career development offices. The counselors there help students assess their interests and can suggest majors that correspond to those interests.

_____ 7. Their mature perspective and real-life experience give academic advisors the ability to help students make wise choices.

_____ 8. Because the choices made in college affect the rest of life, they should be made only after much prayer for God's guidance.

_____ 9. God often guides us into areas of study that we did not originally want to pursue; this demonstrates how God beautifully orchestrates His perfect will.

_____ 10. Rachel told Merideth, "Through various circumstances God has guided me to major in English. Although I used to dislike English, now I love it!"

Name ______________________

Teaching Help 10A: Irregular Comparison

Insert the correct form of the following adjectives and adverbs into the paragraph. Words may be used more than once or not at all.

bad	common	little	many	sick
cheap	good	much	red	well

Last spring I went to a ski resort in North Carolina with some friends. We had the ____________ time even though we faced several out-of-the-ordinary circumstances. First, I taught my friends to ski. Joel and Micah, who are from an island in the Caribbean, learned quickly and were soon skiing ____________ than their sister Janiera even though she said she had skied before. Having been skiing many times, Oran skied very ____________ and even attempted a few jumps. Unfortunately, we had an equipment mishap. On the first trip up the ski lift, one of Micah's poles caught on the lift and bent. I've never felt ____________ than I did at that moment. Fortunately, we didn't have to pay for the pole because it was one of the ____________ rental poles available and wasn't worth anything. Last of all, the snow was the ____________ I have ever skied. Skiing the last night of the season makes for wet, patchy snow. Some sections of the hill had so ____________ snow that we had to slog through mud and puddles of water! I also found that skiing on manmade snow was ____________ difficult than skiing on natural snow and that falling was ____________ than staying on my feet. Throughout the evening we fell ____________ times, got very wet, and laughed at each other. We had a fantastic time!

Name ____________________

Teaching Help 10B: Adjective and Adverb Use

Underline each misused modifier. Rewrite each sentence to correct any misused modifiers. If the sentence is already correct, write *C* in the blank.

1. Forgotten and untouched for hundreds of years, Hiram Bingham discovered Machu Picchu in 1911.

   ____

   ____

2. Machu Picchu was a fortress city of the Inca civilization standing above eight thousand feet.

   ____

   ____

3. Huayna Picchu, near Machu Picchu, is the tallest of the two mountains.

   ____

   ____

4. Many archaeologists have studied the ruins of Machu Picchu, hoping finally to solve the many mysteries surrounding the function of the ancient city.

   ____

   ____

5. There are hardly no satisfactory clues to explain the end of the community living at Machu Picchu.

   ____

   ____

6. Researchers only have discovered hints and not answers to these mysteries.

   ____

   ____

7. The Torreon, thought to be an astronomical observatory, appears to be the center of a pagan worship of nature.

   ____

   ____

Teaching Help 10B: Adjective and Adverb Use (continued)

8. Revering the sun above all, the Intiwatana stone was carefully cut and positioned to act as a type of calendar for religious ceremonies.

9. Despite their most magnificent architectural abilities, the Incas did not glorify God but worshiped His creation and became fools (Rom. 1:21–23).

10. A religiously debased civilization, Francisco Pizarro maliciously conquered the Incas.

Name ________________________________

Teaching Help 11: Capitalization

Underline any words containing capitalization errors in the following letter.

dear Mr. Uptain,

A friend of mine, Rob provenzano, told me about your Bible Camp in the Mountains of wyoming. God has been using Rob's description of your camp to show me the spiritual needs of america's youth. Until he described many of his campers and the ways in which they worship the Gods of this world, i never comprehended the great need for Christian young people to invest their lives in Summer camping ministries.

I am currently a Freshman at a Christian College pursuing a B.S. in biology. Growing up in a chinese home, i was saved out of a buddhist background at age ten. During a vacation on the *victoria* cruise ship, my family heard about God's gift of Salvation from another family. My family and I accepted Christ as Savior during this cruise on the mediterranean sea. Since my salvation i have sought to serve Christ in every aspect of my life.

Though i have never had the privilege of attending a Bible Camp, i believe that the Lord would have me serve him at a camp. Please consider hiring me to work this Summer as a Camp Counselor. My desire is to be a channel, as Mary e. Maxwell describes in the hymn "channels only," through which God's love can shine to the campers.

Jesus, fill now with thy Spirit
hearts that full surrender know;
that the streams of living water
from our inner man may flow.

thank you for your consideration. I will continue in Prayer, as i am sure you will do.

in Christ,

Dashan Xue

Name ____________________________

Teaching Help 12A: End Marks

Identify each sentence as a polite request *(PR)*, an imperative *(I)*, a mild imperative *(MI)*, a direct question *(DQ)*, or an indirect question *(IQ)*. Then place the correct end mark at the end of each sentence.

______ 1. May we please take a tour of the United States Capitol

______ 2. Were you surprised to hear the tour guide welcome everybody to the Capitol in his own language

______ 3. Please feel free to take as many pictures as you like

______ 4. Wow! Look at the Rotunda

______ 5. Who painted the *Apotheosis of Washington*

______ 6. The tour guide asked us if we knew why Washington is surrounded by thirteen women in the painting

______ 7. My friend asked if we would see the National Statuary Hall Collection

______ 8. Will you please tell me which statues are from the state of Wyoming

______ 9. Do you know why some of the statues are not in the National Statuary Hall

______ 10. For security purposes, do not take mace or pepper spray on your tour of the Capitol

Name ________________________________

Teaching Help 12B: Commas with Adjectives

In the blanks write a pair of adjectives for each sentence. Use a variety of coordinate and cumulative adjectives. Insert any necessary commas in your answers. Be prepared to explain your answers.

1. On a ________________ ________________ evening, my friend and I went to a play in the park, Shakespeare's *Much Ado About Nothing*.
2. Because we were not sure of the exact location of the park, we drove up and down ________________ ________________ roads before we found it.
3. Arriving somewhat late, we carried our ________________ ________________ chairs to the back of the crowd and sat down.
4. Some of the ________________ ________________ spectators sat on blankets near the stage.
5. Most people had ________________ ________________ dinners, but my friend and I had forgotten to take anything to eat or drink.
6. The ________________ ________________ stage consisted of a castle front, a platform, an elevated pier, and a few small boats.
7. From our position we sometimes could not hear the ________________ ________________ voice of the actress playing Hero.
8. Of course, we were in stitches over the ________________ ________________ antics of Dogberry.
9. I was surprised by the ________________ ________________ marriage at the end of the play.
10. The ________________ ________________ play combined with the enjoyable atmosphere of the park made for an experience that my friend and I will never forget.

Name ____________________

Teaching Help 12C: Commas with Restrictive and Nonrestrictive Elements

Identify each italicized phrase or clause as restrictive *(R)* or nonrestrictive *(NR)*. Insert any missing commas.

______ 1. The United States Chess Federation (USCF) *a nonprofit organization* is committed to promoting the game of chess in America.

______ 2. The competitor *with the white chess pieces* moves first.

______ 3. The most powerful chess piece is the queen *which can move in all directions and for any number of spaces.*

______ 4. The trend *that prefers sudden death matches over lengthier matches* often frustrates players who have a definite advantage over their opponents but do not have sufficient time to checkmate them.

______ 5. *When he has only five minutes left* a player may ask the director to declare the game a draw to avoid losing the match due to time constraints.

______ 6. Most of the students *who won the National Chess Championship this year* are from a different school district than previous winners.

______ 7. Women's world champion *Zsuzsa Polgar of Hungary* first became the champion in 1996.

______ 8. Larry Christiansen earned the title of grandmaster *after winning the Malaga tournament in 1977.*

______ 9. Novice tournaments *which involve only a minimal fee* provide beginners with an opportunity to experience chess tournaments.

______ 10. Benjamin Franklin *one of America's greatest philosophers* praised the game of chess as a stimulant for the mind.

Name______________________

Teaching Help 13: Punctuation Placement

Identify each statement as true *(T)* or false *(F)*. Then rewrite each false statement to make it correct.

______ 1. Make the possessive form of singular nouns ending in *s* and plural nouns ending in *s* or *es* by adding an apostrophe followed by *s*.

____

____

____

______ 2. Ellipses taking the place of the end of a sentence and the beginning of another are preceded by a period.

____

____

____

______ 3. Periods and commas always go inside closing quotation marks.

____

____

____

______ 4. Set off an internal appositive series with dashes.

____

____

____

______ 5. Exclamation points and question marks precede the closing quotation mark if the entire sentence is an exclamation or question.

____

____

____

______ 6. While commas set off short phrases and clauses, parentheses signal less formal but important material and dashes indicate that the enclosed material is less important.

____

____

____

Teaching Help 13: Punctuation Placement (continued)

_______ 7. To set off material within a set of parentheses, use another set of parentheses.

____

____

____

_______ 8. In a sentence containing divisions set off by parenthetical numbers, commas or semicolons are still necessary between items in the list.

____

____

____

_______ 9. Never enclose the title of your own essay or paper in quotation marks on the title page.

____

____

____

_______ 10. Use a hyphen to divide a word at the end of a line according to the following guidelines: between syllables, with at least three letters and the hyphen on the first line, and with at least two letters on the second line.

____

____

____

Name ____________________

ESL Help 2A: Positions of Adjectives

Adjectives from different meaning categories are usually placed in a specific order before a noun. (Their order in the sentence may sometimes vary, however, especially with words describing shape.) Usually no more than three or four adjectives are used together. The typical order of adjectives as they appear from left to right in a noun phrase can be described as follows:

- **Articles, possessives, cardinal numbers, and most other determiners** (*a/an/the, your/Jonathan's, three/four, many/this, no*)
- **Ordinal (order) determiners** (*first, second, third, last, next*)
- **Evaluative (opinion) words** (*unusual, considerate, strange, kind, talented*)
- **Size** (*large, little, gigantic, long*)
- **Shape** (*round, circular, tall, broad*)
- **Condition** (*messy, flimsy, rusty, tattered, faded, tired*)
- **Age** (*childish, mature, old, juvenile*)
- **Color** (*beige, red, yellow*)
- **Nationality or origin** (*Irish, German, Peruvian, Spanish*)
- **Religion** (*Baptist, Catholic, Islamic*)
- **Modifying nouns describing material makeup** (*silk, gravel, marble, hardwood*)
- **Other modifying nouns** (*garden* path, *summer* home, *computer* handbook)

Name ______________________________

ESL Help 2B: Exercise in Positions of Adjectives

Rewrite the sentences, placing the adjectives in the correct order to modify the noun that immediately follows the adjectives. Do not forget to capitalize the first word of each sentence.

1. *(sweet, the, elderly)* teacher reached for the phone.

____

____

2. She checked *(old, faded, yellow, the)* phone book for the number.

____

____

3. *(yellow, the, bright)* sun was just peeping over the horizon.

____

____

4. The teacher hoped that it was not too early to call the mother of Victoria, one of *(fifth-grade, shyest, her)* students.

____

____

5. Earlier in the week some of the other fifth graders had asked their teacher for permission to hold *(little, a, surprise)* party for Victoria's birthday.

____

____

6. They wanted to bring *(fancy, chocolate, some)* cupcakes for the whole class.

____

____

7. One student even planned to serve *(pink, cold, delicious)* lemonade.

____

____

8. Hence, the teacher thought she should check with Victoria's mother to make sure that she had made *(no, special)* plans already.

____

____

ESL Help 2B: Exercise in Positions of Adjectives (continued)

9. As soon as the phone was answered, the teacher immediately began to explain *(big, elaborate, the)* plans that had been made.

____

____

10. However, it was Victoria who had answered *(the, phone, early)* call, and to this day she has kept her secret.

____

____

Name____________________________

ESL Help 2c: Defining and Using Determiners

Determiners, which come before descriptive adjectives, are very important in English. The most common determiners are articles, possessives, and demonstratives. Other determiners are used to indicate counting, numbering, and amount. Determiners come before nouns, not after them or in place of them.

Articles

The English language has one definite article *(the)* and two forms of the indefinite article *(a* and *an)*.

Possessives

When possessives modify nouns, possessives are considered determiners. Possessive nouns are made up either of a noun (in its singular or plural form) and *'s* or of a noun (in its plural form already ending in *s*) and an apostrophe.

Singular	Singular Possessive	Plural	Plural Possessive
car	car's	cars	cars'
lady	lady's	ladies	ladies'
Mrs. Taylor	Mrs. Taylor's	the Taylors	the Taylors'

Examples The *car's* door is red.
The *lady's* coat was bright red.
The *Taylors'* camper had a flat tire.

English has eight possessive determiners made from pronouns.

Person	Singular	Plural
First	my	our
Second	your	your
Third	his, her, its	their

Examples *My* friends understand *my* decision and give *their* approval.
Our family wants to give *your* mother a gift.

Demonstratives

English has four demonstratives that can be used as determiners before nouns.

Position	Singular	Plural
Near	this	these
Far	that	those

Examples *This* class is easy; *that* one is hard.
These directions are much clearer than *those* others were.

Some Other Determiners

Words such as *one, two, several, many, more, most, some, any, first, second, next,* and *last* can be determiners. Most of these determiners can be used alone before a noun, but sometimes one of them comes after an article, a possessive, or a demonstrative determiner.

EXAMPLES *Many* times people have a hard time determining a vacation spot.

A person should always follow *several* guidelines.

I believe that if *more* people planned ahead, there would be fewer disappointments.

One decision a vacationer should make is the amount of money he wishes to spend.

He also should have *some* idea of how far he wants to go.

Finally, he should ask *many* friends for their advice.

Using Determiners

A singular count noun must have at least one determiner before it.

WRONG | I ate apple.

RIGHT | I ate *an* apple.

I ate *one* apple.

I ate *the* apple.

Name____________________________

ESL Help 2D: Article Usage

1. Proper Nouns

1.1 Always use *the* before a plural proper noun.

***The** Martins* built a new house.

1.2 Usually, do not use an article before a singular proper noun.

Christianity is based on the teachings of Christ.

1.3 Do not use an article before most geographic names.*

Chicago is located in *Illinois.*

*Exceptions include collective names and plurals (***the*** *Philippines* or ***the*** *Adirondack Mountains*), land masses (***the*** *Hawaiian Islands*), bodies of water (***the*** *Pacific Ocean*), and geographic regions (***the*** *North*, ***the*** *Caribbean*, or ***the*** *Far East*).

2. Specific Count and Noncount Nouns

2.1 Use *the* when both you and the hearer know what is referred to.

***The** dessert* is sweet.
***The** road* is rough.

2.2 Use *the* before a noun that has been mentioned before.

George bought *a car*. ***The** car* is a convertible.

2.3 Use *the* before a noun modified by a superlative or ordinal adjective.

***The** cutest* boy I know is my neighbor.
***The** first* person to answer gets a gold star.

3. General Singular Count Nouns

3.1 Use *a* or *an* when representing one member of a class.

Miranda has ***a** kitten.*

3.2 Use an article unless a possessive or a demonstrative is used with the noun.

Miranda loves ***her** kitten.*

3.3 Use *the* in some general statements. See 4.1 and 5.1 for more common generalizations.

***The** dingo* is a kind of canine.

4. General Plural Count Nouns

4.1 Usually, do not use an article with plural count nouns used in a general sense.

Dingoes are canines.

5. General Noncount Nouns

5.1 Usually, do not use an article with noncount nouns used in a general sense (languages, school subjects, etc.).

Water is necessary for life.

5.2 Use *the* if a modifier follows the noun.

***The** water* in the teakettle is hot.

Name ______________________________

ESL Help 2E: Exercise in Article Usage

Choose the correct article *(a, an,* or *the)* to put in each blank. If no article is needed, put an *X* in the blank. Above each answer list the appropriate rule number from the Article Usage sheet.

When someone visits another country, he must learn to communicate with ______ inhabitants of that country. Sometimes it is possible to know ______ language spoken in that country and still have ______ problems. At other times one is able to communicate even without words. In one particular instance a couple from ______ United States went to visit ______ France. ______ Stowes had studied ______ French for only one semester. After a pleasant airplane flight, the couple arrived at ______ Charles de Gaulle Airport barely able to understand ______ traffic signs and menus. While in ______ airport, they had to pick up their luggage, decipher transportation options, and purchase the necessary tickets to travel to their hotel. Having a limited use of ______ French, they began ______ their challenge of traversing ______ maze of bus, rail, and subway lines. Getting on and off at ______ right stops, hauling luggage up and down stairs, and trying not to stare at various musicians along the way were all challenges. After riding ______ third subway train, the couple arrived at ______ metro stop closest to their hotel. They still had to make their way to street level with all their bags and then decide which way to walk to ______ hotel. Evidently they looked somewhat bedraggled because ______ kind French woman helped them. ______ door that she identified led to ______ hidden escalator. The French woman rode with them and asked in ______ halting English what hotel they wanted to go to. After they informed her, she flagged down ______ bus and told ______ driver where to take them. While trying to convey their deep gratitude, the couple hurried onto ______ bus. As its door closed, they heard their newfound friend say, "No thank, I'm ______ Christian!"

Name________________________________

ESL Help 2F: Adverb Placement

Adverbs of Manner

Adverbs of manner answer the question *How?*

EXAMPLES *loudly, quickly, slowly, happily, brightly, enthusiastically, gratefully*

Placement: Adverbs of manner usually come in one of three places:

1. They may come directly before the subject when the subject is not preceded by any introductory information (such as a prepositional phrase).

WRONG	*Loudly* in the distance the train whistle blew. In the distance *loudly* the train whistle blew.
RIGHT	*Loudly* the train whistle blew in the distance.

WRONG	*Brightly* through the window the sun shone. Through the window *brightly* the sun shone.
RIGHT	*Brightly* the sun shone through the window.

2. They may come with the verb.
   - If there are any auxiliaries, place the adverb after the first auxiliary.

     The toddler was *energetically* running from place to place.
     The aroma had *slowly* filled the kitchen.

   - If there is no auxiliary, place the adverb before the main verb.

     Jennifer *gently* rocked the baby.
     Ted *quickly* darkened the lights.
     Grandpa *quietly* strummed his guitar.

3. They may come after the direct object (especially if the direct object is the end of the clause).

   Mother called her child *anxiously.*
   The child printed her name *neatly.*

   Note: Adverbs of manner should not be placed between the verb and its direct object.

   WRONG | The child printed *neatly* her name.

Adverbs of Place

Adverbs of place answer the question *Where?*

EXAMPLES *anywhere, inside, down, southward, everywhere, above, there*

Placement: Adverbs of place usually come after the verb or at the end of the clause.

The toys were strewn *everywhere.*
Please put the book *there.*
The dog was lying *outside.*

Note: Although these rules will be helpful for placing adverbs correctly in a sentence, they are somewhat variable. Exceptions are possible, especially for emphasis.

ESL Help 2F: Adverb Placement (continued)

Adverbs of Time (Including Frequency)

Adverbs of time answer the questions *When?* and *How often?*

EXAMPLES *daily, lately, often, rarely, seldom, then, usually, never*

Placement: Adverbs of time usually come in one of three places:

1. They may come before the subject (exception: *never*).

   Later Dad will lock the door.
   Sometimes he forgets to do it.

2. They may come with the verb.
   - If there are any auxiliaries, place the adverb after the first auxiliary.

     The children will *often* stop here after school.
     They are *usually* looking for something to eat.

   - If there is no auxiliary but there is a *be* verb, place the adverb after the *be* verb.

     Anne is *never* bothered when people visit.
     Guests are *always* welcome in Anne's home.

   - If there is no auxiliary and no *be* verb, place the adverb before the main verb.

     Cindy *seldom* orders water without ice.
     She *frequently* drinks two glasses with a meal.

3. They may come at the end of the sentence if not too far removed from the verb (exception: *never*).

RIGHT	John washes his pickup truck *often.*
TOO FAR REMOVED	His wife polishes her brand-new BMW convertible *habitually.*
BETTER	His wife *habitually* polishes her brand-new BMW convertible.

Qualifiers

A **qualifier** is a special kind of adverb that modifies an adjective or an adverb by either strengthening or weakening the idea of that adjective or adverb. Qualifiers answer the question *To what extent?* about an adjective or an adverb.

EXAMPLES *very, slightly, rather, even, quite, much, extremely, almost, kind of, sort of* (The last two are somewhat informal.)

Placement: A qualifier is placed directly in front of the adjective or adverb that it modifies.

He discovered that the measurements were not *quite* exact.
Therefore, he measured *very* carefully again.

Note: Unlike adverbs that modify verbs, qualifiers cannot be moved around in a sentence.

Name ____________________

ESL Help 2G: Exercise in Adverb Placement

Decide whether the italicized adverbs are placed correctly. If the placement is correct, write *C* in the blank to the left. If the placement is incorrect, write *I* in the blank and then rewrite the sentence correctly.

______ 1. The mountain climber lost *almost* his way in the heavy fog.

____

______ 2. Delphino *outside* peered at the crowd gathered at the train station.

____

______ 3. Malea was *happily* working in her garden.

____

______ 4. The father takes *usually* his daughter along when he goes jogging.

____

______ 5. Campers will *often* exchange addresses.

____

______ 6. Duke wagged his tail *very* energetically when we arrived.

____

______ 7. *Yesterday* she searched for buttons to match her dress.

____

______ 8. *Methodically* at the crime scene the police questioned all bystanders.

____

______ 9. Jana is *seldom* late for class.

____

______ 10. The sun is always *somewhere* shining.

____

Name ____________________

ESL Help 2H: Making Sentences Negative Using *Not*

In English, sentences are usually made negative by adding *not.* English has three basic rules for correctly placing *not* in sentences.

1. If there is an auxiliary (such as *will, have, may, do,* or *is*) in the sentence, place *not* after the first auxiliary.

   Barret *has gone* to bed.
   Steve *has* ***not*** *gone* to bed.

   His portrait *will be painted* soon.
   My portrait *will* ***not*** *be painted* soon.

2. If there is no auxiliary but there is a *be* verb *(am, is, are, was, were),* place *not* after the *be* verb.

   Michelle *was* very studious.
   Although Michelle was studious, she *was* ***not*** athletic.

   This candy is sweet.
   That candy *is* ***not*** sweet.

3. If there is no auxiliary and no *be* verb, add *do, does,* or *did* according to the form of the main verb. Place *not* between the *do* auxiliary and the main verb. The main verb then changes to the first principal part of the verb because the *do* auxiliary will show the number and the tense for the complete verb. The part of the sentence in parentheses may be omitted if it is clearly understood by both the reader and the writer.

   Clarence *plays* minor league baseball.
   Martin *does* ***not*** (*play* minor league baseball).

   Marissa *wanted* to go to the beach.
   Sandy *did* ***not*** *want* to (go to the beach).

   The queen bee *lays* eggs in the hive.
   The worker bees *do* ***not*** (*lay* eggs in the hive).

Name ______________________________

ESL Help 21: Exercise in Making Sentences Negative Using *Not*

Rewrite the following sentences to make them negative. Follow these steps:

A. If there is a word or phrase in parentheses, use it to replace something from the original sentence.
B. Add *not* to each sentence.
C. Change the form of the verb and add an auxiliary if necessary.

EXAMPLE Tyler enjoys working in the garden. *(Zachary)*
Zachary does not enjoy working in the garden.

1. Spring months are usually rainy. *(fall)*

____

2. Sometimes it rains three or four days a week.

____

3. However, "April showers bring May flowers." *(March)*

____

4. Of course, along with spring comes tornado season. *(hurricane)*

____

5. The weatherman's forecast of late afternoon showers often includes tornado watches. *(morning)*

____

6. Occasionally a watch becomes a warning. *(often)*

____

7. A tornado watch suggests the possibility of a tornado forming. *(certainty)*

____

8. However, the spotting of an actual tornado prompts a warning. *(tornado conditions)*

____

9. Some tornadoes have been particularly devastating.

____

10. Strong winds and huge hailstones often accompany tornadoes. *(small thunderstorms)*

____

Name ______________________________

ESL Help 2J: Using Prepositions

General Rules

1. Do not leave necessary prepositions out of a sentence.

WRONG	Pierce looked the squirrel.
RIGHT	Pierce looked *at* the squirrel.

2. *During* is a preposition that signals a prepositional phrase. *While* is a conjunction that usually introduces a dependent clause; it cannot be followed by a noun phrase. *During* and *while* cannot be used interchangeably.

PREPOSITION	She had an accident *during* the rainstorm. (OP: rainstorm)
CONJUNCTION	She had an accident *while* it was raining. (S: it; InV: was raining)

3. Do not use a preposition when *home* is used with a verb of motion or direction. The same rule applies to *downtown* and *uptown*.

WRONG	He went *to* downtown.
RIGHT	After he went downtown, he came home.

If the verb is not a verb of motion or direction, the preposition is usually necessary with *home*.

A writer may work *at* home.
I'll be *at* home after school.

4. Do not use a preposition when *here* or *there* is used after the verb.

WRONG	We are lodging *at* here during June, but we're going *to* there the rest of the summer.
RIGHT	We are lodging here during June, but we're going there the rest of the summer.

5. Use *at* for the most specific time or location, *on* for a more general time or location, and *in* for the most general time or location.

The recital starts *at* 7:00 P.M.
The recital is *on* Friday.
The recital is *in* the evening. It is *in* July.

Josiah lives *at* 315 Greene Street.
He lives *on* Greene Street.
He lives *in* Toronto.

6. Many verbs and adjectives, and even some nouns, must be followed by particular prepositions. Sometimes changing the preposition changes the meaning.

Todd is engaged *to* Maria.
(Todd and Maria plan to marry.)

Maria is engaged *in* painting the shed.
(Painting is her current activity.)

Name ____________________

ESL Help 2K: Exercise in Using Prepositions

Choose the correct word for each blank from the choices in parentheses. If none of the suggested words is correct or if no preposition is needed, put an *X* in the blank.

1. Rich asked me if the chess tournament would be played ____________ there. *(at, on)*
2. I told him that I thought it was being held ____________ downtown somewhere. *(in, at)*
3. The tournament is supposed to be ____________ the Memorial Day weekend. *(during, while)*
4. The games are scheduled ____________ different times throughout the day. *(on, at, in)*
5. Rich hopes to play early ____________ the morning. *(on, in)*
6. Everyone should be very quiet ____________ the games are being played. *(during, while)*
7. Rich said he needed to come ____________ here to practice before the tournament. *(at, to)*
8. Winning the tournament would be a sign ____________ great ability. *(of, at)*
9. The winner will be announced at 5:00 P.M. ____________ Monday. *(on, at, in)*
10. It would be wonderful if Rich brought ____________ home the winning trophy. *(at, to)*

Name________________________________

ESL Help 3A: Inverted Subject and Predicate

English has two basic types of questions: *yes/no* questions and *wh* questions. Some questions use inverted order, and others do not. ("Inverted order" means that the order of the subject and the predicate is reversed.)

Yes/No Questions

(questions that require *yes* or *no* for an answer)

- If a sentence contains an auxiliary verb, move the first auxiliary before the subject.

  Nathan *is playing* a soccer game tonight.
  Is Nathan *playing* a soccer game tonight?

  Nathan *has scored* ten goals this season.
  Has Nathan *scored* ten goals this season?

- If a sentence contains no auxiliary but does have a *be* verb, move the *be* verb before the subject.

  Nathan *is* a good soccer player.
  Is Nathan a good soccer player?

  He *was* on the All-Star Team last year.
  Was he on the All-Star Team last year?

- If there is no auxiliary and no *be* verb, add a form of the auxiliary *do* (*do, does,* or *did*) before the subject. Notice that *do* takes the tense of the verb and the main verb is in its first principal part.

  Nathan *played* half a game with a sprained ankle.
  Did Nathan *play* half a game with a sprained ankle?

  He now *thinks* it was unwise to play with an injury.
  Does he now *think* it was unwise to play with an injury?

Wh Questions

(questions that ask for information using *who/whom/whose, which, what, when, where, why,* or *how*)

- When questioning the subject or something in the subject, do not use inverted order. Replace the word in question with an interrogative pronoun.

  Nathan scored the winning goal. → Who scored the winning goal? *(Nathan)*
  The game yesterday was his first game. → Which game was his first game? *(the game yesterday)*

- When questioning something in the complete predicate, use these three steps:
  1. Replace the word(s) in question with an interrogative pronoun.
  2. Move the interrogative pronoun before the subject.
  3. Follow one of the next three steps.
     - If there is an auxiliary, move the first auxiliary before the subject.

Original	Nathan's last game was played in Carrboro.
Step 1	Nathan's last game was played *where?*
Step 2	*Where* Nathan's last game was played?
Step 3	*Where* was Nathan's last game played?

Original	He was impressed with the playing field.
Step 1	He was impressed with *what?*
Step 2	*What* he was impressed with?
Step 3	*What* was he impressed with?

ESL Help 3A: Inverted Subject and Predicate (continued)

- If there is no auxiliary but there is a form of *be* (*am, is, are, was,* or *were*), move the form of *be* before the subject.

ORIGINAL	The name of Carrboro's team is the Patriots.
STEP 1	The name of Carrboro's team is *what?*
STEP 2	*What* the name of Carrboro's team is?
STEP 3	*What* is the name of Carrboro's team?

- If there is no auxiliary and no *be* verb form, insert the correct form of the auxiliary *do* (*do, does,* or *did*). Then move the form of *do* before the subject.

ORIGINAL	Carrboro's team possesses last year's state championship trophy.
STEP 1	Carrboro's team possesses *what?*
STEP 2	*What* Carrboro's team possesses?
STEP 3A	*What* Carrboro's team does possess?
STEP 3B	*What* does Carrboro's team possess?

Notice the changes when *do* is added.

possess	do possess	What do the teams possess?
possess*es*	do*es* possess	What does the team possess?
possess*ed*	*did* possess	What did the team possess?

The main verb (*possess*) has no ending; the auxiliary *do* must show the correct present or past tense form.

Name ______________________

ESL Help 3B: Exercise in Inverted Subject and Predicate

Change each sentence to a *yes/no* question. Remember to look at the verb tense for each sentence. Then use that same tense for the question.

1. The field trip to the zoo was a successful experience.

   ____

2. Everyone arrived on time for departure.

   ____

3. The students were excited about the day.

   ____

4. They sang songs during the entire bus trip.

   ____

5. They had been looking forward to this field trip all year.

   ____

Change each sentence to a *wh* question. Use the word in parentheses to form the question. Write the question and its short answer in the blank.

6. The buses arrived at the zoo around 10 A.M. (*when*)

   ____

7. Mr. Parker's group entered the zoo first. (*whose*)

   ____

8. The animal they liked most was the elephant. (*what*)

   ____

9. Mrs. Lewis led the most enthusiastic group. (*who*)

   ____

10. They showed their enthusiasm by cheering each time they saw a different animal. (*how*)

    ____

Name ______________________________

ESL Help 3C: Inverting Subjects and Verbs

When any of the following structures are placed at the front of a sentence, the subject goes after the first auxiliary of the independent clause. (If there is no auxiliary and no form of the main verb *be,* then the appropriate form of the auxiliary *do* is supplied—*do, does,* or *did.*)

adverbs of extent or degree	NON-INVERTED INVERTED	The **poet had become** *so* frustrated that he gave up writing for a year. *So* frustrated **had** the **poet become** that he gave up writing for a year.	
negative adverbs of frequency	NON-INVERTED INVERTED NON-INVERTED INVERTED	This **poet had** *rarely* **reached** a standstill in his writing. *Rarely* **had** this **poet reached** a standstill in his writing. **He had** *never before* **stopped** writing for any extended amount of time. *Never before* **had he stopped** writing for any extended amount of time.	Others: *never, hardly ever, seldom, scarcely*
other negative adverbs or adverbial phrases	NON-INVERTED INVERTED	**Writer's block had** *in no way* **hindered** him before. *In no way* **had writer's block hindered** him before.	Others: *in no case, under no circumstances, not until* [time], *not since* [time]
conditional clauses with *only*	NON-INVERTED INVERTED	The **poet would begin** writing again *only if he could write a poem in one month.* *Only if he could write a poem in one month* **would** the **poet begin** writing again.	
comparatives	NON-INVERTED INVERTED	**Many** of his new poems **are** *more interesting than his previous poetry.* *More interesting than his previous poetry* **are many** of his new poems.	

Participles with modifiers of location also cause inversion, but in this case the subject follows the complete verb.

NON-INVERTED	A small pot of flowers should be *sitting on the windowsill.*
INVERTED	*Sitting on the windowsill* should be a small pot of flowers.

Finally, if a location adverbial begins a sentence, inversion of subject and verb is optional. When inversion does occur, the subject follows the complete verb.

NON-INVERTED	The potted geraniums sat *under the sun's heat.*
	Under the sun's heat the potted geraniums sat.
INVERTED	*Under the sun's heat* sat the potted geraniums.

NON-INVERTED	The graceful swan floated *across the water.*
	Across the water the graceful swan floated.
INVERTED	*Across the water* floated the graceful swan.

Name ______________________

ESL Help 5A: How to Combine Sentences

There are seven common formulas for combining clauses. These formulas are listed in the right column, and they use the following abbreviations: IC (independent clause), DC (dependent clause), cc (coordinating conjunction), sc (subordinating conjunction), and ca (conjunctive adverb). Pay close attention to the punctuation included in each formula. Notice that because the subordinating conjunction introduces the dependent clause, these two elements are enclosed in parentheses as a unit.

EXAMPLE Jenna attended music class. Bill fixed the car.

	Sample Combinations	Formulas
1.	**IC , cc IC .** Jenna attended music class, but Bill fixed the car.	IC, cc IC.
2.	**(sc DC), IC .** While Bill fixed the car, Jenna attended music class.	(sc DC), IC.
3.	**IC (sc DC).** Bill fixed the car while Jenna attended music class.	IC (sc DC).
4.	**IC . ca , IC .** Bill fixed the car. Moreover, Jenna attended music class.	IC. ca, IC.
5.	**IC ; ca , IC .** Bill fixed the car; moreover, Jenna attended music class.	IC; ca, IC.
6.	**IC . IC , ca , IC continued .** Bill fixed the car. Jenna, however, attended music class.	IC. IC, ca, IC continued.
7.	**IC . IC , ca .** Bill fixed the car. Jenna attended music class, however.	IC. IC, ca.

Notice the correct placement of commas in the sentences above:

- Place the comma after an adverbial clause that comes at the beginning of a sentence.
- Do not use a comma before an adverbial clause that comes at the end of a sentence.

Name ______________________

ESL Help 5B: Exercise in How to Combine Sentences

The following chart shows meaning similarities among the three main types of connecting words.

Coordinating Conjunctions	Conjunctive Adverbs	Subordinating Conjunctions
and	besides, likewise, moreover, also	—
or	otherwise	—
so	accordingly, consequently, then, therefore, thus	because, since
but, yet	however, nevertheless, still	while, whereas, although, even though

Combine the following sentences using the formulas indicated. Rewrite each sentence, adding a correct connecting word and the correct punctuation. You may leave the words in parentheses out of the sentence.

EXAMPLE Brian borrowed his father's boat. (In addition,) Charles rented some water skis.

IC, cc IC. (Formula 1): Brian borrowed his father's boat, and Charles rented some water skis.

IC; ca, IC. (Formula 5): Brian borrowed his father's boat; moreover, Charles rented some water skis.

IC. ca, IC. (Formula 4): Brian borrowed his father's boat. Moreover, Charles rented some water skis.

1. Brian is muscular. (In contrast,) Charles is very thin.

IC, cc IC. (Formula 1): ______________________

IC. IC, ca, IC continued. (Formula 6): ______________________

IC (sc DC). (Formula 3): ______________________

2. Charles practices skiing often. (As a result,) He now has been chosen for the local ski team.

IC, cc IC. (Formula 1): ______________________

(sc DC), IC. (Formula 2): ______________________

IC; ca, IC. (Formula 5): ______________________

Name ______________________

ESL Help 5C: Multiword Prepositions

Fragments

Fragments created by multiple-word prepositions can be difficult to identify. When using one of these prepositions, make sure the phrase it introduces is attached to an independent clause.

according to
along with
as a result of
as compared with
as for
aside from
as well as
because of
contrary to
due to
except for
for the sake of
in contrast with
in favor of
in spite of
instead of
on account of
regardless of
relative to
up until
with respect to
with the exception of

Name ______________________

ESL Help 6A: Using *Some* Correctly

When a sentence containing the word *some* is made negative using the word *not, some* is replaced with *any.* Replace the words in the left column with the words in the right column when making a sentence negative using the word *not.*

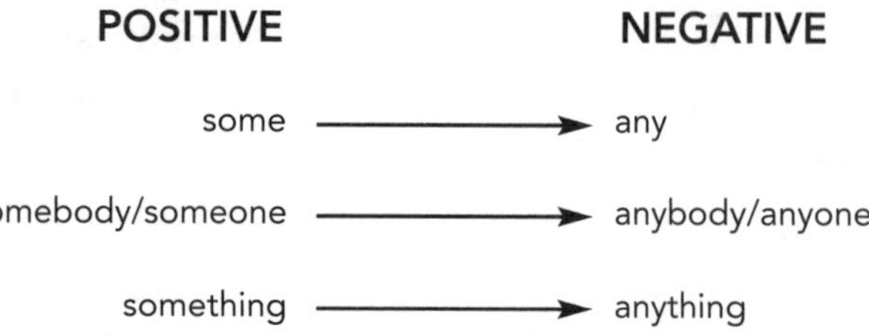

POSITIVE
NEGATIVE
some
any
somebody/someone
anybody/anyone
something
anything

EXAMPLES Oscar wants *some* string for his kite.
Oscar does *not* want *any* string for his kite.

Mark asked *somebody/someone* to volunteer.
Mark did *not* ask *anybody/anyone* to volunteer.

The teacher needed *something* to tell her students.
The teacher did*n't* need *anything* to tell her students.

To make the sentence negative without using the word *not,* use a word that already has a negative meaning.

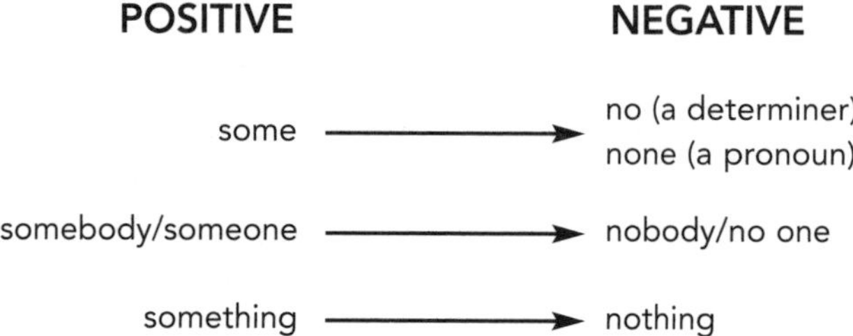

POSITIVE
NEGATIVE
some
no (a determiner)
none (a pronoun)
somebody/someone
nobody/no one
something
nothing

EXAMPLES Oscar wants *some* string for his kite.
Oscar wants *no* string for his kite.

The famous artist painted *some* of the pictures in the exhibit.
The famous artist painted *none* of the pictures in the exhibit.

Somebody/Someone has volunteered for the project.
Nobody/No one has volunteered for the project.

The teacher needed *something* to tell her students.
The teacher needed *nothing* to tell her students.

Name ______________________________

ESL Help 6B: Exercise in Using *Some* Correctly

Read the sentences containing the word *some*. Make each sentence negative by using *not* along with *any, anybody/anyone,* or *anything.*

1. Christian attended a birthday party for someone.

   ____

2. He told somebody about the party.

   ____

3. Christian took someone with him to the party.

   ____

4. While he was at the party, he ate something.

   ____

5. The honored guest opened some gifts.

   ____

Read the sentences containing the word *some*. Make each sentence negative by using *no, none, nobody/no one,* or *nothing.*

6. Some gifts were wrapped in bright paper.

   ____

7. Somebody arrived late to the party.

   ____

8. After the opening of the gifts, someone led the group in games.

   ____

9 The hostess announced something about prizes to be given.

   ____

10. Some of the guests went home with multiple prizes.

   ____

Name________________________________

ESL Help 7A: Using the Auxiliary *Do* Correctly

Do is generally used in three ways:

1. *Do* is used to add emphasis.
   - Add the correct form of the auxiliary *do* only if the clause does not already have an auxiliary or a *be* verb.

     PRESENT TENSE | *does* (third-person singular subjects)
do (all other subjects)

     PAST TENSE | *did* (all subjects)

     WRONG | Maria *does can* ride a unicycle.

     RIGHT | Maria *can* ride a unicycle.

     WRONG | Maria's brother Bob *did was* her teacher.

     RIGHT | Maria's brother Bob *was* her teacher.

   - Place *do* before the main verb. Notice that *do* takes the tense of the verb.

     In the morning Maria *rides* to school.
     In the morning Maria *does ride* to school.

     Her friends *liked* to watch her.
     Her friends *did like* to watch her.

     In a sentence that repeats information, the part that contains repeated information is often omitted.

     When it rained, Bob told Maria that she should not walk to school, but she *did*. (walk to school)
     Bob thought that Maria would arrive wet and muddy, but she *did* not. (arrive wet and muddy)

   - Place the stress, or loudness, on *do* for oral emphasis.

     She <u>*did*</u> *prove* that she could stay dry.
     Her friends <u>*do*</u> *believe* that Maria is wonderful.

2. *Do* is used to help make a sentence negative.
   - Add the correct form of the auxiliary *do* only if the clause does not already have an auxiliary or a *be* verb.

     WRONG | Some people *do* not *may like* to pay taxes.

     RIGHT | Some people *may* not *like* to pay taxes.

     WRONG | Some claim that taxes *do* not *be* fair.

     RIGHT | Some claim that taxes *are* not fair.

   - Place *not* between *do* and the main verb. Notice that *do* takes the tense of the verb.

     Hannah *naps* in the afternoon.
     Hannah *does* not *nap* in the afternoon.

     Alex *painted* his room bright red.
     Alex *did* not *paint* his room bright red.

3. *Do* is used to help ask a question.

   Some questions require the use of *do*. Notice again that *do* takes the tense of the verb.

     Hannah has a baby sister.
     What *does* Hannah *have?*

     Alex wanted a new video game.
     Did Alex *want* a new video game?

Name ________________________________

ESL Help 7B: Verb Tenses

When speaking or writing about events before or after your current situation, use different tenses based on which tense you are already using for general reference.

- If you are speaking or writing from a present-tense perspective, refer to previous events by using the present perfect and to events that will happen later by using the future.

PRESENT	Scott *works* at Pizza Palace.
PRESENT PERFECT	He *has worked* there every week this summer.
FUTURE	He *will work* there on Friday night.

- If you are speaking or writing from a past-tense perspective, refer to previous events by using the past perfect and to events that happen later by using the simple past again.

PAST	Scott cautiously *placed* the pizza into the oven.
PAST PERFECT	Earlier he *had* carefully *added* the correct toppings.
PAST	At closing time he *scrubbed* the floor.

- If you are speaking or writing from a future-tense perspective, refer to previous events by using the future perfect and to events that happen later by using the future again.

FUTURE	It *will take* almost two hours to clean the kitchen.
FUTURE PERFECT	By the end of the summer, he *will have gotten* faster at cleaning.
FUTURE	Scott *will* definitely *be* glad when school starts again.

Name________________________________

ESL Help 7c: Tense Check

Present Perfect

Use the present perfect tense when referring to something completed (finished) during the time period you are in or when referring to something that has continued until the present moment.

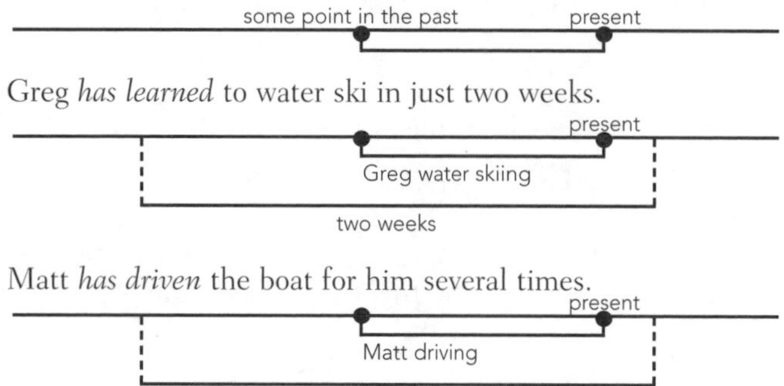

Greg *has learned* to water ski in just two weeks.

Matt *has driven* the boat for him several times.

Past Perfect

Use the past perfect tense when referring to *X*, the first of two points in past time.

Before Tim heard about the skiing, he *had* (already) *asked* his dad whether he could go sometime.

Tim *had* already *swum* for a while before his dad arrived.

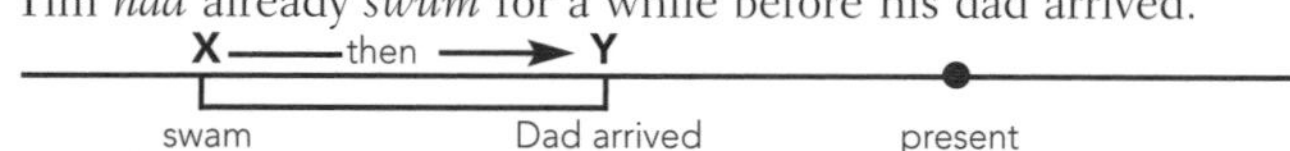

Note: In informal usage, the past tense sometimes substitutes for the past perfect when the time relationships are clear.

Tim *swam* in the lake for a while *before* his dad arrived.

Before is sufficient to make the time relationship clear.

Future Perfect

Use the future perfect tense when referring to X, the first of two points in future time. In this case the perfect tense emphasizes that something happens before another future time or event.

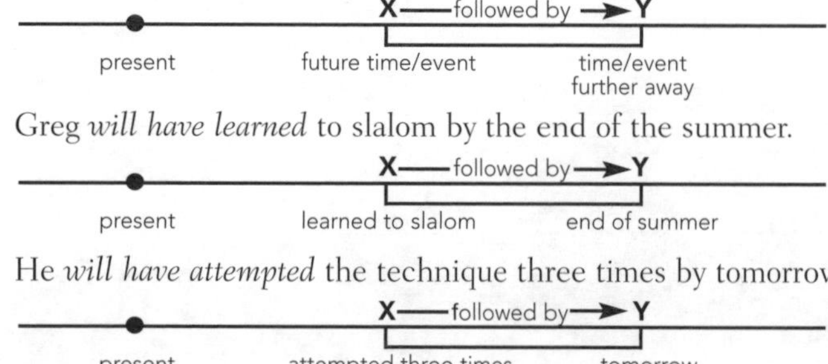

Greg *will have learned* to slalom by the end of the summer.

He *will have attempted* the technique three times by tomorrow.

Name ____________________

ESL Help 7D: How to Use English Tense Forms

In this listing, the tenses are grouped according to grammatical *aspects*—first the *simple* tenses, then the *perfect* tenses, then the *progressive* tenses, and last the *perfect progressive* tenses. For each individual tense, the more frequent uses appear first. Therefore, for an overview you can read just the first two or three uses of each tense. (If four or more uses are listed, read the first three.) For more detail about a tense, you can consult the rest of the list. Each of the uses has at least one example sentence.

The Simple Tenses—Past, Present, and Future

In all the simple tenses, each event is seen as complete in itself. There is no allowance for future development or change. Consider the difference between the simple present and the present progressive.

> Joshua *plays* piano for Sunday School. (*Simple present expressing habitual action not expected to change.*)
> Joshua *is playing* piano for Sunday School. (*Present progressive indicating that the activity may be temporary, allowing for change.*)

1. **Simple Past:** The simple past refers to events and situations as completed wholes that are somehow remote from the present. The remoteness can be that of time (historical distance), or it can refer to an event's being complete at last, as in just finishing a big project.

   - A single, completed event or action:

     > The couple *had* a garden wedding.

   - Habitual/customary action or event in the past:

     > I *taught* three days a week last semester.

   - A state in the past:

     > The dog *appeared* friendly.
     > Last month some people *thought* the rain would never stop.

   - An event with duration in the past but completed before the present:

     > Gary *attended* college for eight years.

   - Contrary-to-fact condition in the dependent clause (referring to present time and considered the present tense, subjunctive mood):

     > If he really *wanted* to win, he would not arrive late for the game.

   - Social distancing for politeness:

     > *Did* you *wish* to sign the guest book?

2. **Simple Present:** In addition to being a complete whole, simple present also contains the idea of immediate factuality. The event or state is true or factual right now. (Note that present states are expressed in the simple present, but present actions are almost always reported in the present progressive.)

   - Habitual or customary action in the present:

     > He *calls* from the office every day.

   - General timeless truths, such as physical laws:

     > Jesus Christ *is* the same, yesterday, today, and forever.
     > Most people *believe* the earth to be round.

- Present states, with *be* and other stative verbs:

  The sunset *is* unbelievably beautiful.
  The car *seems* sluggish.
  He *prefers* root beer sherbet.

- Future scheduled events, usually with a future-time adverbial:

  My aunt's plane *arrives* at 3:40 Saturday afternoon.

- Future time in dependent adverbial clauses of time or condition (the main clause contains a future-tense verb):

  When the doors *open,* seats will be available on a first-come basis.
  If I *work* hard now, I will be free for the weekend.

- Present event or action, usually in sporting events or how-to demonstrations:

  Mia *gets* a breakaway, and now she *scores* a goal!
  Then you *braid* all three ribbons together.

- Speech acts in process, the action being accomplished in the speaking of it:

  Now I *give* you my blessing.

- Conversational historical present, referring to certain past events vividly in oral narration:

  After the accident we were fearing the worst—when both girls *climb* out of the car and *yell,* "We're fine!"

3. **Simple Future:** Simple future sees events as conceptualized wholes, using *will* to express certainty or strong prediction.

- An action expected at some definite future time:

  No one *will come* to work on July 4.

- A future habitual action:

  After today I *will* not *eat* dessert.

- A future state:

  By next year they *will have* nine grandchildren.

- Result predicted in an independent clause accompanied by a future-time condition:

  If the rain doesn't stop, the building project *will be* behind schedule.

The Perfect Tenses—Past, Present, and Future

The perfect tenses express prior actions or states in relation to some other event or time. The speaker refers to a time that is earlier than the main time being expressed.

1. **Past Perfect:** Past perfect is used when needed to show that an event occurred before something else in the past. Sometimes when the time reference is clear because of a word, such as *after,* beginning a time clause, simple past rather than past perfect is used to express prior action in the past. However, the more formal the context, the more likely the past perfect will be used even when the time is already clear.

- An action completed in the past prior to some other past event or time:

  She *had left* for the mall before I could give her the message.

- Contrary-to-fact condition in the dependent clause (referring to past time and considered the past tense, subjunctive mood):

  If the mayor *had made* that speech yesterday, I would have voted differently.

2. **Present Perfect:** In general, the present perfect deals with an action or state that began in the past and has continued up to the present (or very close to the present) or with an action that has continuing effects in the present. If a time period is named with the present perfect, it must be a time period that the speaker is presently in.
   - An action or state that began in the past and continues into the present:

     I *have attended* church all my life.
   - A very recently completed action, often with *just:*

     He *has* just *left*.
   - An action that took place at an unspecified earlier time but with current relevance:

     They *have* already *purchased* their tickets.
   - An action that occurred over a prior time period and is already complete at the moment of speaking:

     The stock market *has risen* several points in the last two months.
   - With verbs expressing prior action in certain dependent clauses of time or condition:

     When you *have finished* your meal, you may leave the table.
3. **Future Perfect:** The future perfect expresses prior time in relation to a named event or time in the future.
   - A future action that will be completed before a specified future time:

     School *will have ended* by the time you get this letter.
   - A state or accomplishment that will be completed before a specified future event or time:

     By next May he *will have taught* thirty-eight years.

The Progressive Tenses—Past, Present, and Future

The progressive aspect expresses an action or situation that is incomplete, ongoing, or temporary. The progressive cannot be used for generic statements (general truths) but only for specific events.

1. **Past Progressive:** Statements with the past progressive focus on an action as ongoing in the past—often as being in progress when something else happened.
   - An action in progress at a specified time in the past:

     The potatoes *were boiling* over when I went to check them.
   - Past action that provides the frame for some other event that is usually stated in the simple past:

     I *was* busily *typing* when my boss stopped by.
   - A repeated past action:

     Margaret *was taking* phone calls the whole time.

- Social distancing for politeness (combining the remoteness of the past tense and the tentativeness of the progressive):

  I *was hoping* that you could possibly leave early.

2. **Present Progressive:** The most important use of the present progressive is to express ongoing action in the present time. If English treats a verb as an action verb (rather than a verb that expresses a state or situation), then for present time it must be in the present progressive tense. (State verbs express present time by using the simple present tense.)

   "I *have* twin sons [*state verb*], and they *are* continually *entertaining* each other [*action verb*]."

   - Action in progress in the present or in the present time period:

     At present he *is swimming* in the pool outdoors.

   - A temporary situation in the present:

     I'*m taking* five subjects this semester.

   - Repeated actions in the present:

     Joyce *is working* for her father this month.

   - A future planned event or action, usually with a future-time adverbial:

     Todd and Drew *are leaving* for France in a week.

   - A negative emotional comment on a present habit, usually with the frequency adverbs *always, constantly,* or *forever:*

     That cat *is forever stalking* chipmunks and birds in our yard.

3. **Future Progressive:** The future progressive combines future time with the ongoing nature of the progressive.

   - An action that will be in progress at a specified time in the future:

     Mason *will be playing* in his first concert this evening.

   - Duration of a future action:

     I *will be attending* two games a week until soccer season ends.

The Perfect Progressive Tenses—Past, Present, and Future

These tenses include both the "prior" meaning of the perfect aspect and the "incomplete" meaning of the progressive aspect. They show that one event is in progress until or immediately before another time or event. Sentences with a perfect progressive verb often include an adverbial expression of duration, such as "for three days" or "since Thursday."

1. **Past Perfect Progressive:** The past perfect progressive speaks of an action in progress before another event or time in the past.

   - An action that took place over a period of time in the past before some other past event or time:

     Kate *had been enjoying* herself so much that she forgot about the time.

   - A past action in progress that was interrupted or ended by a more recent action:

     We *had been roasting* hot dogs, but at Grant's suggestion we got out the marshmallows.

ESL Help 7D: How to Use English Tense Forms (continued)

2. **Present Perfect Progressive:** A statement with a present perfect progressive verb tells about an action or state in progress up to the present time. It may or may not continue into the future.
   - A habitual action or a state that began in the past and continues up to the present (and possibly into the future):

     The yearbook staff *have been proofreading* this year's annual.
     He *has been saying* for some time that he'd like to go.
   - An action in progress and not yet completed:

     This week I *have been sleeping* really well.
3. **Future Perfect Progressive:** The future perfect progressive expresses action in progress up to a specified time in the future or through that time.
   - Action in progress in the present that will continue in the future through or until a specific time:

     By midnight I *will have been driving* for twelve hours straight.
   - Habitual action that will continue through or until a specific time:

     On Friday we *will have been living* here for six months.

Name________________________________

ESL Help 7E: Active and Passive

Active voice is usually the better voice to use, especially in writing. However, as a general rule, writers rely on passive voice when one of the following is true.

1. The doer of the action is redundant or easy to supply.

   Cats *are known* to be very independent. *(cat owners/people in general)*

2. The doer of the action is unknown.

   A goal *was scored* in the fourth quarter. *(unidentified player)*

3. The doer of the action is very general.

   Liver and onions *is* not particularly *known* for its widespread appeal. *(people who dislike liver)*

4. The speaker/writer is being tactful about others.

   The clothes *were strewn* about the dormitory room. *(college student)*

5. The speaker is being evasive about oneself or one's group.

   We had good intentions, but somehow the work *wasn't finished* on time. *(we)*

In passive sentences, the doer of the action is often not mentioned at all. However, there are three main instances in which the doer of the action is almost always named.

1. The doer of the action is new information.

   The power outage *was triggered* by an inquisitive squirrel. *(squirrel)*

2. The doer of the action is nonhuman.

   The camera's malfunction *was caused* by weak batteries. *(batteries)*

3. The doer of the action is a well-known person.

   In the United States the interstate highway system *was initiated* by Dwight D. Eisenhower. *(President Eisenhower)*

Name ____________________

ESL Help 7F: Exercise in Active and Passive

Change one sentence or part of one sentence in each paragraph so that the new portion uses the passive voice instead of active voice. Use the principle in parentheses as a guide to know which sentence to change. Write the new sentence with passive voice in the blank.

Around 1864 a slave woman bore a son, George Washington Carver, who was probably most famous for his research with peanuts. He began life as a slave in Diamond Grove, Missouri, on a plantation owned by Moses Carver. Hence, "George Washington" gained the last name of Carver, a common practice in the days of slavery.

(The doer of the action is redundant or easy to supply.)

____

____

Carver never knew his father, who had died before Carver's birth, and his mother was a kidnap victim of slave raiders while Carver was still an infant. Being a frail child, Carver served with the household staff, probably helping with the gardening. As a result, he gained a keen interest in plants. Because no one provided a school for African Americans in Diamond Grove, the plantation owners tutored young Carver in reading and writing.

(The writer wants to be tactful about slaves not having a school.)

____

____

Even though Carver lacked a formal education, he soon gained a reputation for being a "healer" of sick plants. Carver's frailty actually helped him. His not having to work in the fields allowed him time to roam the woods and learn about the local vegetation.

(The doer of the action is nonhuman.)

____

____

During the next several years, Carver moved to other towns in Missouri and Kansas while trying to get an education. In 1890 he finally began Simpson College in Indianola, Iowa, and later transferred to Iowa State Agricultural College. His initial fields of study were painting and piano, but a teacher later directed him toward agriculture.

(The doer of the action is redundant or easy to supply.)

____

____

ESL Help 7F: Exercise in Active and Passive (continued)

After Carver completed both his bachelor's and master's degrees, Booker T. Washington asked him to teach at Alabama's Tuskegee Institute. As well as teaching his students to understand the basics of nature, Carver taught them to be gentle and to promote education for the common man.

(The doer of the action is a well-known person.)

____

____

In his lifetime Carver created over three hundred products from peanuts, including such items as soap, ink, and face powder. He also made numerous products from both sweet potatoes and pecans. These crops helped give the South an alternative to cotton.

(The doer of the action is nonhuman.)

____

____

After receiving many prestigious honors, Carver died in 1943. In addition to these honors, he left a valuable legacy of work with interracial relations and the YMCA. In 1994 Iowa State posthumously awarded Carver the degree Doctor of Humane Letters, an honor he would have especially appreciated.

(The doer of the action is new information.)

____

____

Name ____________________

ESL Help 10: Showing Comparison

In a sense, each of the four major parts of speech can be compared, each one with its own comparative sentence pattern. Here are the patterns along with two sample sentences for each. (Symbols and words in parentheses may be omitted. *LV* stands for linking verb, and *Vb* refers to the same verb as appears in the main clause.)

ADJECTIVE | **Noun^1 LV *more/less* Adj *than* Noun^2 (Vb/*does*)**

Florida seems *more desirable* for a vacation than Kansas (seems/does).

Lake Hartwell is *larger* than Lake Robinson (is).

The second adjective example above and the second adverb example below show that some adjectives and adverbs are compared with the suffix *er* instead of with the word *more*.

ADVERB | **Noun^1 Verb *more/less* Adv *than* Noun^2 (Vb/*does*)**

Catherine skis *less often* than Virginia (skis/does).

Kent runs *faster* than Lane (runs/does).

NOUN | **Noun^1 Verb *more/less* Noun *than* Noun^2 (Vb/*does*)**

Leah washes *more dishes* than Serena (washes/does).

My savings account makes *less interest* than yours (makes/does).

VERB | **Noun^1 Verb *more/less* *than* Noun^2 (Vb/*does*)**

Roger *eats less* than Rebecca (eats/does).

The baby *sleeps more* than her older sister (sleeps/does).

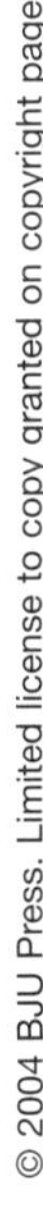

Name________________________________

ESL Help 12A: The Most Common Punctuation Marks in English

Mark	Name	Example
.	period	Kelli works in a crafts store**.**
!	exclamation point	Making certain crafts can be hazardous**!**
?	question mark	Why would making crafts be dangerous**?**
,	comma	Hot glue**,** nails**,** and metal are just a few of the possible dangers.
( )	parentheses	Kelli will attempt any kind of project **(**within reason**)**.
'	apostrophe	She**'**s always looking for new ideas.
" "	quotation marks	Often people will ask her, **"**How did you make that?**"**
;	semicolon	Sometimes her projects take several hours**;** they can even take days.
:	colon	Kelli does have a favorite project**:** making magnolia blossoms from balloons.

Name________________________________

ESL Help 12B: Spacing of Punctuation

If you speak a language with a non-Roman writing system, you probably need to be especially careful about the spacing of your English punctuation.

- End punctuation (a period, a question mark, or an exclamation point) follows immediately after the last word of the sentence. When using a word processor or a computer, leave one blank space before the next sentence. When writing or using a typewriter, leave two blank spaces before the next sentence.

WRONG	The snowcapped mountains glistened in the bright sunshine .
RIGHT	The snowcapped mountains glistened in the bright sunshine.

- Most punctuation inside the sentence (a comma, a semicolon, or a colon) has no space before it and one space after it.

WRONG	When the hikers reached the top of the mountain , they rested for an hour.
RIGHT	When the hikers reached the top of the mountain, they rested for an hour.

- Parentheses (like these) "hug" the words they enclose, and so do quotation marks.
- A hyphen comes inside a word, with no spaces (e.g., *open-ended*). A dash—which is longer—comes between words, with no spaces. (A dash can also be typed with two unspaced hyphens--like this.)

A few special uses, such as the unspaced colon between a chapter and verse in Bible references (e.g., I John 1:9), are noted in your student worktext.

Name________________________________

ESL Help 12c: Cumulative and Coordinate Adjectives

Adjectives that come from different meaning categories are called **cumulative adjectives** because they build on one another. They are usually placed in a specific order before the noun. (See ESL Help 2A for more information about the positions of adjectives.)

EXAMPLES My *faded old* couch looked out of place with the *new leather* chair.
The rabbit nibbled on the *leafy green* lettuce.

Sometimes speakers of English may use two descriptive adjectives from the same meaning category (e.g., two evaluative words, two condition words, etc.). When two such adjectives from the same category have similar meanings, they are usually separated with a comma. These adjectives are called **coordinate adjectives.** There is never a comma between a determiner and another adjective. Also, there is never a comma between a modifying noun and another adjective.

EXAMPLES The *energetic, enthusiastic* cleaning lady attacked the *dirty, cluttered* room.
The *frisky, playful* kitten got entangled in the lacy curtain.

Look at the adjectives in italics. If the adjectives are from the same meaning category, write *coordinate* in the blank and add a comma between the adjectives. If the adjectives are from different meaning categories, write *cumulative* in the blank.

________________ 1. My relatives live in an *old Victorian* house in Illinois.

________________ 2. Their *large shady* yard is very inviting.

________________ 3. The smallness of the town fosters a *close-knit helpful* community.

________________ 4. Many families live all their lives in this *quaint picturesque* town.

________________ 5. The town has only *one neighborhood grocery* store.

________________ 6. The *friendly considerate* employees there always greet you by name.

________________ 7. The *dilapidated brick* schoolhouse has been replaced by a new consolidated one.

________________ 8. Now students come from *four small* towns to attend.

________________ 9. The students are offered *many extracurricular* activities.

________________ 10. The *mile-long oval* track is especially nice.

Name ________________________________

ESL Help 13: Direct and Indirect Quotations

Because a direct quotation reports the exact words of the speaker, pronouns and words for time and place are naturally used from the point of view of the speaker. However, an indirect quotation uses pronouns, tense, and time/place words from the point of view of the reporter.

Direct Quotation	The pastor spoke enthusiastically, "*Rejoice* with *me*. *We are* seeing God's blessings."
Indirect Quotation	The pastor told *us* to rejoice with *him* because *we were* seeing God's blessings.

Many questions require inversion of the subject and the first auxiliary. (See p. 151 for a list of auxiliaries.) However, in an indirect *yes/no* question, no question inversion should be used because the sentence is not really a question.

Direct Question	The choir director asked, "*Would you like* to sing a solo Sunday?"
Indirect Question	The choir director asked whether *I would like* to sing a solo Sunday.

Notice that the word *whether* (or, informally, *if*) begins an indirect *yes/no* question. No question mark is used.

Similarly, indirect *wh* questions use normal subject-verb order, not question inversion.

Direct Question	He also asked, "What kind of accompaniment *would you like?*"
Indirect Question	He also asked what kind of accompaniment *I would like.*

Name ____________________

ESL Help 15: Types of Dictionaries

You have four types of dictionaries to help you: monolingual for native English speakers, monolingual for non-native English speakers, monolingual in your native language, and bilingual. Listed below are descriptions of the dictionaries and some advantages and disadvantages of using each type in your classes and for your homework. (*Mono-* means *one; bi-* means *two;* and *-lingual* means *language.*)

Dictionary	Description	Advantages	Disadvantages
Monolingual for native English speakers	This dictionary is the most common English dictionary. It uses only English.	This dictionary allows you to use English to define new words in English.	If you have advanced English ability, this dictionary will help you even more. If you do not have advanced English ability, this dictionary may be frustrating.
Monolingual for non-native English speakers (ESL dictionary)	This dictionary uses only English, but the English is easier. Also, it contains many useful sections for the ESL learner.	This dictionary is very helpful for learning English vocabulary, grammar, and usage. Also, it helps you to use English to learn more English.	This dictionary may have fewer words. Also, you will probably need to order it.
Monolingual in your native language	This dictionary is entirely in your native language. You use this when you use only your own language.	You can understand this dictionary very well.	This dictionary does not help you with learning English or doing your English homework.
Bilingual: English plus your native language	This dictionary uses one language to translate words to or from the other language.	This dictionary is helpful if you know very little English.	You can become too dependent on the dictionary and not really learn the English words.

Name ________________________________

Chapter 2: Using Parts of Speech

Practice A

In the first blank identify each italicized noun as count *(C)* or noncount *(N)* and in the second blank identify each italicized pronoun as demonstrative *(D)* or relative *(R).*

______ ______ 1. Most people anticipate *vacations* as fun and exciting, but sometimes *that* isn't the case.

______ ______ 2. Last Christmas, for example, a *couple* visited Paris, *which* is particularly famous for the Eiffel Tower.

______ ______ 3. After an earlier *visit* to the Palace of Versailles, the two, *who* were enjoying their first trip abroad, wanted to close out the day at the Tower.

______ ______ 4. Despite the rainy, gray day's not lending itself to panoramic *sightseeing*, they determined to ascend the famed icon, *whatever* the outcome.

______ ______ 5. The time spent standing in line during a soggy *rain* didn't dampen their spirits at all, and *those* around them didn't seem to mind either.

Practice B

Identify each italicized word as adjective *(Adj)*, adverb *(Adv)*, or preposition *(Prep).*

______ ______ 6. Finally, the two were standing on the Tower, peering *out* at the *ethereal* scene.

______ ______ 7. The majesty of the *foggy* city lay *below*.

______ ______ 8. *After* gazing for several minutes, they departed and headed for the *nearby* subway.

______ ______ 9. They boarded *amidst* a crowd and settled *in* for a trip to the outskirts of Paris.

______ ______ 10. It was *there* that the *unexpected* incident occurred.

Practice C

Underline each coordinating conjunction once and each subordinating conjunction twice.

11. Just as the train departed, the husband felt his pocket, realizing it was empty.

12. He had been pickpocketed while he was boarding the train.

13. At the next station, they disembarked, retraced their steps, and found a police officer to report the incident to.

14. The police officer questioned the couple in his broken English but gave them little hope of ever retrieving the money, passport, and credit card.

15. Although the spending money was a bit sparse, nothing could destroy their enjoyment of the trip.

Name ______________________

Chapter 3A: Sentences

Practice A

Identify each sentence as *declarative, interrogative, imperative,* or *exclamatory.* Place an appropriate punctuation mark at the end of each sentence.

__________ 1. Do you know what an idiom is

__________ 2. It is generally a group of words, such as *fly off the handle,* whose meaning cannot be derived from the literal meanings of the individual words

__________ 3. Many idioms actually get their derivations from a similar source, like the use of nautical terms

__________ 4. "I passed that history quiz *with flying colors*"

__________ 5. Do you think the speaker realized that when passing each other, sailing ships identify themselves by their colors or flags

Practice B

Underline each simple subject once and each simple predicate twice.

6. All of us have experienced being *under the weather* at various times.
7. During rough weather ship passengers sometimes become seasick and go below deck for shelter from the storm and violent rocking.
8. These same passengers might not be too interested in getting *a square meal.*
9. However, most of us thoroughly enjoy having such a meal.
10. Old British warships served two very sparse meals, but the third one was larger, requiring a square tray to hold it.

Practice C

Write a sentence of the kind indicated in parentheses about the suggested idiom.

11. Toe the line *(interrogative)*

12. Round robin *(exclamatory)*

13. Aboveboard *(imperative)*

14. Stem to stern *(imperative)*

15. Clean bill of health *(declarative)*

Name ____________________

Chapter 3B: Sentence Patterns

Practice A

Label the sentence patterns *S-TrV-DO, S-TrV-IO-DO,* or *S-TrV-DO-OC.*

1. Most English courses include the study of literature.
2. Teachers often assign students works by American authors, such as Twain, Hawthorne, and Melville.
3. What student doesn't enjoy Huckleberry Finn's adventures?
4. An assignment in Shakespeare might make a student nervous about the old-fashioned language.
5. Other students call Shakespeare their favorite author.

Practice B

Label the sentence patterns *S-LV-PN, S-LV-PA,* or *S-be-Advl.* If the adverbial is a prepositional phrase, underline it.

6. A study of English grammar is surprisingly helpful.
7. Some students even become scholars of the language.
8. The mastery of grammar and usage may seem unnecessary, but it can be of great value to a writer.
9. Knowing whether to say "he doesn't" or "he don't" is an important skill.
10. A writer's strength may be in his knowledge of the language.

Practice C

Rewrite each item as a sentence with the sentence pattern indicated in parentheses.

11. Elementary schools offer little choice in courses. *(S-LV-PA)*

    ____

12. High schools, however, usually allow some options for a student. *(S-TrV-IO-DO)*

    ____

13. Some subjects are not options but requirements for all students at the school. *(S-TrV-DO-OC)*

    ____

14. A typical high school offers history, math, and science among its courses. *(S-be-Advl)*

    ____

15. Schools almost always require an English class too. *(S-LV-PN)*

    ____

Name ________________________________

Chapter 4A: Phrases

Practice A

Identify each italicized phrase as a verbal phrase *(V)*, a prepositional phrase *(P)*, or an appositive phrase *(A)*.

_______ 1. The TGV *(pronounced tay jay vay)* is a high-speed train in France connecting major cities.

_______ 2. *Living up to its reputation,* the train travels at speeds of 185 mph and faster.

_______ 3. *Despite the speed,* the inside of the train is as quiet as a whisper.

_______ 4. This bullet train, *another name for the TGV,* leaves approximately every half an hour from the station.

_______ 5. In fact, at times it is faster *to take the TGV* than it is to fly.

Practice B

Identify each italicized phrase as a gerund phrase *(Ger)*, a participial phrase *(Part)*, or an infinitive phrase *(Inf)*.

_______ 6. *Boarding the train,* one finds storage for luggage immediately inside the door.

_______ 7. A passenger must check his ticket *to see if his assignment is to the upper or lower level.*

_______ 8. *Once settled,* he waits quietly for the train's departure.

_______ 9. *Leaving the station* is done slowly; the train gradually picks up speed once outside the city.

_______ 10. In *keeping with the French culture,* no one speaks loudly, if at all.

Practice C

Identify each italicized phrase as a participial phrase *(Part)* or an absolute phrase *(Abs)*.

_______ 11. Bullet trains are not new, *having originated in Japan in 1964.*

_______ 12. *Safety being a concern to some,* passengers should be encouraged to know these trains are extremely safe.

_______ 13. In fact, the Japanese Shinkansen Line has gone over one billion kilometers, *having never been derailed.*

_______ 14. *The train having such a good safety record,* over three billion passengers have ridden this line.

_______ 15. It seems that many big cities in the United States, *characterized by snarled traffic jams,* could profit from such a train.

Name______________________________

Chapter 4B: Verbals

Practice A

Place parentheses around each participial phrase. Underline each present participle once and each past participle twice.

1. Puppets, enjoyed by both adults and children, have existed for centuries.
2. Seventeenth-century Holland was entertained by *Jan Klaasen en Katrijn,* better known in other places as Punch and Judy.
3. India employs an interesting twist to its puppets, making the face color of the puppets reveal their character: orange is usually a woman, black is a bad person, and green is a hero.
4. Turkey has a famous gypsy puppet, Karagoz, characterized by a black beard and turban.
5. However, one particular puppet, Guignol, originating in France, has achieved worldwide popularity and influence.

Practice B

Underline each gerund phrase and identify its function as subject *(S)*, direct object *(DO)*, predicate noun *(PN)*, object of the preposition *(OP)*, or appositive *(App)*.

_______ 6. At first making puppets was just a sideline for Guignol's creator, Laurent Mourguet.

_______ 7. Mourguet, being a professional tooth puller, wanted a gimmick to attract patients. The solution was puppeteering.

_______ 8. One of his early successes involved creating the puppet Gnafron (from *gnaffre,* meaning shoemaker), who was dressed in a top hat and leather apron.

_______ 9. Mourguet's avocation, designing puppets, soon became his passion.

_______ 10. In the process of sculpturing Guignol, Mourguet dressed him in a gold-buttoned brown jacket, red bow tie, and leather hat sporting earflaps.

Practice C

Rewrite each sentence to incorporate at least one infinitive phrase.

11. To this day no one knows why Mourguet chose the name of Guignol.

____

____

12. Guignol favors the underdog, especially the poor, often to the detriment of local landlords or policemen.

____

____

13. Guignol is a regular participant in all the shows.

____

____

14. Guignol is one of the participants in the *Moisson d'Avril,* a puppet festival hosted by Lyon, France, each April.

____

____

15. Truly Guignol has appealed to many throughout the years.

____

____

Name______________________________

Chapter 5A: Clauses

Practice A

Place parentheses around each noun clause and identify its function as subject *(S)*, predicate noun *(PN)*, direct object *(DO)*, indirect object *(IO)*, object of preposition *(OP)*, or appositive *(App)*.

______ 1. A present-day visitor, wandering the streets of Perouges, France, might be surprised to learn that Perouges dates back to at least the thirteenth century.

______ 2. Whether it gives a truly historic picture of an old feudal village is not certain, but it's quite impressive to a casual tourist.

______ 3. The person, whoever he or she might have been, who configured the narrow cobblestone streets was a great architect.

______ 4. A common conclusion is that these streets would quickly destroy the suspension of cars and trucks today.

______ 5. Nevertheless, for whoever is interested, the streets, along with the flower boxes on windowsills and porch stoops, give a certain picturesque quaintness to the town.

Practice B

Place parentheses around each dependent clause and identify it as adjectival *(Adj)* or adverbial *(Adv)*.

______ 6. The entire town, which is surrounded by fortress-like walls, gives the appearance of strength.

______ 7. When one approaches the town, the first thing noticed is two entrances with huge gates; one pair was almost totally destroyed during a siege in 1468.

______ 8. Although the gates were damaged in that siege, the town did not fall.

______ 9. Artisans, many who are continuing with the trade of their ancestors, can be found throwing pottery, weaving cloth, or baking bread.

______ 10. The village square, which is called *Place de Tilleul,* is named for a lime tree.

Practice C

Identify each sentence as simple *(S)*, compound *(Cd)*, complex *(Cx)*, or compound-complex *(Cd-Cx)*.

______ 11. One of the most interesting sights is the old feudal church, which is directly inside one of the gates.

______ 12. At the front of the church is a statue of Saint George, the dragon slayer.

______ 13. The windows, which are a part of the exterior village walls, were designed as long vertical slits; these slits allowed archers to shoot at enemies through the windows.

______ 14. In spite of the burning candles, the interior was cold and lifeless, and a visitor would have no desire to linger there.

______ 15. This village, located high on a hill just twenty-one miles from Lyon, is a great place to visit.

Name ______________________

Chapter 5B: Avoiding Sentence Errors

Practice A

Identify each group of words as a sentence *(S)* or a fragment *(F)*.

______ 1. Most high-school seniors either dread or greatly anticipate the thought of graduating.

______ 2. They as well as their parents looking forward to graduation and future opportunities.

______ 3. If a student is a Christian, he must prayerfully consider the Lord's will for his life.

______ 4. Several options like going to work, attending college, or learning a trade.

______ 5. Whereas the choice that is made will influence a person for life.

Practice B

Identify each group of words as a sentence *(S)*, a fragment *(F)*, a comma splice *(CS)*, or a fused sentence *(FS)*.

______ 6. Many students apply to several colleges, some apply to only one.

______ 7. Whether or not they will be accepted at the college of their choice.

______ 8. Some even want their friends to attend the same college, making the decision more difficult.

______ 9. In a few weeks they will become acclimated to college life anyway whether their friends are there isn't deemed very important.

______ 10. But everyone wants to succeed.

Practice C

Identify each group of words as a sentence *(S)*, a fragment *(F)*, a comma splice *(CS)*, or a fused sentence *(FS)*. If the item is a sentence error, rewrite the sentence correctly.

______ 11. Seniors often wonder what lies ahead, they're apprehensive about the unknown.

____

____

______ 12. One of their fears is whether they will pass or fail in college.

____

____

______ 13. Because not all students have the same abilities.

____

____

_____ 14. A few students even want to go to summer school they hope to graduate early.

_____ 15. Most, though, desire to leave summers free, a time for making money is often a necessity.

Name ______________________________

Chapter 6A: Subject-Verb Agreement

Practice A

Underline the simple subject(s) of each sentence. Then underline the correct verb from the choices in parentheses.

1. Starting around 1914, the 4-H club—referring to head, heart, hands, and health—*(is, are)* still in existence today.
2. The concern for rural education and the promotion of technologically advanced agricultural techniques *(was, were)* the reasons for creating these clubs.
3. Some of the farmers *(was, were)* slow to adopt these new methods.
4. Also at that time nearly everybody in the farming communities *(was, were)* skeptical of full-time formal schooling.
5. Involved in these 4-H clubs *(was, were)* people from both the public and private sectors.

Practice B

Underline the simple subject of each clause. Then rewrite each sentence that has a subject-verb agreement error to correct it.

6. The year 1948 brought a move to advance the 4-H club to international status, a development that is still active today.

____

____

7. Plans for a foreign exchange program involving young 4-Hers' staying with a host family was implemented.

____

____

8. Approximately forty thousand youth from all over the country is involved presently in this undertaking.

____

____

9. One of the changes that has occurred since 1960 is that over half of those involved in 4-H clubs is from the larger cities rather than the rural areas.

____

____

10. Each year volunteer leaders for these clubs exceeds more than two billion dollars in time and out-of-pocket expenses.

____

____

Practice C

Write the correct form of the italicized verb in the blank.

__________ 11. At least one quarter of all children in grades 1–8 *have* been involved in 4-H at some time during those eight years.

__________ 12. The 4-H leadership *offer* many different projects for boys and girls to participate in.

__________ 13. Cooking projects or some kind of sewing *be* among the more popular choices.

__________ 14. Working with animals *be* another kind of project one might choose.

__________ 15. Taking projects to a county or state fair *delight* many 4-H members.

Name________________________________

Chapter 6B: Pronoun-Antecedent Agreement

Practice A

Underline the correct pronoun from the choices in parentheses.

1. Undoubtedly most men decry the day that the common necktie was created for *(him, them)*.
2. Although most historians date ties to the mid-1600s, some trace *(it, them)* back as far as Chinese emperor Qin Shi Huang in 210 B.C.
3. The more readily accepted origin, however, stems from Louis XIV's admiration of the Croatian soldier, who wore soft scarves around the neck as part of *(his, their)* uniform.
4. In fact, most believe the word *cravat* (a soft necktie) gets *(its, their)* name from the word *croat*.
5. King George II of England introduced the tie to the English when *(he, they)* returned to the throne from exile.

Practice B

Underline each personal pronoun and draw an arrow from it to its antecedent.

6. Sometimes cravats were so stiff that a man had to turn his body instead of his neck in order to see.
7. Cravats could be embroidered, plaid, tasseled—as different as the men who wore them.
8. No gentleman would have considered going anywhere without a cravat around his neck.
9. The 1840s experienced the bow tie; of course, it was the hand-tied kind, not a clip-on.
10. Nearly a hundred different knots could be used for tying, with one, the four-in-hand, getting its origin from the knotted reins a coach driver might use.

Practice C

Questions 11–15: Underline the five incorrect pronouns and then write the correct pronoun above each error.

Neither Qin Shi Huang nor Louis XIV could have foreseen the long-range effects of their use of neckties on men's fashion. These ties change its "look" almost as often as women's dress styles change. In the '60s and '70s ties expanded to 5 inches wide in order to keep pace with the wider lapels on men's suits. To be both safe and stylish, a man can always conform his ties to the 2½ to 3½ inch width, regardless of current trends. Length of a tie might be anywhere from 52 to 58 inches, with their tip just touching the waistband of the slacks. Of course, some men prefer bow ties. In fact, one particular college basketball coach, Jim Phelan, always wore it. During the last game of his final season at Mount St. Mary's, several other coaches also donned the bow tie. Everyone wanted to honor their colleague Phelan. Ties, regardless of the kind, seem to have become a permanent fixture in menswear and allow every man a chance to demonstrate his individuality.

Name________________________________

Chapter 7A: Verb Tense

Practice A

Underline the complete verb and identify its tense as *present, past,* or *future; present perfect, past perfect,* or *future perfect;* or *one of these tenses in the progressive.*

__________________ 1. John Calvin, born on July 10, 1509, in Noyon, France, has become well known as one of the foremost theologians of the Reformation.

__________________ 2. A brilliant student, Calvin had been born again at the age of twenty-three.

__________________ 3. Previously a Catholic, Calvin was working for the reform of Catholicism shortly following his conversion.

__________________ 4. His passion for reform caused him to be exiled from Paris.

__________________ 5. Even today people will remember his *Institutes of the Christian Religion,* presenting a systematic explanation of the Protestant position.

Practice B

In the blank, write each italicized verb in the correct tense.

__________________ 6. In 1559 Calvin *begin* a school now known as the University of Geneva.

__________________ 7. Students *carry* Reformation theology across Europe.

__________________ 8. Even today Calvin's work *continue* to influence evangelical Christianity.

__________________ 9. Calvin *preach* at the famous St. Peter's Cathedral, the oldest building in Geneva, and *be* influential in the conversion of the church to Protestantism in 1536.

__________________ 10. Calvin's original chair and his ornate pulpit, reached by a winding staircase, *be* still *grace* St. Peter's and *continue* to attract tourist in years to come.

Practice C

Underline each verb in incorrect tense and write an appropriate correction in the blank.

__________________ 11. A small chapel is to the right of the main door of St. Peter's, and visitors enjoyed seeing it.

__________________ 12. Written above the pulpit in this chapel one found the words *Post Tenebras Lux,* meaning "after darkness, light" or "after ignorance, understanding [of the Bible]."

________________ 13. About a block from the cathedral stands the Reformation Wall, which is built in 1917.

________________ 14. Sculptors had chiseled statues of Calvin, Bèze, Knox, and Farel, all Protestant reformers.

________________ 15. One also finds the Mayflower Compact on that wall, written in both French and English.

Name________________________________

Chapter 7B: Voice and Mood

Practice A

Identify each italicized verb as active voice *(A)* or passive voice *(P).*

_______ 1. Any snow skiing enthusiast *would recognize* the name of Mont Blanc, which is the tallest mountain in the Swiss Alps.

_______ 2. This mountain boasts twelve ski areas and includes a lift that *goes* above 12,500 feet.

_______ 3. Mont Blanc *has been described* as the most famous extreme ski area in the world.

_______ 4. *Included* in extreme skiing *is* going off piste, skiing where no trail exists.

_______ 5. Those who attempt this type of skiing *should* always *check* the avalanche bulletins and ski in groups of three or more.

Practice B

Rewrite each sentence, changing the passive-voice verbs to active voice.

6. Although the name *Chamonix* is used for the valley that is occupied by Mont Blanc, it is also used for a Swiss village.

____

____

7. The picturesque restaurants and shops become breathtaking when the backdrop of the Swiss Alps is added.

____

____

8. The town is also occupied by a pristine brook, and many restaurants have been built overlooking it.

____

____

9. Colored lights are hung above the streets, and Americans are reminded of Christmastime in the United States.

____

____

10. Wonderful Swiss chocolate is sold in many of the picturesque shops along the brick streets.

____

____

Practice C

Identify the mood of each italicized verb as *indicative, imperative,* or *subjunctive.*

_______________ 11. If you are traveling in this area of the world, *be* careful not to overindulge in the delicious sweets.

_______________ 12. If a traveler *would* plan carefully, he could counterbalance the food temptations with the various kinds of exercise available here.

_______________ 13. Skiing, mountain biking, ice skating, and mountain climbing *are* available to the Mont Blanc tourists.

_______________ 14. Children might wish that they *were* involved in riding summer toboggans or go-carts.

_______________ 15. A visit to Chamonix and Mont Blanc *offers* a trip of a lifetime.

Name ______________________________

Chapter 8A: Correct Use of Pronoun Case

Practice A

Underline the correct pronoun from the choices in parentheses.

1. C. S. Lewis was born to *(him, his)* parents, Albert and Flora Lewis, on November 29, 1898.
2. Although C. S. Lewis's full name was Clive Staples Lewis, *(he, him)* was referred to as "Jack" by most of his friends.
3. Lewis's mother died on August 23, 1908, after a battle *(she, her)* had with cancer.
4. "Jack" married Joy Davidman Gresham in December 1956, but a few years later she died after *(she, her)* own battle with cancer.
5. About three years after his wife's death, Lewis died as a result of various health problems, but *(we, us)* still read his work.

Practice B

Underline each personal pronoun and identify it as subjective *(S)*, objective *(O)*, possessive *(P)*, or independent possessive *(IP)*.

______ 6. Lewis made his name known through a variety of writings ranging from children's fantasy to Christian apologetics.

______ 7. *The Chronicles of Narnia* are possibly Lewis's best-known books, and they have captured children's imaginations for years.

______ 8. Lewis wrote quite a number of letters to close friends, and many of them have been published as part of Lewis's collection of writings.

______ 9. One of Lewis's works is known for its similarities in style to John Bunyan's *The Pilgrim's Progress.*

______ 10. Several writers have written stories inspired by *The Pilgrim's Progress.* Lewis's *The Pilgrim's Regress* is the title of his.

Practice C

Insert an appropriate personal pronoun in each sentence.

________________ 11. *The Chronicles of Narnia* began when four children stayed with Lewis at ? home during World War II.

________________ 12. The children had not been exposed to many imaginative stories, so Lewis began writing one for ?.

________________ 13. As Lewis wrote the *Chronicles,* he made the concept of time in Narnia's world very different from the concept of time in yours and ?.

________________ 14. The writing and publishing of the seven books in the series moved quickly. ? were all published between 1950 and 1956.

________________ 15. While writing the first few Narnia tales, Lewis thought *The Voyage of the Dawn Treader* would be ? last book of the series, but soon found he had several more to write before finishing.

Name______________________________

Chapter 8B: Pronoun Usage

Practice A

Evaluate the pronoun usage and then identify each sentence as correct *(C)* or incorrect *(I)*.

______ 1. Many people who visit Charleston, South Carolina, discover numerous attractions to occupy your time.

______ 2. Much of the city itself has been historically preserved and gives tourists a sense of days gone by.

______ 3. Last summer, me and my family traveled to Charleston for a week of vacation.

______ 4. Us staying there was quite a treat because we had never vacationed along the East Coast before.

______ 5. My family and I had a lovely view of the historic section of Charleston from the window of our room in one of the local bed and breakfast inns.

Practice B

Underline the correct pronoun from the choices in parentheses.

6. Throughout the week, my brother and *(I, me)* each enjoyed different aspects of our visit in Charleston.
7. He enjoyed our evening boat ride around the Charleston Harbor more than *(I, me)*.
8. I had a better time than *(he, him)* when we went on an afternoon shopping excursion to the Old City Market.
9. We both thoroughly enjoyed *(ourself, ourselves)* at one of the seafood restaurants downtown.
10. *(He and I, Him and me)* hope to go back to Charleston soon to see the attractions we did not have time to see last summer.

Practice C

Choose the letter that corresponds to the correct pronoun(s).

______ 11. While we shopped at the market, _?_ picked out souvenirs to take home to our grandparents.

A. my family and I

B. my family and me

______ 12. _?_ else should we buy gifts for?

A. Who

B. Whom

______ 13. We decided to buy handmade sweetgrass baskets for the rest of _?_ friends.

A. our

B. their

Chapter 8B: Pronoun Usage (continued)

_______ 14. Our parents enjoyed picking out the baskets, but _?_ children were even more enthusiastic than _?_.

A. we, they

B. us, them

_______ 15. Before we left the market in Charleston, I decided to buy _?_ a basket as well.

A. myself

B. me

Name________________________________

Chapter 8C: *Who* and *Whom*

Practice A

Identify each sentence as correct *(C)* or incorrect *(I)*.

_______ 1. Whom was the first writer of the American short story?

_______ 2. It is difficult to determine exactly who was the first American author to write a short story.

_______ 3. Early American magazine publishers who were willing to include fiction in their magazines exposed the American people to short fiction beginning in 1789.

_______ 4. Washington Irving, a writer who modeled elements of the short story in his tales, preceded the authors who established the short story in its modern form.

_______ 5. Nathaniel Hawthorne and Edgar Allan Poe were the writers whom established the modern form of the American short story in the 1830s and 1840s.

Practice B

Underline the correct pronoun from the choices in parentheses.

6. *(Who, Whom)* were Nathaniel Hawthorne and Edgar Allan Poe?
7. Nathaniel Hawthorne was the author *(who, whom)* brought the short story to the American people in his collection entitled *Twice-Told Tales*, published in 1837.
8. Edgar Allan Poe is the author to *(who, whom)* we are grateful for printing his definition of the short story in a review in *Graham's Magazine* in 1842.
9. *(Who, Whom)* did Hawthorne and Poe influence through their writing?
10. Robert Louis Stevenson and Rudyard Kipling, *(who, whom)* were both British authors, were directly affected by Hawthorne and Poe.

Practice C

Choose the letter that corresponds to the correct pronoun.

_______ 11. _?_ is the author you like better, Hawthorne or Poe?
A. Who
B. Whom

_______ 12. Hawthorne, _?_ was best known for his novel *The Scarlet Letter,* often used guilt as a theme in his writing.
A. who
B. whom

_______ 13. Poe was the author _?_ we consider to be the father of the modern American short story.
A. who
B. whom

_______ 14. ? were some of the well-known American writers to follow the short story form begun by Poe?

A. Who

B. Whom

_______ 15. Ernest Hemingway, Katherine Anne Porter, and Sherwood Anderson are just a few of the writers ? wrote using the modern form of the short story.

A. who

B. whom

Name ______________________________

Chapter 9: Pronoun Reference

Practice A

Underline each pronoun once and each clear antecedent twice. Identify the pronoun reference in each sentence as clear *(C)*, ambiguous *(A)*, or remote *(R)*.

_____ 1. Although marble games are not as prevalent as they once were, most children have some game requiring marbles.

_____ 2. As children, Mark often played a game of Aggravation with Todd, and he always hoped to be the winner.

_____ 3. After the game Todd would ask Mark to give him another chance.

_____ 4. Usually he was willing to play again.

_____ 5. One old marble game that is still played is Chinese checkers.

Practice B

Underline each pronoun that demonstrates a reference error and write an appropriate correction in the blank. Avoid informal English.

______________________ 6. It says to divide the marbles evenly.

______________________ 7. If the game's main purpose is to shoot marbles, then practice will be needed to play it well.

______________________ 8. In other games you must rely on chance, not skill, to win.

______________________ 9. Mousetrap is an interesting one that uses only one ball or marble.

______________________ 10. Playing the same game several times becomes boring, which is not good.

Practice C

Underline the five pronoun reference errors in the following paragraph and rewrite the paragraph correctly.

Although you would think that marbles are made from marble, most are made from glass, a much cheaper material. Other marble materials of the past have been clay, wood, stone, or even steel, which seems a little strange. As a person might expect, the earliest glass marbles were made in Venice prior to 1800, where they would blow each marble individually. Not until approximately 1920 were they made in America. The alleys (the expensive marbles) are hard to find; their scarcity means that they have become collectors' items. The expression "knuckling down" comes from a method marble experts use when shooting them.

Name________________________________

Chapter 10A: Adjective and Adverb Use

Practice A

Underline each adjective once and each adverb twice.

1. The Butchart Gardens, considered one of the world's most famous and beautiful gardens, covers fifty acres.
2. Located on Vancouver Island, it is only a few miles from Victoria.
3. The name comes from Robert Pim Butchart, who owned and operated a cement company on Tod Inlet, the present site of the gardens.
4. However, it was definitely his wife, Jennie, who decided to reclaim the dismal limestone pit after it had been depleted of useful limestone.
5. Currently, that pit has been transformed into the gorgeous Sunken Garden.

Practice B

Underline each incorrectly used adjective or adverb and write the correction in the blank.

________________ 6. The earlier garden in the entire collection is the Japanese Garden.

________________ 7. Its picturesque pagodas, rustic footbridges, and whimsical statues provide a most unique experience.

________________ 8. Some visitors do not have no interest in leaving this garden.

________________ 9. Nevertheless, most all of them eventually continue to view the other gardens on Tod Inlet.

________________ 10. One of the famousest smaller gardens is the English Rose Garden.

Practice C

Underline the correct adjective or adverb from the choices in parentheses.

11. The (*most perfect, most nearly perfect*) time to visit the Gardens is late afternoon and early evening.
12. Nighttime provides a whole new perspective for (*real, really*) good viewing.
13. The Saturday night fireworks are choreographed especially (*good, well*).
14. Not a note of music that sounds (*bad, badly*) will ever be heard at this display.
15. Visitors may go home (*some, somewhat*) fatigued, but they'll have enjoyed an experience of a lifetime.

Name ____________________

Chapter 10B: Misplaced and Dangling Modifiers

Practice A

Underline each misplaced modifier.

1. Young Brandon enjoys thoroughly hearing Grandpa ask, "Would you like to explore the nearby stream?"
2. The question has hardly been completed before the child is standing at the door impatiently ready to go.
3. Grandpa and grandchild head for the local park, wearing old tennis shoes.
4. Of course Sam, the yellow lab, begs pleadingly to also be allowed to go.
5. In this particular case three grandchildren fall into step quickly looking ahead with wonderful anticipation.

Practice B

Underline each incorrect modifier and identify it as a misplaced modifier *(M)* or a dangling modifier *(D)*.

_______ 6. Upon reaching the stream, chatter grows to a crescendo.

_______ 7. Six small feet try to precariously balance upon the midstream rocks.

_______ 8. Leaving caution to the wind, a huge splash hits Grandpa as Sam leaps into the water.

_______ 9. Everyone laughs until Sam happily shakes water upon one and all, causing a mild panic.

_______ 10. Trying to flee quickly causes each child to tumble into the water.

Practice C

Rewrite each sentence, correcting any misplaced or dangling modifiers.

11. Squeals of either delight or dismay follow, depending upon the child's personality.

____

____

12. Hoping to distract the children from their wet plight, a school of beautiful red minnows is pointed out by Grandpa.

____

____

13. Fascinated by the fish, all six eyes peer into the stream's crystal depths.

____

____

14. Even adults wander by curiously wondering what has transfixed the attention of the children.

15. While exploring at the local park, the stream proved an exciting focal point for Grandpa and the children.

Name ____________________

Chapter 11: Capitalization

Practice A

Underline every word that demonstrates a capitalization error.

1. Nearly every child—even from other parts of the World—has owned a Piggy Bank at one time or another.
2. Many times at birth the child will receive such a bank, often silver, from Grandma or aunt Sarah or even from the Hospital where the child was born.
3. Interestingly, these Banks were not always in the shape of a pig; In fact, they probably had nothing to do with pigs.
4. The origin of the piggy bank probably comes from the middle ages when people had storage jars made from an orange clay called "Pygg."
5. Another theory (probably my Grandmother's) is that leftovers of one's change were fed to the "pig" until it was fat enough to be smashed and its money used for something special.

Practice B

Rewrite each italicized word correctly. If the word is already capitalized correctly, write C in the blank.

______ ______ 6. These piggy banks probably originated in *Europe* sometime during the *sixteenth century.*

______ ______ 7. Even *today* in some European countries, "lucky pigs" are a part of the *new year's* celebration.

______ ______ 8. Piggy banks can now be found nearly everywhere as prizes at *State Fairs*, in Hallmark *card* stores, in hospital gift shops, and in many other places.

______ ______ 9. Children in *Camp* often construct piggy banks as a craft project, sometimes in conjunction with *Holidays*.

______ ______ 10. Many piggy banks are smashed to get money for such things as Walt Disney *world* or the *World* of Coca-Cola.

Practice C

Rewrite the following paragraph, correcting the ten errors in capitalization. (Multiple capitalization errors in a proper noun count as only one error.)

Piggy banks have even become Collectibles. Banks sometimes give them away to encourage a child to save. One Bank in the uk held such a promotion in 1983. For a new account of at least three Pounds, children could receive Baby Woody, the youngest in a family of five pigs. As the accounts grew, Annabel, Maxwell, lady Hillary, and Sir Nathaniel Westminster could be added to the collection. Nathaniel required an investment of one hundred pounds or more, so relatively few british children acquired him. Five years later the offer ended, only to be resurrected in 1998 when cousin Wesley came on the scene. The bank was responsible for six little pigs, quite a different scenario from the famous "three little pigs" story. anyone interested in following the continuing saga should contact the Wade Collectors club.

Name ____________________

Chapter 12A: End Marks and Other Periods

Practice A

Label the end punctuation of each sentence as correct *(C)* or incorrect *(I)*.

______ 1. The AMF Bowling Worldwide icon is easily recognizable today, but few people realize that bowling might be the first sport ever played!

______ 2. Historians wonder whether some form of bowling dates back to the ancient Egyptians of 3200 B.C.?

______ 3. The contents of an Egyptian pyramid included a round ball-like object and marble bars.

______ 4. Can you believe that German monks even partook of the sport around A.D. 300.

______ 5. During the time of Julius Caesar, bocce (a kind of lawn bowling) was a popular pastime for Roman soldiers and continues to be popular in Italy today.

Practice B

Insert any necessary periods.

6. By AD 1650 the Dutch colonists had transported bowling to America

7. Of course, Rip Van Winkle found little men playing nine pins near Catskill, New York

8. In 1895 the ABC (American Bowling Congress) was formed

9. In the early 1900s Skee-Ball, similar to bowling and invented by J D Estes, arrived on the scene

10. These facts would not be taught by Dr Riebe in History 101, but they are still quite interesting to me.

Practice C

Insert any necessary end marks or other periods.

11. The earliest ten-pin bowlers used candlepins, which lost their popularity about 1850 but were reintroduced in 1881 by Justin P White

12. These candlepins stood about 11 in high and narrowed on both ends

13. Getting a strike with the 3 lb ball was extremely difficult

14. No one has ever scored a perfect game

15. I wonder whether anyone ever will

Name ______________________________

Chapter 12B: Commas

Practice A

Identify each sentence as correctly punctuated *(C)* or incorrectly punctuated *(I)*.

______ 1. Any budding writer, who is studying writing techniques in school knows that writing can be a very rewarding job.

______ 2. One might be a technical writer, a fiction writer, or even a textbook writer.

______ 3. However despite one's inherent skills, writing requires much concentration and self-discipline.

______ 4. While being factual a newspaper reporter must write and revise his articles in order to conserve space.

______ 5. The supervisor of any newspaper, the editor, may work overtime to finalize an edition of the paper.

Practice B

Insert any necessary commas.

6. In addition to inherent talent writers must have a practical in-depth knowledge of the computer.
7. An understanding of word processing which is assumed by an employer is only the beginning.
8. To do any research writers must be adept at accessing the Internet and also at giving official credit for quotations and other borrowings.
9. Then too a writer must learn specific formats of spacing font size and styles which are often complex.
10. No a career in writing is not all glamour and fame.

Practice C

Rewrite the following paragraph, inserting any necessary commas. There are ten errors.

Children believe it or not are very discerning readers. Therefore writing literature for children may seem to be an easy vocation but it is actually quite complex. The writer must first have an original idea but thinking of one can be difficult. To be successful a story usually also requires realistic characters and dialogue. Knowing how to get a story published whether it is short or book length requires an understanding of how publishing works. Most successful stories were "kid-tested" read to or by children before they were submitted to a publisher. Dedicated children's authors are involved in a true labor of love.

Name ______________________________

Chapter 12c: Commas, Semicolons, and Colons

Practice A

Identify the use of semicolons in each sentence as correct *(C)* or incorrect *(I)*.

______ 1. Most people claim to be somewhat knowledgeable about a few kinds of cars; but everyone has at least heard of the Volkswagen.

______ 2. Regardless of one's attitude toward the VW; the car is extremely popular.

______ 3. In the 1930s, Adolph Hitler influenced the design and purpose of the Volkswagen; he contracted Ferdinand Porsche to make a car for the common man.

______ 4. Hitler wanted a motor mounted in the rear; a speed of sixty-two miles per hour; and a capacity of two adults and three children.

______ 5. Driving over forty miles per hour was considered fast; quite a feat for that era.

Practice B

Insert any necessary colons. If the sentence is already correct, write *C* in the blank.

______ 6. Throughout their history Volkswagens have had some unusual names Beetles, Things, and Rabbits.

______ 7. In 1960 Volkswagen even produced the Volks-Liner a small wooden boat using a Beetle motor.

______ 8. However, the boat was short-lived, with only a few actually in existence.

______ 9. Albert Klein claims to have driven his 1960s Beetle over one million miles, making one wonder whether he had to replace motors, tires, and brakes several times.

______ 10. A few Volkswagen owners, however, are disenchanted with their vehicles and claim "I wouldn't buy another Volkswagen if it were the last car on Earth!"

Practice C

Insert the ten necessary commas, semicolons, or colons in the following paragraph.

During the 1970s the Guthrie family eagerly purchased a used Volkswagen camper which they affectionately labeled their "camp mobile." The camper included a sink, a refrigerator, a table and beds. Even the roof lifted, so an adult could stand upright. Believing that they had acquired an economical camper they tested it a few times close to home. Soon they decided to take it on a longer trip a Christmas trek from South Carolina to Illinois. The family anticipated going through Knoxville, Tennessee Lexington, Kentucky and Indianapolis, Indiana. However, anticipation faded on I-40 in the North Carolina mountains about 100 A.M. when the camper decided that hauling luggage, Christmas packages, two adults, and four children was simply too much to ask. Dying on a sharp curve the camper rolled to a stop. Mr. Guthrie managed to get it to a gas station where the family waited several hours while he acquired another car finally, they continued the trip. On the return trip the family had to pick up the camper and tow it back to South Carolina. Consequently, the Guthrie family decided that a Volkswagen camper was not the right vehicle for them.

Name________________________________

Chapter 13A: Quotation Marks, Ellipses, and Underlining for Italics

Practice A

Identify each sentence as correctly punctuated *(C)* or incorrectly punctuated *(I)*.

_______ 1. Last week in music class, we studied Frances Ridley Havergal, the British hymn writer who wrote "Take My Life and Let It Be."

_______ 2. Mr. Spaulding told us "that Havergal wrote the hymn as a result of a visit with some friends during which two of the friends were saved."

_______ 3. Larissa asked, "Doesn't one of the lines of that song say, 'Take my silver and my gold; not a mite would I withhold'?"

_______ 4. "Yes," answered Mr. Spaulding, "that is a line in the hymn. Miss Havergal learned a very important lesson from those exact words."

_______ 5. Mr. Spaulding explained that Frances Havergal gave her jewelry to the "Church Missionary House" because of that line from her hymn.

Practice B

In the blank indicate whether the sentence has an error with ellipses *(E)* or underlining *(U)*. If the sentence is correct, write *C* in the blank.

_______ 6. This text says, "Frances Havergal showed her talent...when, at the age of seven, she began writing poetry."

_______ 7. Some of her early poetry was published in a periodical called Good Words.

_______ 8. During her lifetime, she wrote several <u>volumes of hymns</u>, some of which were published after her death.

_______ 9. <u>The Ministry of Song</u>, one of Miss Havergal's books of hymns, was published in 1869.

_______ 10. "In addition to her interest in music," Mr. Spaulding concluded, "Miss Havergal also studied modern languages, Latin and um. . . . Hebrew."

Practice C

Insert any missing quotation marks or underlining. If the sentence is already correct, write *C* in the blank.

_______ 11. In 1851 during her teenage years, Miss Havergal trusted Christ as her Savior.

_______ 12. Concerning her salvation experience, she said, I committed my soul to the Savior. . . . Earth and heaven seemed brighter from that moment; I did trust the Lord Jesus.

_______ 13. Miss Havergal wrote several devotional books in the years following her salvation; one of these is entitled Kept for the Master's Use.

_______ 14. The title of the first chapter in Havergal's book Kept for the Master's Use is Our Lives Kept for the Master.

_______ 15. In this chapter, Miss Havergal emphasizes the need for each Christian to be fully consecrated to Christ.

Name ______________________________

Chapter 13B: Apostrophes

Practice A

Identify each item as correctly punctuated *(C)* or incorrectly punctuated *(I)*.

______ 1. Charles Dickens' family background greatly influenced his writing.

______ 2. Dickens's father, who worked as a clerk in the Navy Pay Office, struggled financially and was eventually imprisoned for debt.

______ 3. The Dickenses' lives were affected in different ways. Charles worked at a blacking factory to earn money for the family while his sister Fanny continued her studies at the Royal Academy of Music.

______ 4. Charles's education was put on hold because his family could'nt afford for him to stop working.

______ 5. Fanny's and Charles's younger siblings lived with their father and mother in the prison, but Fanny and Charles didn't join them.

Practice B

Rewrite each italicized word, correcting any apostrophe errors. If the italicized word is already correct, write *C* in the blank.

______________ 6. Eventually, his father was released from prison, and Dickens attended Wellington House Academy for a few years during the *1820s*.

______________ 7. Dickens spent some of his time at school making up stories and acting out scenes for the other *childrens'* enjoyment.

______________ 8. After leaving school, he worked as a clerk in various *lawyers's* offices, but he soon turned to reporting instead.

______________ 9. To prepare for a job as a court reporter, Dickens learned shorthand with all *it's* intricacies.

______________ 10. After a few years in the field of court reporting, *Dickens's* career took another turn when he switched to newspaper journalism.

Practice C

Questions 11–15: Correct the five apostrophe errors in the following paragraph.

The first published stories of Dickens appeared in *Monthly Magazine*. A few years later, Dickens began writing novels with characters who resembled his acquaintances. Many of the characters idiosyncrasies reflect the behaviors of a family member, a friend, or an employer. Dickens also regularly included scenes drawn from his memorys storehouse. For example, *David Copperfield* is a partially autobiographical account of the authors troubles as a child and a young man. Its not accurate, however, to say that every adventure in *David Copperfield* really happened in Dickens life.

Name ____________________

Chapter 13c: Brackets, Hyphens, Dashes, and Parentheses

Practice A

Identify each sentence as correctly punctuated *(C)* or incorrectly punctuated *(I)*.

_______ 1. Sleep deprivation—a serious lack of sleep, creates several negative results.

_______ 2. Individuals (often teenagers) who are sleep deprived may experience health problems as well as difficulty completing normal tasks properly.

_______ 3. There are numerous reasons [some of which are valid] behind the lack of sleep experienced by so many people today.

_______ 4. Parents with babies who are 0—2 months old often get little sleep because their babies do not sleep on a regular schedule.

_______ 5. On the other hand, teenagers often inflict a less-than-desirable amount of sleep on themselves by choosing to stay up late at night.

Practice B

Identify the punctuation missing from each sentence. In the blank write the letter that corresponds to the correct answer. If the sentence is already correct, write *C* in the blank.

A. brackets
B. dashes
C. hyphen
D. parentheses
E. correct

_______ 6. The amount of sleep necessary to function properly throughout the day varies from person to person.

_______ 7. Toddlers require an average of thirteen fourteen hours of sleep each day.

_______ 8. Some adults although they are rare may be able to cope with as little as four hours of sleep per night.

_______ 9. Other individuals especially teenagers may need as much as ten hours of sleep to feel rested.

_______ 10. A sleep expert has written, "The average recommended amount of sleep for individuals to recieve *sic* each night is eight hours."

Practice C

Questions 11–15: Insert five missing hyphens, dashes, and parentheses. (Punctuation marks used as a pair count as a single error.)

Sleep deprivation a common problem today has a strong effect on teenagers. Some experts believe a lack of sleep can cause school related problems among teens. Low concentration, lack of effort, and behavior problems each of these is a possible consequence for adolescents who receive inadequate sleep. In order to combat these problems, experts suggest that teens allow themselves about nine and one half hours of sleep each night. This change which some may find difficult would greatly benefit teenagers in their school performance and fulfillment of daily tasks.

Name ______________________________

Chapter 2: Descriptive Essay

Planning

Use the following chart to organize the elements you wish to describe in your essay. List vivid expressions that will stimulate sensations in your audience similar to those that you experienced when you saw the scene you are describing.

	Literal Sensation	Creative Expression
Taste		
Touch		
Smell		
Sight		
Hearing		

Determine your audience (someone other than your teacher); then describe a scenario in which the audience would read your essay. Consider things such as the age and interests of your audience and their familiarity with the place or event you are describing.

____

____

____

____

State your purpose in writing this essay. For example, your purpose may be to evoke in your reader the excitement that you experienced when your high-school basketball team scored the winning point during the final thirty seconds of the championship game.

____

____

Based on the three options described on pages 31–32 of the student text, decide how you can organize your essay to best achieve your purpose. State your method below. Then give general guidelines that can aid you in the outlining and drafting stages.

____

____

____

____

Name ____________________________

Chapter 3: Comparison-and-Contrast Essay

Brainstorm

Label the columns below with the subjects you have chosen for your essay. Below each subject heading, list general and specific facts about each subject. You may wish to keep related facts across from each other. Write down ideas as soon as you think of them even if you cannot think of a related item for the other subject. Leave a blank in the opposite column so that you can add a related item later. Using different colored pens or pencils, underline similar pairs with one color and differing pairs with another color.

Name ____________________

Chapter 4A: Interior Monologue

Character Web

Use the following worksheet to create a character web for a fictional or historical character. First, place the character's name in the center of the oval. Second, around the oval write words and phrases describing the character's likes, dislikes, and character qualities. Third, decide what chief trait the fictional character will possess or what trait best represents the historical character.

Name ____________________

Chapter 4B: Interior Monologue

Thought Train

Use the following example of a thought train to help you create one for your own character.

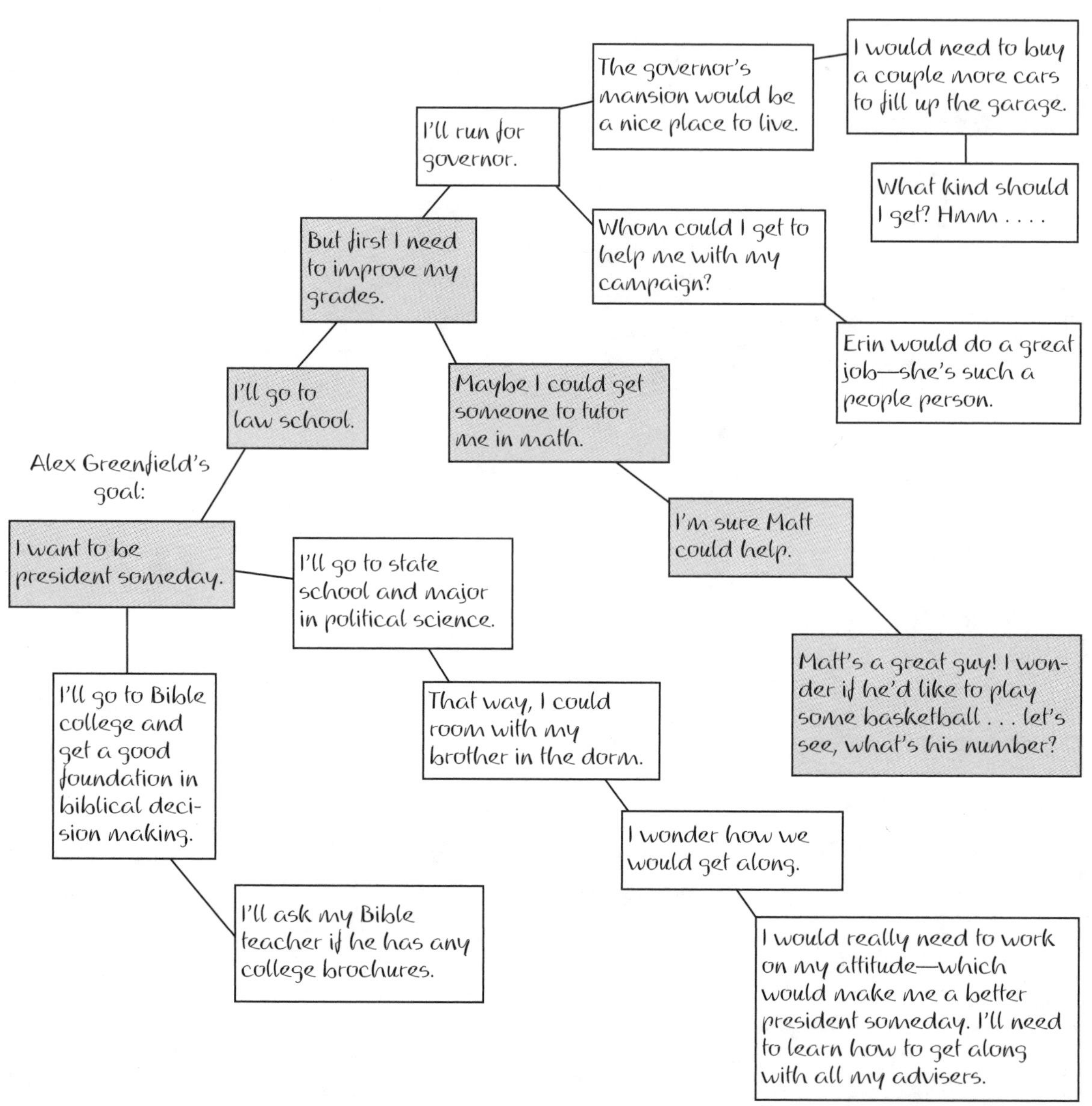

Name ____________________

Chapter 5: Persuasive Essay

Revising

Use the following questions to evaluate a peer's essay or your own.

	Questions	Evaluation and Suggestions
Organization	Are the thesis statement and restated thesis placed correctly?	
	Are the paragraphs organized logically, with the strongest point last?	
Content	How effective is the introduction in getting the reader's attention?	
	List the concrete examples used to support the thesis.	
	What denotative and connotative language does the writer use? Is the connotative language effective or overused?	
	Can you identify any stereotypes in the essay?	
Purpose	What action is the writer urging the reader to take?	
	Is the argument clear and convincing?	
	Is the action valid for the audience?	
Style	Is the thesis clear, concise, and controversial?	
	Is the essay written in active voice?	

Name ______________________________

Chapter 6A: Writing a Dramatic Scene

Sample Scene Map

Conflict: Rebecca struggles between her desire to please her friends and her desire to please God.

Resolution: Rebecca realizes that doing God's will sometimes means making choices that others will not understand. She determines not to give in to the taunts of her friends.

Setting: present day; Duncan's Diner, the after-school hangout for "cool" students

Characters: REBECCA, high-school senior and dedicated Christian

TRISH, DAN, MANUEL } REBECCA's friends, also seniors in high school

	Stage Business	Dialogue
Beginning	• Rebecca sits down at a table with friends. • They are looking at college brochures and discussing what they want to major in. • Rebecca says she would like to go to a French-speaking country as a missionary.	REBECCA: I was thinking about majoring in French. DAN: I'm definitely majoring in business so I can make some serious money when I graduate. MANUEL: Yeah, like anyone'd hire you. REBECCA: I mean, I'd sorta . . . well, I'd like to be a missionary some day to a French-speaking country—maybe in Africa.
Middle	• Rebecca's friends tease her about choosing French as a major. • Rebecca struggles internally as she hears their comments but boldly interjects her conviction of God's will for her life. • Her friends go on talking about their own goals (fashion designer, business tycoon, and broadcast journalist).	TRISH: French? What kind of major is that? There's no future in it. MANUEL: You could always get a job as a waitress in a French restaurant and correct everyone's pronunciation when they order. REBECCA: But I believe that's where God wants me. TRISH: Where in the Bible does God say you should learn French? DAN: Hey, Becca, how about an order of *French* fries with that Coke? MANUEL: Yeah, or *French* toast?
End	• Rebecca catches the server's attention and orders French fries. After the server brings them in a bag, Rebecca says a quick good-bye and leaves the table. • Rebecca pauses at the door to look back at her friends talking happily. She watches them for a moment and then goes out the door.	REBECCA: An order of fries, please . . . and could I have them to go? TRISH: Hey, where're you goin' so fast? REBECCA: Gotta run, guys. *Au revoir!*

Name ______________________

Chapter 6B: Writing a Dramatic Scene

Scene Map

Conflict:

Resolution:

Setting:

Characters:

	Stage Business	Dialogue
Beginning		
Middle		
End		

Name ____________________

Chapter 7: Extemporaneous Essay

Follow these steps as you write your essay.

Planning

1. On another piece of paper, brainstorm the topic assigned by your teacher.
2. Decide on a purpose, an audience, and a specific topic for your essay. Write a statement of intent incorporating each of these elements.
3. Write a clear, concise thesis that communicates your subject and your main point about that subject.
4. List the main points and the details you will use to support them.
5. Arrange the main points and the details into an outline in order from strongest to weakest.
6. Plan your conclusion. Restate your thesis and decide what other information, if any, you will use to reiterate your main point.

Drafting

7. Consider your audience and your purpose when choosing the tone for the essay.
8. List some transitional words that you may incorporate into the essay.
9. On another piece of paper, write your first draft. Remember to double space, write on only one side of the paper, and use correct form (thesis, support, restated thesis).

Revising

10. Save enough time to read through your essay at least once. Cross out any unimportant information and neatly add any words that will clarify your meaning.
11. Edit for grammar and mechanics errors.

Name ______________________________

Chapter 8A: Video Report

Script Format

Use the following chart to help you script the video report.

______________________________ (Video Report's Title)	
VIDEO	AUDIO

Name ____________________

Chapter 8B: Video Report

Filming Considerations

Refer to the questions on page 202 of your textbook as you address each of the considerations below. Record your decisions on this planning worksheet.

Camera Movement	
Editing	
Framing	
Lighting	
Music/Sound	
Narration	

Name ______________________

Chapter 9: College Application Essay

The application process allows a college or university to become acquainted with you, your academic history, and your future goals. The following application presents an overview of the information that a college or university asks of prospective students.

Personal Information

Legal Name ______________________
Last First Middle

Mailing Address ______________________
City State Zip Country

Date of Birth ____________ Home Phone ____________ E-mail Address ____________

Major ____________ Minor ____________

Educational Information

High School ______________________

Address ______________________
City State Zip Country

Anticipated Graduation Date ______________________

Is your school a public, private, or home school? ______________________

Scholastic Information

List any academic awards or honors you have earned since entering ninth grade.

____

____

____

____

____

____

____

____

____

Extracurricular Information

List any extracurricular, volunteer, or church-related activities in order of interest, including summer activities. Approximate the time spent on each and check the activities you plan to continue in college.

Activity	Grade 9	Grade 10	Grade 11	Grade 12	Hours per week	Weeks per year	Positions held or honors won	College partici-pation

Application Essay

On a separate sheet of paper, write an essay stating your choice of study and your expectations for success in this program. Your essay will allow the application committee to become acquainted with you as a person and as a student. Type your essay on standard-sized paper and attach it to this application form.

Name ______________________________

Chapter 10A: Sonnet

Sonnet 18

Shall I compare thee to a summer's day?
Thou art more lovely and more temperate:
Rough winds do shake the darling buds of May,
And summer's lease hath all too short a date;
Sometime too hot the eye of heaven shines,
And often is his gold complexion dimm'd,
And every fair from fair sometime declines,
By chance or nature's changing course untrimm'd;
But thy eternal summer shall not fade,
Nor lose possession of that fair thou ow'st,
Nor shall Death brag thou wand'rest in his shade,
When in eternal lines to time thou grow'st.
So long as men can breathe or eyes can see,
So long lives this, and this gives life to thee.

Sonnet 130

My mistress' eyes are nothing like the sun;
Coral is far more red than her lips' red;
If snow be white, why then her breasts are dun;
If hairs be wires, black wires grow on her head.
I have seen roses damask'd, red and white,
But no such roses see I in her cheeks;
And in some perfumes is there more delight
Than in the breath that from my mistress reeks.
I love to hear her speak, yet well I know
That music hath a far more pleasing sound;
I grant I never saw a goddess go;
My mistress, when she walks, treads on the ground.
And yet, by heaven, I think my love as rare
As any she belied with false compare.

Questions about Sonnet 130

1. What kind of picture is Shakespeare presenting in the first twelve lines of this sonnet?

2. Why do you think the speaker describes the object of his love in this manner?

3. What hints prepare the reader for the shift of thought in the couplet?

4. What is Shakespeare communicating about love in this sonnet?

5. Does the resolution of the couplet satisfy you? Why or why not?

Name ______________________________

Chapter 10B: Sonnet

Get an Idea

Creativity springs from thoughtful observation. Use the following questions to spark ideas as you brainstorm or make a web diagram.

- What interesting event did you observe on your way to school this morning? What emotion do you connect with this observation? How could this event demonstrate an issue or circumstance you feel strongly about?
- Whom do you enjoy spending time with? How does this person influence your life? Why do you appreciate him? What about him do others not know or understand?
- What discoveries have you made in your reading? How do you respond to what you are reading? Why is the work significant? Why is your response to it significant?
- What do you find humorous that others may not think is humorous? Why do you find the situation or occurrence funny when others do not? How can you present the incident so that others will see it from your perspective?

Every author says something through his writing. Consider the message you want to communicate through your sonnet.

- What is your theme?
- Is the theme serious or humorous? Why?
- How will you communicate your theme through the subject you have chosen?
- How will you reveal the theme in the first and second parts of the sonnet?

Review the ideas you have formulated and organize them in the chart below. Decide which topic is most meaningful to you and is most promising for the subject of your sonnet.

Observation	Topic	Possible Theme

Name ____________________________________

Chapter 10C: Sonnet

Peer Evaluation

Use the following questions to evaluate a peer's sonnet.

1. Does the sonnet read smoothly?
2. What is the form of the sonnet? Is the form correct?
3. Are the rhyming words natural, or are they forced to be there just for the sake of rhyme?
4. Do the sounds and images contribute to the theme or draw attention away from it?
5. What metaphoric relationship does the author create, if any? Is it effective?
6. How does the sonnet affect you?
7. What theme does the sonnet communicate?
8. Does each line support the theme?
9. Does the sonnet realistically resolve the tension that it creates?
10. Is there a definite shift of thought in the closing couplet or sestet?
11. Is the closing couplet or sestet convincing? Why or why not?
12. What do you especially like about the sonnet?
13. How could the author strengthen this sonnet?

Name ______________________

Chapter 11A: Research Report

Primary and Secondary Sources

Assume that you are writing a research report about the repercussions of Operation Desert Storm. Identify each source as a primary source *(P)* or a secondary source *(S)*.

_______ 1. a website honoring soldiers from the Gulf War

_______ 2. an encyclopedia entry on Desert Storm

_______ 3. a book co-authored by someone who was an air force commander during the war

_______ 4. a magazine article discussing the "Gulf War Syndrome"

_______ 5. an interview with a corporal from the Gulf War

_______ 6. a copy of a TV speech by General H. Norman Schwarzkopf

_______ 7. a newspaper article discussing the use of nerve gas during the war

_______ 8. a diary from a nurse involved in the Gulf War

_______ 9. a taped radio program giving a news commentator's view of the war

_______ 10. a historian's notes about the impact of the Gulf War on China

Name________________________________

Chapter 11B: Research Report

Avoiding Plagiarism

Every time you paraphrase or quote a source in your report, you must carefully evaluate the accuracy of the statement. Use the following questions as a guide for this research report and for any other research writing you do in the future.

1. Have I paraphrased thoroughly (changing the words, sentence structure, and order of ideas)?

2. Have I accurately represented the meaning of the source in my paraphrase?

3. Have I used quotation marks for all wording (words, phrases, or sentences) taken from a source?

4. Have I accurately quoted my source?

5. Have I correctly punctuated any additions to or deletions from the original source?

6. Have I carefully given source information for all paraphrases and quotations?

Name ______________________________

Chapter 11c: Research Report

Planning Your Research Report

Use the questions below to evaluate the effectiveness of your report.

Formulating a thesis

- Does your thesis state both the topic and your particular slant on that topic?
- Is the topic specific enough to be covered adequately in a five-paragraph paper?
- Does the thesis suggest only one main idea? (If you have a compound sentence, you will want to put one of the main ideas into a subordinating construction, leaving the most important one as the independent clause.)
- Is the thesis verifiable, declarative, and possibly controversial?
- Is the wording of the thesis clear and devoid of all-inclusive terms such as *all, always, every,* and *never?*

Identifying supporting points

- Does each main supporting point relate directly to the thesis? (If the main point discusses some minor side issue, then it should be restructured.)
- Does the main point summarize the supporting idea of the whole paragraph, or is it merely one of several details included in the paragraph? (If there is no statement to summarize the main idea of the paragraph, write one that encompasses the details that support the main idea.)
- Are the supporting points distinct from each other, or do they overlap? (Make sure that each supporting point covers an area of its own and not some extension or evaluation of another point.)
- Have you limited your support to three main ideas? (If not, you may want to reorganize the supporting material into three main points. You may have to omit a few details if they do not fit under one of the three main headings.)

Outlining the report

- Have you used the same format—topic or sentence—consistently throughout the outline? (Remember that a topic outline requires parallel grammatical form within each point.)
- Do you have a total of three main points, corresponding to each of the three supporting paragraphs?
- Do you have a *II* for every *I*, a *B* for every *A*, and so on?
- Have you divided your subpoints into groups pertaining to the main points?
- Do you have sufficient support for each of the main points? (If not, you may need to seek out additional information for your report, or you may wish to reassess the content of the main supporting points.)

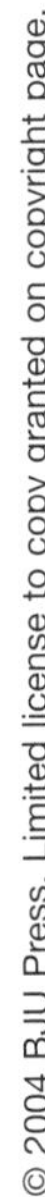

Name________________________________

Chapter 12: Issue Analysis Essay

Propaganda Devices

Ad Hominem: attacking a person rather than an issue

- **Statement:** "Don't listen to Mr. Brown (board member at University USA). He only wants you to go to University USA so that he can impress the other board members with a high number of recruits."
- **Error:** Mr. Smith, a board member at University America, wants to recruit more students, so he uses unsupported criticisms of Mr. Brown's character instead of discussing the qualities of each university.

Hasty Generalization: basing a conclusion on too little evidence

- **Statement:** "University America's football team has won the championship five years in a row. It's obvious that University America has a stronger sports program than any other university."
- **Error:** University America has failed to reach the semifinals in any other sport for the past five years. The strength of their sports program cannot be based solely on the performance of their football team.

Bandwagon or **Popular Opinion:** encouraging others to join an allegedly overwhelming majority

- **Statement:** "Everyone knows that University America is the place to go, so join in and enroll in University America!"
- **Error:** Apparently, if a person does not enroll in University America, he is completely out of step with everyone else. But who is *everyone?*

Card Stacking: intentionally presenting only one side of an issue

- **Statement:** "University USA doesn't offer students good academic or social opportunities. University America, however, offers widespread academic, social, and extracurricular opportunities."
- **Error:** This statement fails to mention that University USA is twenty-five years younger than University America and is therefore still building some of its programs.

Testimonial: citing a well-known personality as an authority on an issue that he or she is not qualified to speak about

- **Statement:** "Mr. Mayor stated, 'University America is the best choice around. I'm sending both my children to University America for their college education!'"
- **Error:** Mr. Mayor did not attend either University America or University USA; he has visited University America only once and has never visited University USA. Even though Mr. Mayor is a well-known voice among the people, he does not know enough about either university to state that University America is better, let alone the "best choice around."

Straw Man: simplifying the opponent's argument into something that can be easily refuted

- **Statement:** "University USA is concerned only about being wealthy. The university raised tuition this year just to get more money from the students."
- **Error:** University USA is actually trying to build a stronger science program and raise the professors' salaries, so an increase in tuition is necessary.

Name ______________________________

Chapter 13: Response to a Dramatic Scene

Avoiding Plagiarism

Read the following excerpt from Edmond Rostand's *Cyrano de Bergerac*, translated by Gladys Thomas and Mary F. Guillemard.

RAGUENEAU Monsieur de Cyrano is not here? 'Tis strange.

LIGNIÈRE Why so?

RAGUENEAU Montfleury plays!

LIGNIÈRE Ay, 'tis true
That that hippopotamus is to take Phedon's part tonight;
But what is that to Cyrano?

RAGUENEAU How? Know you not? He has got a hot hate
For Montfleury, and so has forbidden him strictly
To show his face on the stage for one whole month.

LIGNIÈRE Well?

RAGUENEAU Montfleury will play!

. . . .

FIRST MARQUIS Who is this Cyrano?

CUIGY A fellow well skilled in all tricks of fencing.

SECOND MARQUIS Is he of noble birth?

CUIGY Ay, noble enough.
He is a cadet in the Guards.

. . . .

CUIGY Is it not true that he is the most excellent of men?

LE BRET True that he is the choicest of earthly beings!

RAGUENEAU Poet!

CUIGY Soldier!

BRISSAILLE Philosopher!

LE BRET Musician!

LIGNIÈRE And how fantastic a presence!

RAGUENEAU Whimsical, wild, the maddest fighter
Of all the Gascon crew—with his triple-plumed hat
And six-pointed doublet—
The sword-point sticking up 'neath
His mantle like an insolent cocktail!
And above his ruff he carries a nose!
Ah, good my lords, what a nose is his!
When one sees it one is fain to cry aloud,
"Nay! 'tis too much! He plays a joke on us!"
Then one laughs, says, "He will soon take it off."
But no! Monsieur de Bergerac always keeps it on.

Chapter 13: Response to a Dramatic Scene (continued)

When quoting a source be careful not to misrepresent the meaning of the source. Quoting words out of context or leaving out key words in a quotation may change the meaning of the source and is a type of plagiarism.

INCORRECT	Ragueneau observes that Montfleury will act in the play because Cyrano wants him "to show his face on the stage for one whole month."
CORRECT	Ragueneau reminds Lignière that Cyrano "has forbidden [Montfleury] strictly / To show his face on the stage for one whole month."
INCORRECT	Cuigy describes Cyrano as a man "well skilled in all tricks."
CORRECT	Along with Cyrano's other good qualities, he is "a fellow well skilled in all tricks of fencing."

Identify the statements that faithfully represent the source.

______ 1. A. Cyrano, "the choicest of earthly beings," portrays a "fantastic . . . presence" in his abilities, dress, and fighting skill.

B. Cyrano, "whimsical, wild, [and] the maddest fighter / Of all the Gascon crew . . . [acts] like an insolent cocktail."

______ 2. A. With great delight Cyrano "plays a joke on" all by wearing a fake nose.

B. Cyrano's nose, "above his ruff," attracts the attention of all who see him.

DESCRIPTIVE ESSAY 2

	MESSAGE
	Tone and Purpose 3 Essay sparks reader interest and draws attention to the main idea, using a detail or figure of speech to set the tone. 2 Essay includes a detail or figure of speech that sets the tone but does not clearly draw attention to the main idea. 1 Essay does not begin with a specific detail or figure of speech or begins with one that does not set the tone or clearly identify the main idea.
	Descriptive Language 3 Essay contains details and figures of speech that make the description interesting and unique. 2 Essay contains details and figures of speech that are clichèd. 1 Essay contains details and figures of speech that are inappropriate, or essay does not use details or figures of speech.
	Organization 3 Essay demonstrates a clear progression of ideas through the use of a specific form of organization (e.g., spatial, chronological, order of importance). 2 Essay demonstrates some clarity of ideas but does not consistently use a specific form of organization. 1 Essay does not demonstrate any specific form of organization.
______	**MESSAGE SCORE**

	MECHANICS
	Grammar and Usage 3 Writer displays a command of grade-level skills (e.g., agreement, verb and pronoun usage, sentence structure). 2 Writer displays a basic knowledge of grade-level skills (e.g., agreement, verb and pronoun usage, sentence structure). 1 Writer displays little or no knowledge of grade-level grammar skills.
	Spelling 3 Writer uses and spells words above grade level. 2 Writer spells words on grade level. 1 Writer misspells grade-level words.
	Capitalization and Punctuation 3 Writer demonstrates a command of grade-level capitalization and punctuation. 2 Writer demonstrates an understanding of grade-level capitalization and punctuation. 1 Writer misuses grade-level capitalization and/or punctuation.
______ ______	**MECHANICS SCORE** **TOTAL SCORE (Message plus Mechanics)**

A 16–18 B 14–15 C 12–13 D 10–11 F 6–9

Overall, this writing . . .

CHAPTER 3 RUBRIC

COMPARISON-AND-CONTRAST ESSAY 3

	MESSAGE
	Subjects and Purpose 3 Essay contains two subjects that are somewhat related and a clear purpose that gives direction to the essay. 2 Essay contains two subjects that are somewhat related, but the essay shows no clear purpose. 1 Essay contains two subjects that are not related or contains only one subject.
	Thesis 3 Essay contains a clear thesis that presents each subject and the point of comparison or contrast and is worded as a statement. 2 Essay contains an inexact thesis that presents the two subjects but either fails to state the point of comparison or contrast or is not worded as a statement. 1 Essay lacks a thesis statement that presents the two subjects clearly or states the point of comparison or contrast.
	Support 3 Essay contains relevant supporting ideas that are specific and are placed in order from least to most important. 2 Essay contains relevant supporting ideas that are specific but are not placed in order from least to most important. 1 Essay contains irrelevant supporting ideas or ideas that are neither specific nor placed in order from least to most important.
	Organization 3 Essay uses block arrangement or point-by-point arrangement and maintains the same order to present information within the points. 2 Essay uses block arrangement or point-by-point arrangement but does not maintain the same order to present information within the points. 1 Essay lacks consistent arrangement.
______	**MESSAGE SCORE**

	MECHANICS
	Grammar and Usage 3 Writer displays a command of grade-level skills (e.g., agreement, verb and pronoun usage, sentence structure). 2 Writer displays a basic knowledge of grade-level skills (e.g., agreement, verb and pronoun usage, sentence structure). 1 Writer displays little or no knowledge of grade-level grammar skills.
	Spelling 3 Writer uses and spells words above grade level. 2 Writer spells words on grade level. 1 Writer misspells grade-level words.
	Capitalization and Punctuation 3 Writer demonstrates a command of grade-level capitalization and punctuation. 2 Writer demonstrates an understanding of grade-level capitalization and punctuation. 1 Writer misuses grade-level capitalization and/or punctuation.
______ ______	**MECHANICS SCORE** **TOTAL SCORE (Message plus Mechanics)**

A 16–18 B 14–15 C 12–13 D 10–11 F 6–9

Overall, this writing . . .

CHAPTER 4 RUBRIC

INTERIOR MONOLOGUE 4

	MESSAGE
	Purpose 3 Interior monologue includes a clear goal and distinguishable character traits that complement that goal. 2 Interior monologue includes a somewhat clear goal but no distinguishable character traits that complement that goal. 1 Interior monologue includes no clear goal or distinguishable character traits.
	Style 3 Interior monologue displays a sense of naturalness through a meaningful yet seemingly random train of thought. 2 Interior monologue displays a sense of naturalness through a meaningful train of thought but lacks any elements that seem random. 1 Interior monologue does not display a sense of naturalness because the train of thought is irrational and unconnected.
	Technique 3 Interior monologue uses a variety of techniques (i.e., direct thoughts, indirect thoughts, speech, action, or description) to communicate the character's thoughts. 2 Interior monologue uses only two techniques to communicate the character's thoughts. 1 Interior monologue uses only one technique to communicate the character's thoughts.
______	**MESSAGE SCORE**

	MECHANICS
	Grammar and Usage 3 Writer displays a command of grade-level skills (e.g., agreement, verb and pronoun usage, sentence structure). 2 Writer displays a basic knowledge of grade-level skills (e.g., agreement, verb and pronoun usage, sentence structure). 1 Writer displays little or no knowledge of grade-level grammar skills.
	Spelling 3 Writer uses and spells words above grade level. 2 Writer spells words on grade level. 1 Writer misspells grade-level words.
	Capitalization and Punctuation 3 Writer demonstrates a command of grade-level capitalization and punctuation. 2 Writer demonstrates an understanding of grade-level capitalization and punctuation. 1 Writer misuses grade-level capitalization and/or punctuation.
______ ______	**MECHANICS SCORE** **TOTAL SCORE (Message plus Mechanics)**

A 16–18　　B 14–15　　C 12–13　　D 10–11　　F 6–9

Overall, this writing . . .

RUBRICS

CHAPTER 5 RUBRIC

PERSUASIVE ESSAY

	MESSAGE
	Topic 3 Essay contains a topic that is controversial and is argued from either the "pro" or "con" position but not both. 2 Essay contains a topic that is controversial, but the topic is either argued from both the "pro" and "con" positions or not argued at all. 1 Essay contains a topic that is not controversial.
	Thesis and Purpose 3 Essay contains a one-sentence thesis that clearly states the main idea and acts as the primary purpose for the entire essay. 2 Essay contains a one-sentence thesis that clearly states the main idea, but the essay deviates from the thesis. 1 Essay does not contain a clear thesis statement.
	Support 3 Essay includes supporting information that is presented from weakest to strongest and persuades the reader to agree with the position presented and to take a specific action. 2 Essay includes supporting information that is presented from weakest to strongest but does not persuade the reader to agree with the position presented or to take a specific action. 1 Essay does not include strong supporting information to persuade the reader to agree or to take a specific action.
	Style 3 Essay contains an introduction that gains the reader's attention, uses sound evidence and connotative language to persuade without focusing too heavily on emotion, and is written in active voice. 2 Essay contains an introduction that partially gains the reader's attention but either does not use sound evidence, focuses too heavily on emotional appeal to persuade, or is not written in active voice. 1 Essay contains an introduction that does not gain the reader's attention, does not use sound evidence, focuses too heavily on emotional appeal to persuade, and/or is not written in active voice.
______	**MESSAGE SCORE**

	MECHANICS
	Grammar and Usage 3 Writer displays a command of grade-level skills (e.g., agreement, verb and pronoun usage, sentence structure). 2 Writer displays a basic knowledge of grade-level skills (e.g., agreement, verb and pronoun usage, sentence structure). 1 Writer displays little or no knowledge of grade-level grammar skills.
	Spelling 3 Writer uses and spells words above grade level. 2 Writer spells words on grade level. 1 Writer misspells grade-level words.
	Capitalization and Punctuation 3 Writer demonstrates a command of grade-level capitalization and punctuation. 2 Writer demonstrates an understanding of grade-level capitalization and punctuation. 1 Writer misuses grade-level capitalization and/or punctuation.
______ ______	**MECHANICS SCORE** **TOTAL SCORE (Message plus Mechanics)**

A 19–21 B 16–18 C 13–15 D 10–12 F 7–9

Overall, this writing . . .

DRAMATIC SCENE 6

	MESSAGE
	Conflict and Resolution 3 Scene presents a clear conflict at the beginning and has a definite resolution at the end so that the audience is not left wondering about the outcome. 2 Scene presents a clear conflict at the beginning, but there is no resolution or the resolution is unclear so that the audience is left wondering about the outcome. 1 Scene presents no clear conflict (or presents multiple conflicts) or has no clear resolution.
	Style (showing v. telling) 3 Scene portrays the characters realistically through natural-sounding dialogue. 2 Scene portrays the characters somewhat realistically, but the dialogue seems unnatural. 1 Scene does not portray characters realistically, and the dialogue seems unnatural, unmotivated, and awkward.
	Development 3 Scene includes adequate stage directions to aid in picturing setting and characters' actions, but the dialogue provides the primary details. 2 Scene relies heavily on stage directions for setting and characters' actions, and the dialogue does not include much detail. 1 Scene relies almost entirely on stage directions to fill in details about setting and characters' actions rather than relying on dialogue.
______	**MESSAGE SCORE**

	MECHANICS
	Grammar and Usage 3 Writer displays a command of grade-level skills (e.g., agreement, verb and pronoun usage, sentence structure). 2 Writer displays a basic knowledge of grade-level skills (e.g., agreement, verb and pronoun usage, sentence structure). 1 Writer displays little or no knowledge of grade-level grammar skills.
	Spelling 3 Writer uses and spells words above grade level. 2 Writer spells words on grade level. 1 Writer misspells grade-level words.
	Capitalization and Punctuation 3 Writer demonstrates a command of grade-level capitalization and punctuation. 2 Writer demonstrates an understanding of grade-level capitalization and punctuation. 1 Writer misuses grade-level capitalization and/or punctuation.
______ ______	**MECHANICS SCORE** **TOTAL SCORE (Message plus Mechanics)**

A 16–18 B 14–15 C 12–13 D 10–11 F 6–9

Overall, this writing . . .

CHAPTER 7 RUBRIC

EXTEMPORANEOUS ESSAY

	MESSAGE
	Thesis 3 Essay includes a clear, concise thesis statement. 2 Essay includes a somewhat clear thesis statement that lacks conciseness. 1 Essay includes an unclear thesis statement.
	Organization and Development 3 Essay exhibits proper form (thesis, support, restated thesis), includes supporting information that is relevant to the topic, and begins with the strongest supporting point. 2 Essay exhibits proper form but includes supporting information that is irrelevant or begins with a weak supporting point. 1 Essay does not exhibit proper form and includes supporting information that is irrelevant or begins with a weak supporting point.
	Style 3 Essay uses an appropriate, consistent tone throughout and employs transitional words effectively. 2 Essay uses a consistent tone throughout, but the tone is inappropriate for the audience. 1 Essay uses a tone that is neither appropriate nor consistent and may misuse transitional words.
______	**MESSAGE SCORE**

	MECHANICS
	Grammar and Usage 3 Writer displays a command of grade-level skills (e.g., agreement, verb and pronoun usage, sentence structure). 2 Writer displays a basic knowledge of grade-level skills (e.g., agreement, verb and pronoun usage, sentence structure). 1 Writer displays little or no knowledge of grade-level grammar skills.
	Spelling 3 Writer uses and spells words above grade level. 2 Writer spells words on grade level. 1 Writer misspells grade-level words.
	Capitalization and Punctuation 3 Writer demonstrates a command of grade-level capitalization and punctuation. 2 Writer demonstrates an understanding of grade-level capitalization and punctuation. 1 Writer misuses grade-level capitalization and/or punctuation.
______ ______	**MECHANICS SCORE** **TOTAL SCORE (Message plus Mechanics)**

A 16–18 B 14–15 C 12–13 D 10–11 F 6–9

Overall, this writing . . .

CHAPTER 8 RUBRIC

VIDEO REPORT — 8

	MESSAGE
	Topic 3 Report clearly covers the main points of the topic and fills in the necessary details. 2 Report covers most of the main points of the topic but leaves out some necessary details. 1 Report fails to cover the main points of the topic thoroughly and leaves out most or all of the necessary details.
	Style 3 Report contains a consistent angle (shot as an onlooker or participant) and frame (developed as a newscast or documentary) and uses direct, logical speech. 2 Report contains inconsistencies in angle and frame (i.e., switches between styles rather than using one style throughout) and uses some speech that muddles the message. 1 Report does not employ any specific angle or frame and uses confusing speech throughout.
	Special Effects 3 Report uses a variety of shots and sound effects to add to the message. 2 Report hardly varies the shots and some of the sound effects detract from the message. 1 Report uses only one shot and the sound effects detract from the message.
______	**MESSAGE SCORE**

	MECHANICS
	Filming Considerations 3 Reporter displays a thorough treatment of each of the elements on the Filming Considerations chart. 2 Reporter displays only partial treatment of each of the elements on the Filming Considerations chart. 1 Reporter does not adequately treat most or all of the elements on the Filming Considerations chart.
	Grammar and Usage 3 Reporter displays a command of grade-level skills (e.g., agreement, verb and pronoun usage, sentence structure). 2 Reporter displays a basic knowledge of grade-level skills (e.g., agreement, verb and pronoun usage, sentence structure). 1 Reporter displays little or no knowledge of grade-level grammar skills.
	Spelling 3 Reporter uses and spells words above grade level. 2 Reporter spells words on grade level. 1 Reporter misspells grade-level words.
	Capitalization and Punctuation 3 Reporter demonstrates a command of grade-level capitalization and punctuation. 2 Reporter demonstrates an understanding of grade-level capitalization and punctuation. 1 Reporter misuses grade-level capitalization and/or punctuation.
______ ______	**MECHANICS SCORE** **TOTAL SCORE (Message plus Mechanics)**

A 19–21 B 16–18 C 13–15 D 10–12 F 7–9

Overall, this writing . . .

CHAPTER 9 RUBRIC

COLLEGE APPLICATION ESSAY 9

	MESSAGE
	Introduction 3 Essay's introduction catches reader's attention and clearly presents the main idea. 2 Essay's introduction either fails to catch the reader's attention or fails to clearly present the main idea. 1 Essay's introduction neither catches reader's attention nor clearly presents the main idea.
	Style 3 Essay includes specific details and information and avoids sensationalism. 2 Essay includes specific details and information but employs sensationalism or overstatement to bolster its message. 1 Essay includes few specific details and little information and relies on sensationalism or overstatement.
	Organization and Development 3 Essay is direct and succinct, containing only information that is closely related to the topic and reserving the most convincing idea for the conclusion. 2 Essay contains some information that is unrelated to the topic but reserves the most convincing idea for the conclusion. 1 Essay contains information that is unrelated to the topic and does not reserve the most convincing idea for the conclusion.
_____	**MESSAGE SCORE**

	MECHANICS
	Grammar and Usage 3 Writer displays a command of grade-level skills (e.g., agreement, verb and pronoun usage, sentence structure). 2 Writer displays a basic knowledge of grade-level skills (e.g., agreement, verb and pronoun usage, sentence structure). 1 Writer displays little or no knowledge of grade-level grammar skills.
	Spelling 3 Writer uses and spells words above grade level. 2 Writer spells words on grade level. 1 Writer misspells grade-level words.
	Capitalization and Punctuation 3 Writer demonstrates a command of grade-level capitalization and punctuation. 2 Writer demonstrates an understanding of grade-level capitalization and punctuation. 1 Writer misuses grade-level capitalization and/or punctuation.
_____ _____	**MECHANICS SCORE** **TOTAL SCORE (Message plus Mechanics)**

A 16–18 B 14–15 C 12–13 D 10–11 F 6–9

Overall, this writing . . .

CHAPTER 10 RUBRIC

SONNET

	MESSAGE
	Effect 3 Sonnet achieves a specific desired effect with each sound or image contributing to the whole. 2 Sonnet achieves a specific desired effect, but some of the sounds or images detract from the theme. 1 Sonnet does not achieve a specific desired effect.
	Form 3 Sonnet consistently uses iambic pentameter and the rhyme scheme of the English or Italian sonnet form. 2 Sonnet is inconsistent in its use of iambic pentameter and varies somewhat from the English or Italian sonnet rhyme scheme. 1 Sonnet is inconsistent in both its meter and rhyme.
	Resolution 3 Sonnet demonstrates a clear shift in thought in the closing couplet or sestet and a clear resolution to the problem or answer to the question of the first part. 2 Sonnet demonstrates an unclear shift in thought in the closing couplet or sestet and an unclear or contrived resolution to the problem or answer to the question of the first part. 1 Sonnet demonstrates no shift in thought and no resolution.
______	**MESSAGE SCORE**

	MECHANICS
	Grammar and Usage 3 Writer displays a command of grade-level skills (e.g., agreement, verb and pronoun usage, sentence structure). 2 Writer displays a basic knowledge of grade-level skills (e.g., agreement, verb and pronoun usage, sentence structure). 1 Writer displays little or no knowledge of grade-level grammar skills.
	Spelling 3 Writer uses and spells words above grade level. 2 Writer spells words on grade level. 1 Writer misspells grade-level words. .
	Capitalization and Punctuation 3 Writer demonstrates a command of grade-level capitalization and punctuation. 2 Writer demonstrates an understanding of grade-level capitalization and punctuation. 1 Writer misuses grade-level capitalization and/or punctuation.
______ ______	**MECHANICS SCORE** **TOTAL SCORE (Message plus Mechanics)**

A 16–18 B 14–15 C 12–13 D 10–11 F 6–9

Overall, this writing . . .

CHAPTER 11 RUBRIC

RESEARCH REPORT

	MESSAGE
	Thesis 3 Report contains a thesis statement that is both verifiable and declarative; it may also be controversial. 2 Report contains a thesis statement that is either verifiable or declarative but not both. 1 Report contains no clear thesis statement.
	Organization and Support 3 Report is organized into five paragraphs (one introduction, three support, one conclusion), and middle paragraphs include clear topic sentences and a variety of types of support to reinforce them. 2 Report is organized into five paragraphs, and middle paragraphs include clear topic sentences but use only one type of support to reinforce them. 1 Report is not organized into five paragraphs, and supporting information is not varied or is insufficient.
	Research and Sources 3 Report contains abundant information from various sources presented appropriately in both paraphrases and direct quotations, and sources are cited accurately. 2 Report contains adequate information from limited sources presented mainly through paraphrases or direct quotations (not both), and sources are cited accurately. 1 Report lacks adequate information, and sources are cited incorrectly.
______	**MESSAGE SCORE**

	MECHANICS
	Works-Cited Page 3 Writer demonstrates a command of correct and complete format. 2 Writer demonstrates a basic knowledge of correct format. 1 Writer demonstrates little or no knowledge of correct format.
	Grammar and Usage 3 Writer displays a command of grade-level skills (e.g., agreement, verb and pronoun usage, sentence structure). 2 Writer displays a basic knowledge of grade-level skills (e.g., agreement, verb and pronoun usage, sentence structure). 1 Writer displays little or no knowledge of grade-level grammar skills.
	Spelling 3 Writer uses and spells words above grade level. 2 Writer spells words on grade level. 1 Writer misspells grade-level words.
	Capitalization and Punctuation 3 Writer demonstrates a command of grade-level capitalization and punctuation. 2 Writer demonstrates an understanding of grade-level capitalization and punctuation. 1 Writer misuses grade-level capitalization and/or punctuation.
______ ______	**MECHANICS SCORE** **TOTAL SCORE (Message plus Mechanics)**

A 19–21 B 16–18 C 13–15 D 10–12 F 7–9

Overall, this writing . . .

CHAPTER 12 RUBRIC

ISSUE ANALYSIS ESSAY

	MESSAGE
	Thesis 3 Essay includes a thesis that clearly identifies a problem to be analyzed or clearly states the writer's position about a topic. 2 Essay includes a thesis that does not clearly identify a problem to be analyzed or clearly state the writer's position about a topic. 1 Essay does not include a thesis.
	Support 3 Essay contains supporting information that is clearly organized and includes specific information. 2 Essay contains supporting information that is somewhat organized but includes little specific information. 1 Essay contains supporting information that is not organized and includes little or no specific information to aid the support.
	Style 3 Essay contains an appropriate level of informality for the intended audience. 2 Essay contains some elements that are either too formal or too informal for the intended audience. 1 Essay contains an inappropriate level of informality for the intended audience.
______	**MESSAGE SCORE**

	MECHANICS
	Grammar and Usage 3 Writer displays a command of grade-level skills (e.g., agreement, verb and pronoun usage, sentence structure). 2 Writer displays a basic knowledge of grade-level skills (e.g., agreement, verb and pronoun usage, sentence structure). 1 Writer displays little or no knowledge of grade-level grammar skills.
	Spelling 3 Writer uses and spells words above grade level. 2 Writer spells words on grade level. 1 Writer misspells grade-level words.
	Capitalization and Punctuation 3 Writer demonstrates a command of grade-level capitalization and punctuation. 2 Writer demonstrates an understanding of grade-level capitalization and punctuation. 1 Writer misuses grade-level capitalization and/or punctuation.
______ ______	**MECHANICS SCORE** **TOTAL SCORE (Message plus Mechanics)**

A 16–18 B 14–15 C 12–13 D 10–11 F 6–9

Overall, this writing . . .

RESPONSE TO DRAMATIC SCENE

	MESSAGE
	Thesis 3 Essay contains a thesis that clearly analyzes a problem in the text, supports an arguable position from the text, or examines a personal view of the text; thesis also states something that is not readily apparent to the reader. 2 Essay contains a thesis that is too easily proved or is too obvious to the casual reader. 1 Essay contains no clear thesis.
	Support 3 Supporting information provides solid proof and explanations for the thesis and includes no unnecessary details or comments. 2 Supporting information provides solid proof and explanations for the thesis but includes some unnecessary details or comments. 1 Supporting information does not provide solid proof or explanations for the thesis and includes unnecessary details or comments.
	Organization and Development 3 Essay organizes topic sentences with the strongest point last, the second strongest point first, and any other supporting points between those; also uses direct quotations appropriately to support argument. 2 Essay organizes topic sentences with the strongest point last, the second strongest point first, and any other supporting points between those, but essay uses direct quotations inappropriately or awkwardly. 1 Essay does not organize topic sentences effectively and uses direct quotations inappropriately or not at all.
______	**MESSAGE SCORE**

	MECHANICS
	Grammar and Usage 3 Writer displays a command of grade-level skills (e.g., agreement, verb and pronoun usage, sentence structure). 2 Writer displays a basic knowledge of grade-level skills (e.g., agreement, verb and pronoun usage, sentence structure). 1 Writer displays little or no knowledge of grade-level grammar skills.
	Spelling 3 Writer uses and spells words above grade level. 2 Writer spells words on grade level. 1 Writer misspells grade-level words.
	Capitalization and Punctuation 3 Writer demonstrates a command of grade-level capitalization and punctuation. 2 Writer demonstrates an understanding of grade-level capitalization and punctuation. 1 Writer misuses grade-level capitalization and/or punctuation.
______ ______	**MECHANICS SCORE** **TOTAL SCORE (Message plus Mechanics)**

A 16–18 B 14–15 C 12–13 D 10–11 F 6–9

Overall, this writing . . .

Name ______________________

Chapter 2 Pretest: Parts of Speech

I. Nouns

Underline each noun.

1. Have you ever visited the Grand Teton National Park?
2. This park includes land that Congress designated in 1929 as well as land that John D. Rockefeller Jr. donated in 1950.
3. The Grand Teton, the highest mountain in the Teton Range, reaches an elevation of 13,770 feet.
4. The Snake River meanders through the valley on the eastern side of the Teton Range.
5. Several species of wildflowers, such as Indian paintbrush, and wildlife, including marmots, inhabit the park.

II. Pronouns

Underline each pronoun and label it personal *(per)*, indefinite *(ind)*, demonstrative *(dem)*, relative *(rel)*, indefinite relative *(ind rel)*, interrogative *(int)*, reflexive *(ref)*, or reciprocal *(rec)*.

6. Anyone *(ind)* visiting the Tetons in the summer can choose from a variety of activities to amuse himself *(ref)*.
7. Hiking, mountaineering, fishing, and whitewater rafting—these *(dem)* are only a few of the activities that *(rel)* might interest a tourist.
8. Outdoor enthusiasts may hire professionals to guide them *(per)* on climbing and rafting trips, or they *(per)* may venture into the wilderness by themselves *(ref)*.
9. Groups rafting on the Snake River often amuse themselves *(ref)* by having water fights with each other *(rec)*.
10. Whatever *(ind rel)* you *(per)* choose to do will be a blast! Who *(int)* wants to visit the park with me *(per)*?

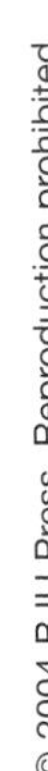

III. Verbs

Underline the main verb of each clause once; underline each auxiliary twice.

11. When the Grand Teton National Park has closed for the winter, the nearby town of Jackson Hole becomes a hub of activity.
12. Jackson is known for its world-famous downhill ski resorts.
13. Those who want to stay warm might try shopping at the Jackson square or visiting a museum.
14. Every tourist should take a sleigh ride through the National Elk Refuge, where thousands of elk congregate for food and shelter.
15. Don't miss the breathtaking view of the sunset behind the Tetons.

IV. Adjectives and Adverbs

Underline each adjective once and each adverb twice.

16. Paul Petzoldt made the first ascent of the Grand Teton when he was only a sixteen-year-old youth.

17. Having a natural inclination for dealing with people, Petzoldt soon began skillfully and safely guiding hikers in the Tetons.

18. Petzoldt deftly traversed the Matterhorn twice in one day and took part in the first American expedition to K2.

19. When a New Tribes Mission plane crashed on Mount Moran in the Tetons, Petzoldt led a recovery team to search for survivors.

20. Petzoldt's most significant accomplishment was founding the National Outdoor Leadership School.

V. Prepositions

Underline each preposition once and the object of each preposition twice.

21. Having gray-green leaves, sagebrush grows abundantly in the Teton valley.

22. Except for aspen and cottonwood trees, most trees inside the Grand Teton National Park are conifers.

23. Only hardy flowers and a few dwarfed shrubs grow above the timberline on the peaks.

24. Lupine, Colorado columbine, and Indian paintbrush brightly carpet meadows with purple, white, and red flowers.

25. Unfortunately, flower picking is not permitted within the park.

VI. Conjunctions and Interjections

Underline each conjunction once. Then label each conjunction as coordinating *(coord)*, correlative *(corr)*, or subordinating *(sub)*. Underline each interjection twice.

26. Both (corr) the Tetons and (corr) Yellowstone display beautiful scenery.

27. Please, do not feed the bears or (coord) other wildlife.

28. In the spring, you may see a bull elk in velvet if (sub) you're lucky.

29. Hey, check out herds of bison while (sub) you're in the area.

30. Because (sub) they range in high alpine meadows, bighorn sheep are difficult to spot.

Name ______________________

Chapter 3 Pretest: Sentences

I. Identifying Types of Sentences

Identify each sentence as *declarative, interrogative, imperative,* or *exclamatory.* Insert the appropriate end punctuation for each sentence.

imperative 1. Discover the fascinating and beautiful lighthouses of America.

interrogative 2. Did you see the incredible sunset at the Pemaquid Point lighthouse in Maine?

exclamatory 3. In 1978 a ferocious blizzard destroyed much of the Boon Island lighthouse, forcing the lightkeepers to take refuge in the lantern room for two days!

declarative 4. Curtis Island lighthouse, named after Cyrus H. Curtis, the founder and publisher of the *Ladies' Home Journal*, is located near Camden, Maine.

declarative 5. Before mesh wiring reinforced the dome, migrating birds often crashed into the lantern of Old Barney in Barnaget, New Jersey.

interrogative 6. Why is the Cape Hatteras lighthouse considered a symbol of lighthouses?

declarative 7. Standing 205 feet high, the Hatteras tower warns ships of the treacherous waters caused by the joining of the Labrador Current and the Gulf Stream.

interrogative 8. Did the famous pirate Blackbeard make his home in Ocracoke, North Carolina, near the future site of a lighthouse?

imperative 9. Notice the octagonal tower of the Sand Island lighthouse on Lake Superior.

exclamatory 10. The Rock of Ages, the brightest of all lighthouses, shines on Lake Superior with a 700,000 candlepower light!

II. Finding Subjects and Predicates

Underline the simple subject once and the simple predicate twice. If the subject of the sentence is understood, write *you* in the blank.

_______ 11. One lightkeeper lost his mind while tending the isolated Stannard Rock lighthouse fifty miles off the coast of Michigan.

_______ 12. Beauty and tranquility characterize the sunset view of Heceta Head lighthouse in Oregon.

Chapter 3 Pretest: Sentences (continued)

you 13. Watch the red-and-white flashing lens in the Umpqua River lighthouse.

_____ 14. What historical event prompted the construction of the Alcatraz lighthouse?

_____ 15. Low-lying fog along the California coast made some early lighthouses ineffective.

you 16. Check out the Golden Gate Bridge from the Point Bonita lighthouse.

_____ 17. Augustin Fresnel invented a unique lens for lighthouses in 1822.

_____ 18. Fresnel lenses are white, red, or green glass.

_____ 19. Why would the center of Fresnel lenses be shaped like a magnifying glass?

_____ 20. This beehive-shaped lens can be up to twelve feet tall.

III. Analyzing Sentence Patterns

Label the sentence patterns *S-InV, S-TrV-DO, S-TrV-IO-DO, S-LV-PN, S-LV-PA, S-TrV-DO-OC,* or *S-be-Advl.* If the adverbial is a prepositional phrase, underline it.

21. Lighthouses (S) in New Brunswick, Canada, are (LV) often square (PA) with red-and-white vertical stripes.

22. Slangkop lighthouse (S) guides (TrV) ships (DO) around the hidden reefs and dangerous rocks in South Africa.

23. Automated lighting systems (S), in lighthouses such as Hangklip, make (TrV) lightkeepers (DO) unnecessary (OC).

24. Vasily Ilchenko (S) is (LV) a lightkeeper (PN) on the Egershelde Peninsula in Russia.

25. *Almagrundet* (S) is (LV) one (PN) of several Swedish lightships.

26. Some lightkeepers' quarters (S), converted into youth hostels, provide (TrV) travelers (IO) a place (DO) to stay.

27. Fastnet lighthouse (S) off the coast of Ireland features (TrV) an annual yacht race (DO).

28. Australia's Cape Wickham lighthouse (S) is (be) on King Island (Advl).

29. Restoration efforts (S) by the Australian government saved (TrV) the octagonal South Channel Pile Light (DO) from decay.

30. Gabo Island's red granite tower (S) stands (InV) firm.

Name ____________________

Chapter 4 Pretest: Phrases

I. Prepositional Phrases

Place parentheses around each prepositional phrase. Draw an arrow from each prepositional phrase to the word it modifies.

1. (On clear nights (with brightly shining stars)) you can identify constellations.
2. The Big Dipper (in the Northern Hemisphere) and the Southern Cross (in the Southern Hemisphere) are the easiest constellations to find.
3. (By beginning (at the Big Dipper,)) you can find other constellations more easily.
4. Dubhe and Merak, two stars (in the cup (of the dipper)) point (to the North Star)
5. Boötes is located (across the sky) (in line (with the handle (of the Big Dipper.)))

II. Appositive Phrases

Underline each appositive or appositive phrase. Draw an arrow from each appositive or appositive phrase to the word it renames.

6. Leo, a constellation visible in both hemispheres, includes the star Regulus.
7. *Cor Leonis*, another name for Regulus, means "Heart of the Lion."
8. Positioned in the mane of Leo, the double star Algeiba is yellow-orange in color.
9. Denebola, the star representing the lion's tail, is a white double star about 1.5 times the diameter of the Sun.
10. According to ancient mythology, the Nemean Lion (memorialized as the constellation Leo) presented a formidable foe to Hercules, the immortal son of Zeus.

III. Verbal Phrases

Identify each italicized verbal phrase as noun *(N)*, adjective *(Adj)*, or adverb *(Adv)*.

__Adj__ 11. *Defeating the Nemean Lion after a month-long battle,* Hercules wore the lion's impenetrable hide as a protective cloak.

__N__ 12. *Knowing the mythical stories* serves as a useful tool for remembering the location of and details about the individual constellations.

__Adj__ 13. The Nemean Lion, Cancer, and Draco are just a few constellations *to associate* with the Hercules myth.

Adj 14. The goddess Hera placed the crab, *crushed by Hercules's heel,* in the stars as the constellation Cancer.

Adv 15. *To memorialize him,* Hera turned the dragon Ladon into the constellation Draco.

IV. Verbal Phrases

Underline each verbal or verbal phrase. Above each verbal or verbal phrase, label it as a gerund *(G)*, a participle *(P)*, or an infinitive *(I)*.

16. Locating the constellations [G] requires obtaining some knowledge of Greek myths [G].

17. One myth to know [I] concerns the famed [P] hunter Orion.

18. Accompanied by his dogs Canis Major and Canis Minor [P], Orion moves across the sky hunting Lepis, the hare, and Taurus, the bull [P].

19. According to Greek mythology, Scorpius, having killed Orion [P], was placed on the opposite side of the sky from Orion by the gods to prevent [I] his hurting Orion again [G].

20. Various names attached to the constellation [P] mean "hunter," "giant," "mighty one," and "fool."

21. The Bible word translated *Orion* [P] is also translated *fool* to refer to one who rejects God [I].

22. Knowing Jewish tradition [G] provides an alternate story of Orion from that of the Greek myth.

23. Nimrod, an acknowledged [P] hunter (Gen.10:9), supposedly called this constellation by his own name.

24. Amos exhorts the Israelites to seek Him who made Orion [I] (5:8).

25. To illustrate God's omnipotence [I], Job cites God's creation of Orion and other heavenly bodies (Job 9:9).

Name__________________________

Chapter 5 Pretest: Clauses

I. Identifying Independent and Dependent Clauses

Identify each italicized clause as independent *(IC)* or dependent *(DC)*.

DC 1. In 1943, *as a naval engineer conducted experiments to develop an antivibration device,* the Slinky was invented.

IC 2. Since its debut at the Gimbels Department Store in Philadelphia, *the Slinky has become famous for its ability to "walk."*

IC 3. Using simple materials and the scientific method, *the Slinky demonstrates how forces are transmitted by waves and other physics principles.*

DC 4. *Though it is an enjoyable toy,* the Slinky has one problem: its propensity to tangle.

DC 5. Have you ever noticed *that a badly tangled Slinky is almost impossible to fix?*

II. Adjective Clauses

Place parentheses around each adjective clause. Write the word it modifies in the blank. Underline each relative pronoun once; underline each relative adverb twice.

limbs 6. Recent research has been conducted concerning the use of springs in prosthetic limbs,(which are normally extremely hard to use.)

reason 7. The incorporation of advanced design springs in prosthetics is the reason(that wearers will expend less effort when using their artificial limbs.)

wearers 8. Prosthesis wearers,(who have many adjustments to make when learning to use artificial limbs,)will greatly enjoy the advanced technology.

things 9. The same technology is used in many things(that we operate on a daily basis, such as cars.)

hinge 10. For instance, the hood of the car usually has a spring at its hinge,(where it can assist us as we lift the hood.)

III. Adverb Clauses

Place parentheses around each adverb clause. In the blank write the word or words it modifies. Underline each subordinating conjunction.

are used 11. (Whereas springs function well for a variety of purposes,)they are frequently used in conjunction with shock absorbers.

were 12. Car and wagon rides were very bouncy(before shock absorbers were invented.)

drive 13. (Since spring suspensions and shock absorbers have been refined greatly,)cars now drive with virtually no vibration.

___are___ 14. (<u>While</u> many bikes have shocks,) suspension systems in cars are much more elaborate than those of bikes.

___may have___ 15. Someday airplanes may have shock absorbers (<u>so that</u> turbulence will cause less trauma for passengers.)

IV. Noun Clauses

Place parentheses around each noun clause. Identify the functions of each noun clause as subject *(S)*, predicate noun *(PN)*, direct object *(DO)*, indirect object *(IO)*, object of the preposition *(OP)*, or appositive *(App)*. Underline each subordinating conjunction, indefinite relative pronoun, or indefinite relative adverb.

___OP___ 16. Every day we use springs in almost (<u>whatever</u> we do.)

___DO___ 17. Some mechanical and electrical devices require (<u>that</u> springs as small as 0.08 mm in diameter provide precise movements.)

___App___ 18. The fact (<u>that</u> the technology for such small springs was not developed until the end of the twentieth century) is amazing.

___S___ 19. (<u>How</u> this technology works) is still a mystery to most people.

___PN___ 20. The coil shape, as well as the elasticity, is (<u>what</u> makes the spring a very useful invention.)

V. Avoiding Sentence Errors

Identify each group of words as a sentence *(S)*, a fragment *(F)*, a comma splice *(CS)*, or a fused sentence *(FS)*.

___F___ 21. Three basic types of springs.

___S___ 22. There are compression springs, torsion springs, and tension springs.

___FS___ 23. The compression spring is designed to be compressed it resists or aids circular movement, depending on the desired direction of motion.

___CS___ 24. The torsion spring twists against a force in a circular motion, productive circular movement results.

___CS___ 25. Pulling two objects or components toward each other, the tension spring holds the objects in place, sometimes the tension moves them together.

Name ____________________

Chapter 6 Pretest: Agreement

I. Subject-Verb Agreement

Underline the subject(s) in each sentence. Then underline the correct verb from the choices in parentheses.

1. Building violins or other stringed instruments (*is, are*) a work of art.
2. Few (*understands, understand*) the time and painstaking work involved in the process.
3. Maple or sycamore (*is, are*) used for the back, ribs, and neck of a violin.
4. Both the spruce for the belly of the violin and the maple (*needs, need*) to air-dry for eight to ten years.
5. The acoustics of each instrument (*depends, depend*) on its intricate, mathematical design and precise construction.
6. Violin makers through the years (*has, have*) used hide glue because it, unlike common wood glue, will come apart when necessary.
7. Gouges, scrapers, and planers (*is, are*) used to carve the wood.
8. Aesthetically beautiful as well as functional, the inlaid ebony purfling around the edge of a violin (*requires, require*) great patience and practice.
9. When mixed and applied correctly, the two-layered varnish (*beautifies, beautify*) the wood but does not stifle its resonance.
10. Precision in all aspects of construction (*affects, affect*) the sound of each violin.

II. Pronoun-Antecedent Agreement

Underline the correct pronoun from the choices in parentheses.

11. Peter Paul Prier, a violin maker and restorer, opened (*his, their*) violin making school in 1972.
12. Though he uses a tough curriculum including physics, sculpture, and music history, Prier encourages (*his, its*) students to persevere.
13. Each beginning student faces discouragement as (*he, they*) makes mistakes and ruins months of work.
14. If a violin's wood is not carefully chosen and prepared, (*he, it*) will crack under the tension of the strings.
15. As a violin maker files away at a piece of maple, blond-colored shavings pile up on (*its, their*) surface.

16. Neither the students nor Prier forget to set aside one day each year to rest from (*his*, *their*) work and ski in the Wasatch Mountains near the school.

17. After months of hard work, the students who don't give up see (*his*, *their*) instruments finished and ready to be sold.

18. Many of the school's graduates have now started (*his*, *their*) own schools.

19. The Violin Making School of America and (*its*, *their*) graduates are serving the needs of musicians in America and around the world.

20. As a result of (*its*, *their*) high quality of workmanship, the school has produced and sold over a thousand instruments, including violins, violas, cellos, and basses.

III. Agreement Overview

Identify each error in the sentences below as a subject-verb agreement error *(SV)* or a pronoun-antecedent agreement error *(PA)*. If the sentence is correct, write *C*.

SV 21. The famed quartet prepare for a concert in honor of the great violin maker Stradivarius.

PA 22. Antonio Stradivarius and Andrea Guarneri, also a famous violin maker, made his homes in Cremona, Italy.

C 23. Actually, Stradivarius and Andrea Guarneri apprenticed themselves to Nicolo Amati.

SV 24. Everybody recognize these three as the masters of violin making.

SV 25. Stradivarius's artistry in decorating instruments are obvious in his intricate purfling designs.

PA 26. Some violinists prefer to use the instruments of Joseph Guarnerius del Gesu, grandson of Andrea Guarneri, because of its variant design and beautiful sound.

C 27. The identification labels inside violins sometimes give people false hope that they own an original Stradivarius violin.

PA 28. Many violins bear the Stradivarius label to acknowledge that its model was a Stradivarius.

PA 29. The 1701 "Servais" cello, a true Stradivarius, bears the name of his owner Adrien Francois Servais, who lived in the nineteenth century.

C 30. In April 2002 someone stole the beautiful 1714 Stradivarius "Le Maurien" in New York City!

Name ____________________

Chapter 7 Pretest: Verb Use

I. Simple and Perfect Tenses

Underline each complete verb. Then identify it as *present, past, future, present perfect, past perfect,* or *future perfect.*

present perfect 1. Have you read Gracia Burnham's book *In the Presence of My Enemies*?

past perfect 2. Gracia and her husband Martin had served as missionaries in the Philippines for fifteen years.

past 3. May 27, 2001, marked an irrevocable change in the Burnhams' lives.

present 4. The Abu Sayyaf, who kidnapped the Burnhams, claims to be part of Osama bin Laden's terrorist group al-Qaeda.

future 5. Gracia will always remember the lessons God taught her during her captivity.

II. Progressive Tenses

Underline each progressive verb. Then identify it as *present progressive, past progressive, future progressive, present perfect progressive, past perfect progressive,* or *future perfect progressive.*

past perfect progressive 6. Martin had been flying supplies to missionaries in the Philippines, and Gracia had been teaching their children.

past progressive 7. Martin and Gracia were vacationing in Dos Palmos Resort to celebrate their eighteenth wedding anniversary.

past perfect progressive 8. The Abu Sayyaf had been using any means necessary to accomplish their goal of instituting a Muslim state in the southern Philippine Islands.

present perfect progressive 9. Reflecting on the Burnham's story, I have been seeing that God does not always do what we think He ought to do but what He knows is best.

future progressive 10. Christians years from now will be learning from the Burnhams' experiences.

III. Tense Sequence and Consistency

Underline each verb written in incorrect tense. Write the correct verb. If the sentence is already correct, write *C* in the blank.

provided 11. During their time of captivity, God provides food—even a Mcdonald's hamburger—for the Burnhams.

Could have eaten 12. Could you have been eating a live minnow straight out of a stream as Gracia did?

abducted 13. The Abu Sayyaf abduct the Burnhams so quickly that Gracia did not have time to grab her Bible.

had sent 14. Gracia's niece will have sent the Burnhams two letters crammed with Bible verses, but only one letter reached them.

C 15. Despite her dangerous and difficult situation, Gracia came to enjoy the fellowship with God that resulted from complete dependence on Him.

IV. Voice

Underline the complete verb in each independent clause. Then identify it as either *active* or *passive*.

passive 16. Gracia was faced with her own rebelliousness and lack of faith in God's guidance.

active 17. God loves and guides His people in difficult times as well as in good times.

active 18. Martin demonstrated his desire to see souls saved by witnessing to his captors and serving them in every way possible.

active 19. Already familiar with the gospel message, the Abu Sayyaf members rejected the Burnhams' witness.

passive 20. The Burnhams' captors have been forgiven by Gracia.

V. Mood

Identify the mood of the italicized verb as *indicative, imperative,* or *subjunctive.*

indicative 21. God *answered* many specific prayers for the Burnhams.

subjunctive 22. If it *had been* God's will, the Abu Sayyaf would have released them.

indicative 23. During the seventeenth gun battle between the Philippine military and the Abu Sayyaf, a bullet *hit* Martin in the chest.

subjunctive 24. God desires that Christians *be* willing to trust Him in all circumstances.

imperative 25. *Read* Gracia's book to learn more about the struggles and triumphs that God allowed her to face.

Name ____________________

Chapter 8 Pretest: Pronoun Use

I. Pronoun Case: Personal Pronouns

Underline each personal pronoun and identify it as subjective *(S)*, objective *(O)*, possessive *(P)*, or independent possessive *(IP)*.

P 1. Adventurous men and women throughout the years have sought to establish their names in history for exploratory firsts.

O 2. Robert Edwin Peary chose Matt Henson to accompany him to the North Pole.

S 3. He designed a special ship, the *Roosevelt,* that would break through the ice of the Arctic.

P 4. Henson, the first black explorer of the Arctic, and Peary's wife, the first white woman to winter in the Arctic, wrote books of their experiences.

IP 5. Peary and Henson finally reached the North Pole in 1909, but theirs was not the first claim.

II. Pronoun Case: Appositives and Comparisons

Underline the correct pronoun from the choices in parentheses.

6. Though Dr. Fredrick Cook argued that he had reached the North Pole a year before Peary and Henson, Cook's account is less believable than *(theirs, him)*.

7. The northern coast of Ellesmere Island was also explored by the team led by Peary—Henson, Dr. Dedrick, some Eskimos, and *(he, him)*.

8. On his fourth expedition Peary reached a personal record of 84° 17' N, but Fridtjof Nansen had reached a point farther north than *(he, him)* three years earlier.

9. *(We, us)* Americans can take pride in the accomplishments of Peary.

10. Several of the men who aided Peary accomplished the same goal as *(he, him)*—reaching the North Pole.

III. Pronoun Case: "Subjects" and Objects of Verbals and *Who* vs. *Whom*

Underline the correct noun or pronoun from the choices in parentheses.

11. *(His, Him)* losing his toes to frostbite did not deter Peary from his goal.

12. Because George Borup would soon return with supplies, Peary wanted *(he, him)* to bring more fuel.

13. Ross Marvin was the man *(who, whom)* Peary had deliver the message to Borup.

14. Seeing *(they, them)* return with the fuel relieved Peary.

15. *(Who, Whom)* knows what would have happened if Peary's supplies had not been restocked.

Chapter 8 Pretest: Pronoun Use (continued)

IV. Courtesy Order and Reflexive and Intensive Pronouns

Underline the correct pronoun(s) from the choices in parentheses.

16. Reaching the Pole, even the team's dogs enjoyed (*themselves*, *them*) with a special meal provided by Peary.
17. Peary double-checked (*him*, *himself*) by crisscrossing the area of the North Pole and by taking multiple measurements.
18. Between (*me and you*, *you and me*), Peary's account of his expedition and the claims of his witnesses are much more convincing than the unfounded claims of Cook.
19. The monument on Peary's grave, which has a star representing the North Pole, came from a suggestion that Peary (*himself*, *hisself*) made to his wife.
20. During the class trip to Washington, D.C., with Mr. Lloyd, did (*you and he*, *he and you*) take a picture with the monument in the background?

V. Pronoun Shift

Underline each incorrect pronoun. In the blank write a correct pronoun. If the sentence is already correct, write *C* in the blank. ***(Answers may vary.)***

___*his*___ 21. Each of the explorers has their own memories of the expedition.

___*we*___ 22. Not only should we honor Peary, but you should also remember the sacrifices his wife Josephine made.

___*her*___ 23. Anyone who will accompany their husband into a freezing world and bear a child there deserves acknowledgment.

___*C*___ 24. Just before Peary retired from the navy in 1911, Congress promoted him to the rank of rear admiral and gave its full recognition of his reaching the North Pole first.

___*their*___ 25. Peary is just one of many explorers who have earned his place in history.

Name ________________________________

Chapter 9 Pretest: Pronoun Reference

I. Ambiguous and Remote Reference

Underline each pronoun that refers to an ambiguous or remote antecedent. Then rewrite the problem sentence correctly, replacing the unclear pronoun with the intended antecedent. ***(Answers may vary.)***

1. Booker T. Washington attended a school founded by General Samuel Armstrong because he had an insatiable desire to learn and improve himself.

   Because he had an insatiable desire to learn and improve himself, Booker T. Washington attended a school founded by General Samuel Armstrong.

2. Hampton Institute's head teacher Mary F. Mackie presented Washington with an unusual entrance examination. It had a classroom that needed to be cleaned, and Mackie told him to sweep it.

   Hampton Institute's head teacher Mary F. Mackie presented Washington with an unusual entrance examination. The Institute had a classroom that needed to be cleaned, and Mackie told him to sweep it.

3. Because Washington saw that Mackie was just like his previous employer Mrs. Ruffner, a woman who insisted on absolute cleanliness, he knew how she wanted the classroom to be cleaned.

   Because Washington saw that Mackie was just like his previous employer Mrs. Ruffner, a woman who insisted on absolute cleanliness, he knew how Mackie wanted the classroom to be cleaned.

4. Not only did he move all the furniture and sweep the floor three times, but he also dusted it inside and out four times so that not a speck of dust remained.

   Not only did he move all the furniture and sweep the floor three times, but he also dusted the furniture inside and out four times so that not a speck of dust remained.

5. Mackie's inspection lived up to Washington's expectations. She checked the corners of the closets and the railing on the wall for dust but found it immaculate. He passed the test, so she admitted him to the school.

   Mackie's inspection lived up to Washington's expectations. She checked the corners of the closets and the railing on the wall for dust but found the room immaculate. He passed the test, so she admitted him to the school.

Chapter 9 Pretest: Pronoun Reference (continued)

II. Reference to an Implied Noun or to a Noun that is a Modifier

Underline each pronoun once and each antecedent twice. If there is no antecedent or if the antecedent is a modifier, supply an appropriate antecedent in the blank. ***(Some answers may vary.)***

the government 6. Washington struggled to get an education because they didn't offer educational opportunities to emancipated slaves after the Civil War.

Washington 7. Washington's mother somehow acquired a spelling book that included the alphabet for him.

______ 8. At their own expense, blacks in Washington's community opened a school for the children. But it did not help Washington because he had to work.

______ 9. Sometimes the only night-school teacher Washington could find lived in a different town, and he had to walk several miles to and from school after working all day.

Attending the Institute 10. One day while working in a dark coal mine, Washington overheard two men talking about the Hampton Institute, where poor but hardworking blacks could receive an education. This became Washington's one passion.

III. Indefinite Reference of Personal Pronouns

Rewrite each sentence to correct any unclear or informal pronoun reference. If the sentence is already correct, write *C* in the blank. ***(Answers may vary.)***

11. Before Washington left home to attend Hampton Institute, it was apparent to him that no one expected him to succeed in his endeavor.

    Before Washington left home to attend Hampton Institute, he realized that no one expected him to succeed in his endeavor.

12. Washington set out for the school to prove to himself and others that you can achieve great things through hard work and determination.

    Washington set out for the school to prove to himself and others that anyone can achieve great things through hard work and determination.

13. During his trip to the school, Washington learned that they didn't like to provide room and board to a person of his race regardless of whether he had money or not.

    During his trip to the school, Washington learned that hotel keepers didn't like to provide room and board to a person of his race regardless of whether he had money or not.

Name ____________________

Chapter 9 Pretest: Pronoun Reference (continued)

14. Washington sought a place to sleep under an elevated portion of the board sidewalk where no one could see him.

    C

15. It was well worth the long, difficult journey when Washington saw the three-storied brick school buildings.

    Seeing the three-storied brick school buildings was well worth the long, difficult journey for Washington.

IV. Reference to a Broad Idea

Identify each sentence as clear *(C)* or unclear *(U)*. If the meaning is unclear, underline the pronoun causing the indefinite or broad reference.

U 16. Washington thought that getting an education meant a life of ease without hard labor, but he learned that this was a misconception.

U 17. The unselfish giving of the teachers at the Institute impressed Washington greatly. It taught him that happiness comes from serving others.

C 18. Miss Natalie Lord taught Washington the importance and relevance of the Bible. This appreciation for the Bible remained with him throughout his life.

C 19. Observing Mary Mackie clean windows and floors taught Washington an important lesson: a good education and high social standing does not exempt a person from hard work.

U 20. After Washington graduated from Hampton, he returned home to begin his lifelong mission of educating other members of the black community, which is a noble goal.

Name ____________________

Chapter 10 Pretest: Adjective and Adverb Use

I. Identification and Comparison of Modifiers

Underline each adjective, including the correct choice from the adjectives in parentheses. Double underline each adverb that modifies a noun.

1. The *(more common, most common)* species of sea turtle is the loggerhead with its exceptionally large head.
2. Because loggerhead turtles are only a threatened species and not an endangered species, they are *(more numerous, most numerous)* than the other species of sea turtles.
3. Having a reddish-brown carapace (upper shell) and a dull brown plastron (lower shell), these *(large, larger)* turtles can weigh up to 350 pounds.
4. A primarily carnivorous animal, the loggerhead uses its *(strong, stronger)* jaw muscles to eat shell-fish, including horseshoe crabs, clams, and mussels.
5. Of the two favorite nesting areas for loggerheads today, Masirah Island in the Middle East and the southeastern coast of the United States, Masirah Island has *(more, the most)* nests—about thirty thousand.

Underline each adverb. Double underline each noun that modifies a verb.

6. In Lewis Carroll's story, the Mock Turtle sighs deeply and sings Alice a song about turtle soup.
7. According to some people, green sea turtles taste curiously good in turtle soup.
8. If you've never had green turtle soup, you've also probably never had a steak from a green sea turtle's calipee.
9. The single pair of scales in front of the eyes of the green sea turtle easily distinguishes it from other turtles that have two pairs of scales.
10. Compared to green sea turtles in the Atlantic Ocean, those in the Pacific Ocean many times appear quite black and small.

II. Problems with Modifiers

Underline each incorrect adjective or adverb and write an appropriate correction in the blank. If the sentence is already correct, write C in the blank. ***(Answers may vary.)***

___*C*___ 11. Moving slowly but steadily up the beach, a female leatherback turtle plans to lay her eggs in a very deep hole.

___*omit very*___ 12. The turtle digs somewhat quickly in her very unique way.

a ______ 13. She is not making no snow angel design, though she moves her front flippers in a wing-like manner as she digs.

omit more ______ 14. Measuring up to 8 feet long and weighing up to 1,300 pounds, leatherbacks grow to be more bigger than all the other sea turtles.

unique ______ 15. Having small bones under their skin, leatherbacks possess a most unique leathery skin rather than a hard shell that other turtles have.

III. Placement of Modifiers

Underline each misplaced or dangling modifier. Then rewrite each sentence, making the modifiers clear and correct. If the sentence is already correct, write *C* in the blank. ***(Answers may vary.)***

16. Breaking free from their buried nest and scurrying toward the ocean, birds love to eat the newly hatched turtles.

    Breaking free from their buried nest and scurrying toward the ocean, newly hatched turtles face many dangers, such as predatory birds.

17. Fishermen who unknowingly use nets to catch fish also trap and drown turtles in their nets.

    Fishermen who use nets to catch fish also unknowingly trap and drown turtles in their nets.

18. All arriving on the same day, hundreds of Kemp's ridleys' nests line the beach near Rancho Nuevo, Mexico.

    All arriving on the same day, hundreds of Kemp's ridleys nest on the beach near Rancho Nuevo, Mexico.

19. Even flies, laying their eggs in Kemp's ridleys' nests, pose a threat to the turtle population as the maggots feed on the unhatched eggs.

    C

20. Many conservationists hope to especially protect the remaining sea turtles and to encourage the growth of their population.

    Many conservationists especially hope to protect the remaining sea turtles and to encourage the growth of their population.

Name________________________________

Chapter 11 Pretest: Capitalization

I. Personal Names, Religions, Nationalities, and Proper Adjectives

Underline each word containing a capitalization error.

1. History recognizes many great Visual Artists, including rembrandt, claude monet, leonardo da vinci, and pierre-auguste renoir.
2. The spanish Pablo Picasso painted in several different styles, such as Cubism and Expressionism.
3. Originally producing sad, dark paintings, vincent van gogh incorporated more color and happiness into his later Works after viewing colorful japanese paintings.
4. The florentine family de Medici patronized the Masterful artist Michelangelo Buonarroti. Michelangelo most often depicted christian subjects in his art, but on one occasion he produced a larger-than-life sculpture of the pagan god bacchus.
5. You can see rembrandt's painting *The Music Party* at the rijksmuseum in Amsterdam.

II. Place Names, Transportation, and Astronomy Terms

Underline each word containing a capitalization error.

6. Astronomical art—the Bayeux Tapestry of A.D. 1073, for example—dates back to early sightings of halley's comet.
7. Giotto, an artist of florence, accurately depicts all the parts of halley's comet in his painting *The Adoration of the Magi*.
8. In 1986 the European space agency launched the spacecraft *giotto* to photograph the nucleus of halley's comet and the Comet grigg-skjellerup.
9. Thomas Rowlandson of england caricatured the drastic reactions of people viewing Comets.
10. While most modern astronomical art utilizes photography and digital art, artist Steven Florides uses gouache to depict a large crater on mimas, one of saturn's moons, in his painting *The Eye of Mimas*.

III. Businesses and Organizations, Cultural and Historical Terms

Underline each word containing a capitalization error.

11. Staying current on art trends is possible through organizations such as the national assembly of state art agencies (nasaa).
12. Modern artists, such as Sculptor Karen McCoy, the head artist for a project commemorating the lewis and clark expedition, contribute to the development of historical and cultural sites.

Chapter 11 Pretest: Capitalization (continued)

13. Recording New Hampshire rural life during the depression, artists Nathaniel Burwash and Herbert Waters were celebrated in an art exhibition of the department of cultural resources from march to june of 2003.

14. The crowning achievement of sculptor Gutzon Borglum is mount rushmore, which memorializes four American presidents.

15. Students attending the university of missouri-columbia have the option of taking serigraphy classes.

IV. Titles, First Words, and Single Letters

Underline each word containing a capitalization error.

16. A taut piece of fabric (Early serigraphers used silk), paint, and a squeegee are necessary to produce a serigraph.

17. "I have printed only one serigraph," my friend Debbie remarked, "Not several. Serigraphy is just one type of printing that I learned in advanced printmaking."

18. With six different screens, Debbie printed a beautiful serigraph called *autumn leaves*.

19. In *cowboy coffee* G. Harvey, a prominent American artist, combines the processes of serigraph and lithograph to produce a beautiful print of brilliant color and subtle shading.

20. To find out more about serigraphy and other forms of printmaking, read *the bevelled edge* magazine.

Name ______________________

Chapter 12 Pretest: Punctuation

I. End Marks and Other Uses of the Period

Insert any missing periods or decimal points, question marks, or exclamation points.

1. Wow! Alaska is a huge state!
2. Did you know that Alaska is 2.3 times the size of Texas and one-fifth the size of all the other states combined?
3. The tour guide asked me if I knew that William H. Seward negotiated America's purchase of Alaska from Russia for only 7.2 million dollars in A.D. 1867.
4. At 9:30 A.M. we will visit the Anchorage Museum of History and Art on 121 W. Seventh Ave.
5. Help me! This king salmon must weigh at least 50 lb.

II. Commas: In a Series and After Introductory Elements

Insert any missing commas. If the sentence is already correct, write *C* in the blank.

_____ 6. While we're still in the Kenai Peninsula area, I'd also like to try some sea kayaking, bear watching, and hiking.

__C__ 7. On one hike a magnificent bald eagle flew out of a tree in front of me, and I snapped a quick picture of him.

_____ 8. Cracking and rumbling loudly, the Holgate Glacier in Kenai Fjords National Park calves into the bay.

_____ 9. I paddle my sea kayak in Aialik Bay, seal families float by on icebergs, and whales swim in the distance.

_____ 10. Finally, my tour of Kenai has ended, and I head to the interior of Alaska.

III. Commas: To Separate

Insert any missing commas.

11. The Alaska Range, home of Denali and Mt. Foraker, is located two hours north of Fairbanks.
12. Denali, not Mt. McKinley, is the original name of the highest mountain in North America.

13. Climbing either of these mountains involves potential dangers; therefore, each climber must pre-register with the Denali National Park rangers and pay a fee to offset the costs of rescue efforts.

14. You've heard that Denali rises 20,320 feet above sea level, haven't you?

15. Rachel, you would enjoy the photography opportunities, as well as many other activities, at the Denali National Park and Preserve.

IV. Commas: In Letters, Quotations, Dates, Addresses, and in Special Constructions

Insert any missing commas.

16. February 26, 1917, marked the beginning of Denali National Park and Preserve.

17. While visiting the park and Fairbanks, Alaska, I observed some strange lights in the night sky and asked what they were.

18. "The Aurora Borealis and Australis are caused by the interaction of solar flares with the earth's magnetosphere," explained scientist Jerry Scott, "and are most active in the fall, winter, and spring."

19. The Aurora Borealis creates a beautiful light show in the north; the Aurora Australis, in the south.

20. For more information about the Aurora Borealis, write to the Nome Convention and Visitors Bureau, P.O. Box 240, Nome, Alaska 99762.

V. Incorrect Commas

Circle any incorrect commas. If the sentence is already correct, write *C* in the blank.

______ 21. Amanda McFarland, and Isabelle Barnette are two women who contributed to Alaskan history.

__C__ 22. Having mushed a dog sled over the Alaska Range, Isabelle Barnette and her husband established a trading post and named it Fairbanks.

______ 23. For her brave work among Alaskan girls, Amanda McFarland earned the name, "Alaska's Courageous Missionary."

Name ______________________

Chapter 12 Pretest: Punctuation (continued)

______ 24. Alaska's first female pilot, Marvel Crosson, died in August, 1929, when her plane's engine failed and her parachute opened too late.

______ 25. Natasha Shelikof, wife of a Russian ruler, was the first white woman to live in Alaska, and, the native Alaskan women learned about manners and cleanliness from her.

VI. Semicolons and Colons

Insert any missing semicolons or colons. If the sentence is already correct, write *C* in the blank.

______ 26. Before leaving Alaska, I want to ride the famous White Pass railway that I have read about in *Alaska/Yukon Railroads:An Illustrated History*.

__C__ 27. The White Pass Summit Excursion includes a three-thousand-foot rise in only twenty miles, several bridges, and even two tunnels; be prepared for some great sights.

______ 28. The White Pass and Yukon Route also offers other options:the Lake Bennett Steam Adventure runs to the end of the Chilkoot Trail;a rail trip of just over an hour runs from Skagway, Alaska, to Fraser, British Columbia;and Chilkoot Trail hikers can catch a ride back to Skagway after their thirty-three-mile hike.

______ 29. Dear Mr. Danielson:

Thank you for the wonderful tour I received on the White Pass and Yukon Route;your employees were pleasant and the scenery was spectacular!

______ 30. Psalm 24:1 comes to mind as I think about all the wonders of Alaska:"The earth is the LORD's, and the fulness thereof; the world, and they that dwell therein."

Name ____________________

Chapter 13 Pretest: More Punctuation

I. Quotation Marks

Insert any missing quotation marks. If the sentence is already correct, write *C* in the blank.

_______ 1. "Do you remember who wrote 'The fog comes / on little cat feet?' " asked Merideth.

_______ 2. "Let's see," replied Drew, "I think it was Carl Sandburg. My teacher said that he lived and worked in Chicago for many years."

_______ 3. "Sandburg's poem 'Chicago' exemplifies his view of the hardworking man as the strength of America," Merideth observed.

___C___ 4. "Doesn't Sandburg personify the city as the 'Hog Butcher, Tool Maker, Stacker of Wheat, Player with Railroads / and Freight Handler to the Nation'?"

_______ 5. "Yes," answered Merideth, "he is often called the 'laureate of industrial America' for this type of imagery."

II. Ellipses and Brackets

Read the paragraph below. Write the letter of the quotation that is properly punctuated.

Carl Sandburg worked hard at whatever job he could find. He also rode the rails as a hobo. During this time Sandburg observed the life and hardship of the average American struggling to succeed. When he attended Lombard College, several teachers reinforce his developing socialistic ideology, which is very prominent in his poetry.

___B___ 6. A. Between the years 1892 and 1897, Sandburg "rode the rails as a hobo . . . [He] observed the life and hardship of the average American."
B. Between the years 1892 and 1897, Sandburg "rode the rails as a hobo. . . . [He] observed the life and hardship of the average American."
C. Between the years 1892 and 1897, Sandburg rode the rails as a hobo. . . . He observed the life and hardship of the average American."

___A___ 7. A. "When he attended Lombard College, several teachers reinforce [*sic*] his developing socialistic ideology."
B. "When he attended Lombard College, several teachers reinforced his developing socialistic ideology."
C. "When he attended Lombard College, several teachers reinforce [sic] his developing socialistic ideology."

___A___ 8. A. "Carl Sandburg [an American poet] worked hard at whatever job he could find."
B. "Carl Sandburg, an American poet, worked hard at whatever job he could find."
C. "Carl Sandburg (an American poet) worked hard at whatever job he could find."

Chapter 13 Pretest: More Punctuation (continued)

Read the poem below. Write the letter of the quotation that is properly punctuated.

The poet in a golden clime was born,
With golden stars above;
Dowered with the hate of hate, the scorn of scorn,
The love of love.

He saw through life and death, through good and ill,
He saw through his own soul.
From "The Poet" by Alfred, Lord Tennyson

__C__ 9. A. Sandburg, "dowered with the hate of hate, ... saw through life and death."
B. Sandburg, "dowered with the hate of hate, ... saw through life and death."
C. Sandburg, "dowered with the hate of hate, . . . saw through life and death."

__C__ 10. A. The student recited, "'The poet in a ... um ... golden clime ... was born.'"
B. The student recited, "'The poet in a, um, golden clime, was born.'"
C. The student recited, "'The poet in a . . . um . . . golden clime . . . was born.'"

III. Underlining for Italics

Underline any words that should be italicized.

11. When the bombing of the battleship USS *Maine* began the Spanish-American War, Sandburg signed on with the army to fight for the freedom of Cuba.
12. During much of his life, Sandburg supported the Socialist Party and wrote articles in several socialist newspapers, especially the *International Socialist Review*.
13. Professor Philip Green Wright published Sandburg's first collection of poems, *In Reckless Ecstasy*. The publishing of six of his poems in *Poetry: A Magazine of Verse* gained him recognition in the literary world.
14. In "Jabberers" Sandburg's use of the word *jabber* implies the significance, and insignificance, of the individual's language to distinguish him from the language of the world around him.
15. Sandburg's personality, interests, and down-to-earth manner made him a *persona grata* to all classes of American society.

Name ________________________________

Chapter 13 Pretest: More Punctuation (continued)

IV. Apostrophe and Hyphen

Insert any missing apostrophes and hyphens. Underline any words that contain unnecessary apostrophes or hyphens.

16. As an older man Sandburg collaborated with his brother-in-law Edward Steichen, a well-known painter and photographer, to produce a 503-picture book entitled *The Family of Man*.

17. This book, promoting Sandburg's humanistic view of a global community, sold more than fifty million copies by the mid-1990's.

18. Sandburg also produced several volume's of children's storybooks during the years 1922–30.

19. Sandburg's multivolume biography of President Lincoln won him the Pulitzer Prize.

20. Lillian Sandburg's passion, goat-raising, led Sandburg to buy Connemara, a 245-acre farm in Flat Rock, North Carolina.

V. Dashes and Parentheses

Insert any missing dashes or parentheses. ***(Some answers may vary.)***

21. The Carl Sandburg National Historic Site (have you visited there?) includes Connemara, a few goats, and hiking trails.

22. The top of Big Glassy Mountain—a gentle 1.3 m hike from the house—provides a spectacular view of the valley below.

23. A tour of the house, a hike up Big Glassy Mountain, and a visit to the goat barn—these will give you a better understanding of the poet and his writings.

24. Park regulations require that pet owners (1) keep pets on leashes at all times, (2) not leave pets unattended, and (3) refrain from taking pets into any buildings or near the goats.

25. Though hailed as a great American poet, Carl Sandburg held and proclaimed a philosophy contradictory to the Bible—belief in the goodness of man.

Name ____________________

Teaching Help 1: The Five-Paragraph Essay

Read the following essay and be prepared to answer questions about its structure and development. Underline the thesis statement, the topic sentence of each supporting paragraph, and the thesis restatement.

At the close of the school day each afternoon, many high-school students head home to relax. For other students, however, the day's activity is far from over as they race across athletic fields, dive into swimming pools, and practice gym relays. For some of these students, the choice to play sports in high school may have been a difficult one, especially as athletic commitments invariably involve much valuable time. However, the benefits of high-school athletics far outweigh the obvious time drawbacks.

First, high-school athletes learn discipline in their use of time. When whole evenings of potential study time are not available, students must carefully allocate several hours for study. Further, having time constraints on an evening's study time encourages students to devote quality, not mere quantity, time to school projects. A busy schedule makes student athletes plan ahead and study in advance or on alternate nights of the week. Time-pressed athletes know that when athletic practice ends, serious studying must begin.

Second, high-school athletes gain valuable social skills through team interaction. Consider the social benefit in learning to get along with others of different backgrounds and abilities. Student athletes learn a healthy tolerance for others and an understanding of their own gifts and limitations. Team sports, such as volleyball, basketball, and football, teach the importance of individuals working together to accomplish tasks: In order to score points all the players must work together. Such a lesson learned early will equip these students to be team players in other organizations, such as the church or workplace. Individual sports like track and swimming also foster teamwork because athletes must work toward collective goals like winning the next meet or gaining the regional championship. In all athletic groups, supportive friendships with coaches and teammates foster development of dedication and teamwork.

Third, high-school athletes set a healthy lifestyle with immediate and future rewards. Students who discipline themselves to stay in shape are stronger and healthier than their nonexercising peers, enjoying greater coordination and physical stamina as well as valuable mental alacrity. Students who exercise need not become dependent on artificial sugars and caffeinated beverages that give them second-rate alertness. Further, the well-being enjoyed by high-school athletes encourages them to continue making healthful fitness choices in the future, and as a result, they experience a better quality of life.

As high-school classes are dismissed each day, students make important decisions regarding their quality of life. For some students, the level of commitment involved in playing on an athletic team may seem too high a price to pay. However, the cost of remaining inactive in organized sports looms still higher in terms of a student's lack of disciplined time use, his loss of valuable social lessons, and his need of a healthy lifestyle. High-school students should take full advantage of the benefits available through athletics.

Name ____________________

Teaching Help 3: Sentence Patterns

Label the sentence patterns *S-InV, S-LV-PN, S-LV-PA, S-TrV-DO, S-TrV-IO-DO, S-TrV-DO-OC,* or *S-be-Advl.* If the adverbial is a prepositional phrase, underline it.

S LV Advl
1. The Metropolitan Opera House is <u>on the corner of West Sixty-second and Sixty-seventh Streets and Columbus and Amsterdam Avenues</u>.

S TrV IO DO
2. For its opening season in 1883, the Metropolitan Opera paid soprano Marcella Sembrich $1,455 for each of fifty-eight performances.

S TrV DO OC
3. The audience of Henry Abby's benefit concert thought Sembrich an accomplished musician.

LV S Advl
4. There were relatively cheap seats <u>in the Family Circle level of the opera house</u>.

S LV PN
5. After the financial loss of its first year, the Metropolitan Opera became a German opera company instead of an Italian one.

S S S InV
6. Cheaper seats, more affordable salaries for the performers, and appeal to the large German-speaking population in New York combined for financial and artistic success in the Metropolitan's second season.

S TrV DO OC OC
7. As the new manager, Edmund C. Stanton made Anton Seidl conductor and music director in 1885.

S TrV DO
8. George Bernard Shaw regarded the Metropolitan's 1884 production of the opera *Hamlet*, which was very different from Shakespeare's play, as being foolish.

S LV PA
9. While performing in San Francisco, the Metropolitan Opera company was devastated by the 1906 earthquake.

S TrV IO DO
10. Struggling with the task of managing the Metropolitan Opera, Heinrich Conried offered Gustav Mahler the position of conductor in 1907.

Name ______________________________

Teaching Help 4A: Absolute Phrases

Identify each introductory element as an *absolute phrase* or a *clause*.

absolute phrase 1. Chinese brush calligraphy differing from western calligraphy, artists elaborate on traditional characters to express their creativity.

clause 2. Because they symbolize good luck and prosperity, a Huishan craftsman molds "Da A Fu" figurines of a plump boy holding a green fish.

absolute phrase 3. Artists having written poems and painted pictures on fans, the elite of China valued fans for their beauty and the relief they provided from the heat.

absolute phrase 4. The Chinese considering poetry and painting to be complementary art forms, the best Chinese artists are also poets who include characters and seals in their pictures.

clause 5. When the Chinese began to cut beautifully colored paper to depict everyday objects and events, they created an art form unique to their culture.

Write a sentence containing an absolute phrase.

6. The dragon symbolizes the emperor. Chinese architects use artful statues to represent power and prestige in royal palaces.

   The dragon symbolizing the emperor, Chinese architects use artful statues to represent power and prestige in royal palaces.

7. Because the Gu Gong palace was the imperial home of the Quin emperors, strict rules governed who could open the ornately carved gates and when they were to be opened.

   The Gu Gong palace being the imperial home of the Quin emperors, strict rules governed who could open the ornately carved gates and when they were to be opened.

8. The Summer Palace is located on the Fine Jade Isle in Kun Ming Hu Lake. Quin emperors enjoyed this elaborate vacation home.

   The Summer Palace being on the Fine Jade Isle in Kun Ming Hu Lake, the Quin emperors enjoyed their elaborate vacation home.

9. While emperors live and vacation in elaborate palaces, the common people of Northwest China live more simply in caves lined with brick or slate.

   Emperors living and vacationing in elaborate palaces, the common people of Northwest China live more simply in caves lined with brick or slate.

10. The herdsmen of Northern China live a nomadic life. Yurts (portable homes made of animal hide) are common.

   The herdsmen of Northern China living a nomadic life, yurts (portable homes made of animal hide) are common.

Name____________________

Teaching Help 4B: Present Participles vs. Progressive Verbs

Underline each present participial phrase once and each progressive verb twice.

1. Do you see that girl climbing high on El Capitan in Yosemite?
2. Lynn is moving effortlessly through a series of reaches and steps toward the top.
3. Deciding on her next move, Lynn confidently executes her plan to reach the next handhold.
4. Photographers hanging from elaborate rope systems snap photos of her graceful movements.
5. Notice how she is controlling her momentum so that her feet don't slip off the miniscule ledges.
6. Ascending the route in record time is one goal propelling Lynn upward.
7. She is using her gear—rope, harness, and carabiners—for safety purposes, not to aid her ascent.
8. Noticing the beauty of the granite, Lynn is enjoying the aesthetics of her climb.
9. The watching crowd cheers her on toward her goal.
10. Reaching the apex, Lynn celebrates her accomplishment!

Name ____________________

Teaching Help 4C: Verbal and Nonverbal Phrases

Label the sentence patterns in each of the following sentences. Identify the italicized phrase as prepositional *(Prep)*, appositive *(App)*, participial *(Part)*, gerund *(Ger)*, or infinitive *(Inf)*. Then identify the function of the phrase as noun *(N)*, adjective *(Adj)*, or adverb *(Adv)*.

S TrV DO
__Ger__ __N__ 1. *Decorating a home with antique furniture* preserves historical objects from damage.

S TrV DO
__Inf__ __Adv__ 2. Some collectors travel abroad *to search for valuable objects.*

S TrV DO DO
__Inf__ __Adv__ 3. Other people visit antique shops or flea markets *to find hidden treasures.*

S TrV DO
__Prep__ __Adv__ 4. *During the summer,* we asked an appraiser to value our collection.

S InV
__Part__ __Adj__ 5. He stated that our grandfather clock, *retaining its original chimes,* sounded beautiful.

S TrV DO
__App__ __N__ 6. The pendulum, *a fascinating device,* has kept precise time for many years.

S InV
__Prep__ __Adv__ 7. This heirloom fits well *in our hallway.*

S InV
__Part__ __Adj__ 8. The 1820s walnut bookcase, *filled with antique books*, came from my great-grandfather's library.

S TrV DO OC
__App__ __N__ 9. The appraiser considered my marble table, *a gift from my grandparents,* the most valuable in our collection.

S LV PA S TrV DO
__Ger__ __N__ 10. *Saying which of our antiques is my favorite* is too difficult; I love all of them.

Name________________________________

Teaching Help 5A: Subordinating Conjunctions and Prepositions

Identify each italicized word (except titles of works) as either a subordinating conjunction *(SC)* or as a preposition *(P)*. Underline the subject of each dependent clause once and the predicate of each dependent clause twice.

__SC__ 1. *Before* Jane Austen was twenty-five years old, she had written *Pride and Prejudice,* a novel published in 1813.

__P__ 2. The heroine, Elizabeth Bennet, forms a poor opinion of Darcy *before* understanding his character.

__P__ 3. Despite Elizabeth's lower social rank, Darcy falls in love with her *because of* her quick wit and charming personality.

__SC__ 4. Elizabeth grows even more contemptuous of Darcy *when* Lieutenant Wickham accuses Darcy of denying Wickham his inheritance.

__SC__ 5. Elizabeth refuses to accept Darcy's offer of marriage *because* he has convinced his good friend Mr. Bingley not to marry her sister Jane.

__P__ 6. *Upon* seeing Pemberley, Darcy's large estate, Elizabeth contemplates living in such a home.

__SC__ 7. Darcy saves Elizabeth and her family from disgrace *as* her youngest sister has eloped with Wickham.

__P__ 8. Unexpectedly, Lady Catherine de Bourgh, Darcy's controlling aunt, arrives accusing Elizabeth *of* tricking Darcy into loving her and demands that Elizabeth promise not to marry Darcy.

__P__ 9. Elizabeth, however, has come to love Darcy *since* his kindness to her family during Lydia's elopement and therefore refuses to make any such promise to Lady Catherine.

__SC__ 10. Darcy and Elizabeth marry in a double wedding with Jane and Bingley *after* Darcy confesses his error of discouraging Bingley from pursuing Jane.

Name________________________________

Teaching Help 5B: *That* as a Relative Pronoun and a Subordinating Conjunction

Identify each italicized *that* as a relative pronoun *(RP)* or a subordinating conjunction *(SC)*. Identify the grammatical function of each relative pronoun within the dependent clause as subject *(S)*, direct object *(DO)*, or object of the preposition *(OP)*.

RP	*S*	1. In one of her novels, Jane Austen portrays Emma, the title character, as a young lady *that* possesses both material wealth and loving friends but is immature in her reasoning and treatment of others.
SC		2. Emma hopes *that* she might arrange a marriage between Harriet Smith, a young lady of low social standing, and Mr. Elton, the village vicar.
SC		3. *That* Emma could place him on the same social level as Harriet greatly offends Mr. Elton.
RP	*DO*	4. The marriage proposal *that* Mr. Elton makes to Emma is as unwelcome to her as the thought of marrying Harriet is to him.
SC		5. Mr. Knightley, appalled *that* Emma would flippantly play with Harriet's emotions, rebukes her for attempting to make matches.
RP	*OP*	6. Frank Churchill proves to be a new acquaintance *that* Emma can entertain herself with.
RP	*DO*	7. By flirting with Emma, Frank succeeds at hiding the love *that* he possesses for Jane Fairfax.
RP	*DO*	8. The death of his aunt provides Frank the freedom *that* he needs to marry Jane.
SC		9. When Harriet tells Emma of her love for Mr. Knightley, Emma finally realizes *that* she loves him herself and cannot bear the thought of anyone else marrying him.
RP	*S*	10. Through all her blunders Emma gains a mature perspective *that* resembles Mr. Knightley's clear judgment.

Name________________________________

Teaching Help 6A: Agreement Rules

Write the correct answer in the blank. Then circle each answer in the word-search box.

Answer		Statement
Amounts	1.	_?_, including periods of time, are considered singular and require singular verbs.
intervening	2.	The true subject, not an _?_ phrase, will agree with the verb.
pronoun	3.	Compound antecedents joined by *and* or *both—and* require a plural _?_.
inverted	4.	Identify the verb with the true subject of an _?_ sentence.
teams	5.	Names of _?_ and organizations that exist in plural form require plural verbs.
plural	6.	Do not use a _?_ personal pronoun to refer to a singular indefinite pronoun.
individuals	7.	A singular collective noun may require a plural verb if the meaning of the sentence emphasizes the _?_ in the group rather than the group as a whole.
antecedent	8.	A relative pronoun has the same number as its _?_.
person	9.	Each verb must agree with its subject in _?_ and number.
of	10.	An indefinite pronoun can be singular or plural depending on the _?_ phrase that modifies it.
title	11.	The _?_ of an individual work of art, music, or literature is always singular.
nearer	12.	For compound subjects joined by *or, either—or,* or *neither—nor,* the subject _?_ the first verb determines the form of the verb.
subject	13.	When the predicate noun differs in number from the subject, the verb agrees with the _?_.
meaning	14.	When determining whether a collective noun needs a singular or plural pronoun, analyze the sentence for its _?_.
singular	15.	When a word ending in *ics* refers to a field of study, use a _?_ verb.

Teaching Help 6A: Agreement Rules (continued)

I A T I T L S D E C E T N A
S N S L A M O U N T S V E M
I E T S A E I H P R O N B O
N A J E R G O N S E A F Q U
D E T R E V N I D R M L G N
I S I Y F X N U P A O N N P
V I T N S G W L O E I G O L
I N L S U T J M B N Y L S U
D G E L B E K E E L O Y R R
U U A P J E R V U A L R E A
A R L V E S R T Q H N A P L
L U N O C E R J B U S I E C
S R A N T E C E D E N T N O
I E W N A E T Y P D F H I G
M S I V N R A S M A E T D N

Name____________________

Teaching Help 6B: Agreement Review

In the blank write the correct form of the verb or pronoun as indicated in the parentheses. Then use your answers to complete the crossword puzzle.

ACROSS

fascinates 1. The history surrounding Lewis and Clark's adventures *(fascinate)* Americans today.

attempts 2. The Lewis and Clark Trail Heritage Foundation *(attempt)* to protect and preserve the historic trail for the enjoyment and education of the public.

are 3. Woolly mammoths, Peruvian llamas, and Welsh-speaking Indians *(be)* all myths about the West that Americans believed in 1803.

were 4. Both Meriwether Lewis and William Clark *(be)* captains in the army and shared command during the expedition.

requires 5. Knowing that the logistics of such a trip *(require)* extensive preparation, Lewis spent months buying supplies and studying science and navigation.

its 6. The Corps of Discovery commissioned by President Thomas Jefferson made *(personal pronoun)* way across the continent in search of the Northwest Passage.

realizes 7. Almost nobody *(realize)* that Lewis took a Newfoundland dog named Seaman on the expedition.

records 8. "A Summary View of Rivers and Creeks," Lewis's first report sent to President Jefferson, *(record)* details of the Missouri River water system.

their 9. Lewis and Clark spent much of *(personal pronoun)* time surveying, mapping, and studying flora and fauna.

their 10. Hired by Lewis to be an interpreter, Toussaint Charbonneau brought with him his Indian wife Sacagawea and *(personal pronoun)* fifty-five-day-old son.

DOWN

would 1. At the end of a long line of interpreters, Sacagawea was the one who *(auxiliary)* translate from Hidatsa into Shoshone.

was 2. One hundred lashes *(be)* the punishment for Private John Newman's mutinous actions at the beginning of the expedition.

traveled 3. Hauling their boats on wheels made from cottonwood, the explorers *(travel)* eighteen miles in five days to avoid waterfalls near modern day Great Falls, Montana.

his 4. Lewis painted *(personal pronoun)* face with red dye as a sign of peace to the Shoshone women that he first encountered.

were 5. Neither the Nez Perce nor the Shoshone tribes *(be)* hostile toward the explorers.

Teaching Help 6B: Agreement Review (continued)

presented 6. Crossing the Bitterroot Mountains on the Lolo Trail *(present)* many hazards to the explorers.

wants 7. No one *(want)* to remember who shot Lewis in the leg: Pierre Cruzatte accidentally hit Lewis while hunting elk.

is 8. Appendicitis *(be)* recorded to be the cause of Sgt. Charles Floyd's death, the only death during the expedition.

believed 9. Though nobody *(believe)* John Colter's description of an area of geysers and boiling mud pits, many people today know of Yellowstone National Park.

his 10. Each American should make it a point to learn about *(personal pronoun)* heritage.

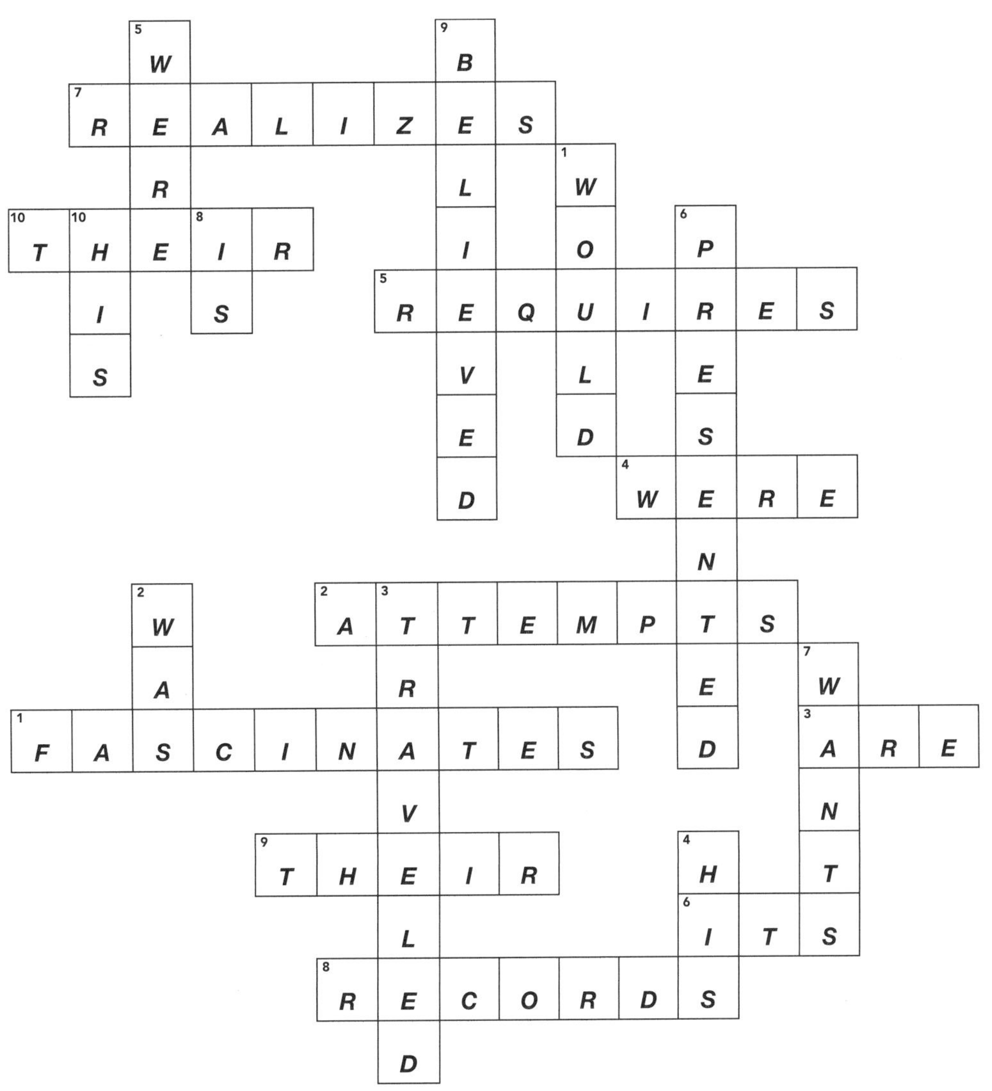

Name ______________________

Teaching Help 7A: Consistency and Sequence of Tenses

Underline each verb in incorrect tense. Then rewrite the paragraph correcting the incorrect verbs.

Last week we study about James Fenimore Cooper in literature class. Miss Rhinier, our teacher, reads part of *Deerslayer* to us, and then we discuss the character Natty Bumppo. Natty, who was an orphan of white settlers, lived with the Delaware Indians. In *Deerslayer* he sets out on a mission to prove himself a man. Though already an accomplished hunter, Natty had never killed another human. He believed that taking scalps was wrong for a white man and that a white man must keep his word. Natty kills a Huron named Le Loup Cervier who wanted Natty's canoe. Because Natty refused to fight unfairly and because of his surprisingly accurate aim, the dying Indian names him Hawkeye. No longer just a good hunter, Natty was now a warrior.

Last week we studied about James Fenimore Cooper in literature class. Miss Rhinier, our teacher, read part of* Deerslayer *to us, and then we discussed the character Natty Bumppo. Natty, who is an orphan of white settlers, lives with the Delaware Indians. In* Deerslayer *he sets out on a mission to prove himself a man. Though already an accomplished hunter, Natty has never killed another human. He believes that taking scalps is wrong for a white man and that a white man must keep his word. Natty kills a Huron named Le Loup Cervier who wants Natty's canoe. Because Natty refuses to fight unfairly and because of his surprisingly accurate aim, the dying Indian names him Hawkeye. No longer just a good hunter, Natty is now a warrior.

Name ______________________________

Teaching Help 7B: Using Active and Passive Sentences

Underline each passive verb once and each retained object or subjective complement twice. Then rewrite the paragraph in active voice, keeping passive voice only when necessary. ***(Answers will vary.)***

During a witty exchange, my friend Lynnelle was told a humorous quotation by her English professor: "If in his study he hath so much care / To hang all old strange things, let his wife beware." Lynnelle decided to find the source of this couplet. Searching the Internet, she found that it had been penned by John Donne to describe an antique collector. As a result of her study, Lynnelle became fascinated by Donne's religious poems. She was challenged by the poem "The Cross," which states, "Since Christ embraced the cross itself, dare I / His image, th' image of His cross, deny?" Lynnelle presented her study to the class and reported that Donne is considered a great metaphysical poet by critics. The class was given an appreciation of Donne and his writing through Lynnelle's presentation.

During a witty exchange, an English professor told my friend Lynnelle a humorous quotation: "If in his study he hath so much care / To hang all old strange things, let his wife beware." Lynnelle decided to find the source of this couplet. Searching the Internet, she found that John Donne had penned it to describe an antique collector. As a result of her study, Lynnelle became fascinated by Donne's religious poems. The poem "The Cross" challenged her with these words: "Since Christ embraced the cross itself, dare I / His image, th' image of His cross, deny?" Lynnelle presented her study to the class and reported that critics consider Donne a great metaphysical poet. Lynnelle's presentation gave the class an appreciation of Donne and his writing.

Name______________________________

Teaching Help 8: Pronouns with Verbals

Write the missing word from each rule in the blank.

possessive 1. The "subject" of a gerund is in the ? case.

function 2. If a pronoun is followed and modified by a participial phrase, not a gerund phrase, the case of the pronoun is determined by its ? within the sentence.

objective 3. The "subject" of an infinitive is in the ? case.

objective 4. A noun or pronoun that follows an infinitive and acts as its object is in the ? case.

same 5. A pronoun that follows a linking verb infinitive must be in the ? case as the earlier word that it is renaming.

Write the correct pronoun in the blank.

his 6. Andrew Campbell's curiosity led to ? discovering the Luray Caverns in 1878.

them 7. After his initial discovery Campbell approached several friends and asked ? to accompany him on an exploratory trip into the cavern.

him 8. Benton Stebbins photographed ? sliding down a rope into the cavern below for the first time.

they 9. These early explorers realized that if anyone was going to develop the caverns for public use, it would have to be ?.

them 10. The cave's features are so captivating that vacationers flock to see ?.

Name ______________________

Teaching Help 9A: Clear Pronoun Reference

Underline the five ambiguous or remote pronoun references. Then rewrite the paragraph, correcting the unclear references. ***(Answers will vary.)***

In a game of cricket, the offensive player attempts to knock over his opponent's wicket with an overhand throw, and the defensive player bats the ball away from the wicket. It is a favorite game among the English and the countries colonized by the English. Robert, who is from England, and Ashish, who is from India, drove to the field to play cricket. He grabbed a bat, ball, and wicket out of the car. While Robert practiced bowling techniques, Ashish practiced various batting techniques. He played cricket professionally in India. They allow the batter to hit the ball in any direction. Eventually the men participated in a close game of cricket. When they finished playing, Ashish told Robert that he had played well.

In a game of cricket, the offensive player attempts to knock over his opponent's wicket with an overhand throw, and the defensive player bats the ball away from the wicket. Cricket is a favorite game among the English and the countries colonized by the English. Robert, who is from England, and Ashish, who is from India, drove to the field to play cricket. Ashish grabbed a bat, ball, and wicket out of the car. While Robert practiced bowling techniques, Ashish, who had played cricket professionally in India, practiced various batting techniques. These techniques allow the batter to hit the ball in any direction. Eventually the men participated in a close game of cricket. When they finished playing, Ashish said, "Robert, you played well."

Name______________________

Teaching Help 9B: Pronoun Reference

Identify each sentence as *clear (C)* or *unclear (U)*. Underline each pronoun causing unclear reference.

___*U*___ 1. They say that most college students change their major several times during their college careers.

___*U*___ 2. A college's course catalog often provides valuable information concerning its majors.

___*U*___ 3. Many college-bound people think you ought to know what to major in right away, but sometimes waiting a year or two is advisable.

___*U*___ 4. Colleges and universities may offer hundreds of majors to choose from, which can be daunting.

___*C*___ 5. A student's interest in a particular subject can help the student to decide if he would like to pursue it as his major.

___*C*___ 6. Most colleges have career development offices. The counselors there help students assess their interests and can suggest majors that correspond to those interests.

___*C*___ 7. Their mature perspective and real-life experience give academic advisors the ability to help students make wise choices.

___*C*___ 8. Because the choices made in college affect the rest of life, they should be made only after much prayer for God's guidance.

___*U*___ 9. God often guides us into areas of study that we did not originally want to pursue; this demonstrates how God beautifully orchestrates His perfect will.

___*C*___ 10. Rachel told Merideth, "Through various circumstances God has guided me to major in English. Although I used to dislike English, now I love it!"

Name ______________________________

Teaching Help 10A: Irregular Comparison

Insert the correct form of the following adjectives and adverbs into the paragraph. Words may be used more than once or not at all.

bad	common	little	many	sick
cheap	good	much	red	well

Last spring I went to a ski resort in North Carolina with some friends. We had the ___***best***___ time even though we faced several out-of-the-ordinary circumstances. First, I taught my friends to ski. Joel and Micah, who are from an island in the Caribbean, learned quickly and were soon skiing ___***better***___ than their sister Janiera even though she said she had skied before. Having been skiing many times, Oran skied very ___***well***___ and even attempted a few jumps. Unfortunately, we had an equipment mishap. On the first trip up the ski lift, one of Micah's poles caught on the lift and bent. I've never felt ___***sicker/worse***___ than I did at that moment. Fortunately, we didn't have to pay for the pole because it was one of the ___***cheapest***___ rental poles available and wasn't worth anything. Last of all, the snow was the ___***worst***___ I have ever skied. Skiing the last night of the season makes for wet, patchy snow. Some sections of the hill had so ___***little***___ snow that we had to slog through mud and puddles of water! I also found that skiing on manmade snow was ___***more***___ difficult than skiing on natural snow and that falling was ___***more common***___ than staying on my feet. Throughout the evening we fell ___***many***___ times, got very wet, and laughed at each other. We had a fantastic time!

Name ______________________________

Teaching Help 10B: Adjective and Adverb Use

Underline each misused modifier. Rewrite each sentence to correct any misused modifiers. If the sentence is already correct, write *C* in the blank. ***(Answers will vary.)***

1. Forgotten and untouched for hundreds of years, Hiram Bingham discovered Machu Picchu in 1911.

   Forgotten and untouched for hundreds of years, Machu Picchu was discovered in 1911 by Hiram Bingham.

2. Machu Picchu was a fortress city of the Inca civilization standing above eight thousand feet.

   Machu Picchu, standing above eight thousand feet, was a fortress city of the Inca civilization.

3. Huayna Picchu, near Machu Picchu, is the tallest of the two mountains.

   Huayna Picchu, near Machu Picchu, is the taller of the two mountains.

4. Many archaeologists have studied the ruins of Machu Picchu, hoping finally to solve the many mysteries surrounding the function of the ancient city.

   Many archaeologists have studied the ruins of Machu Picchu, hoping to finally solve the many mysteries surrounding the function of the ancient city.

5. There are hardly no satisfactory clues to explain the end of the community living at Machu Picchu.

   There are almost no satisfactory clues to explain the end of the community living at Machu Picchu.

6. Researchers only have discovered hints and not answers to these mysteries.

   Researchers have discovered only hints and not answers to these mysteries.

7. The Torreon, thought to be an astronomical observatory, appears to be the center of a pagan worship of nature.

   C

Teaching Help 10B: Adjective and Adverb Use (continued)

8. Revering the sun above all, the Intiwatana stone was carefully cut and positioned to act as a type of calendar for religious ceremonies.

   Revering the sun above all, the Incas carefully cut and positioned the Intiwatana stone to act as a type of calendar for religious ceremonies.

9. Despite their most magnificent architectural abilities, the Incas did not glorify God but worshiped His creation and became fools (Rom. 1:21–23).

   Despite their magnificent architectural abilities, the Incas did not glorify God but worshiped His creation and became fools (Rom. 1:21–23).

10. A religiously debased civilization, Francisco Pizarro maliciously conquered the Incas.

    Francisco Pizarro maliciously conquered the Incas, a religiously debased civilization.

Name ____________________

Teaching Help 11: Capitalization

Underline any words containing capitalization errors in the following letter.

dear Mr. Uptain,

A friend of mine, Rob provenzano, told me about your Bible Camp in the Mountains of wyoming. God has been using Rob's description of your camp to show me the spiritual needs of america's youth. Until he described many of his campers and the ways in which they worship the Gods of this world, i never comprehended the great need for Christian young people to invest their lives in Summer camping ministries.

I am currently a Freshman at a Christian College pursuing a B.S. in biology. Growing up in a chinese home, i was saved out of a buddhist background at age ten. During a vacation on the *victoria* cruise ship, my family heard about God's gift of Salvation from another family. My family and I accepted Christ as Savior during this cruise on the mediterranean sea. Since my salvation i have sought to serve Christ in every aspect of my life.

Though i have never had the privilege of attending a Bible Camp, i believe that the Lord would have me serve him at a camp. Please consider hiring me to work this Summer as a Camp Counselor. My desire is to be a channel, as Mary e. Maxwell describes in the hymn "channels only," through which God's love can shine to the campers.

Jesus, fill now with thy Spirit
hearts that full surrender know;
that the streams of living water
from our inner man may flow.

thank you for your consideration. I will continue in Prayer, as i am sure you will do.

in Christ,

Dashan Xue

Name ____________________

Teaching Help 12A: End Marks

Identify each sentence as a polite request *(PR)*, an imperative *(I)*, a mild imperative *(MI)*, a direct question *(DQ)*, or an indirect question *(IQ)*. Then place the correct end mark at the end of each sentence.

PR 1. May we please take a tour of the United States Capitol**?**

DQ 2. Were you surprised to hear the tour guide welcome everybody to the Capitol in his own language**?**

MI 3. Please feel free to take as many pictures as you like**.**

I 4. Wow! Look at the Rotunda**!**

DQ 5. Who painted the *Apotheosis of Washington***?**

IQ 6. The tour guide asked us if we knew why Washington is surrounded by thirteen women in the painting**.**

IQ 7. My friend asked if we would see the National Statuary Hall Collection**.**

PR 8. Will you please tell me which statues are from the state of Wyoming**?**

DQ 9. Do you know why some of the statues are not in the National Statuary Hall**?**

I 10. For security purposes, do not take mace or pepper spray on your tour of the Capitol**.**

Name ______________________

Teaching Help 12B: Commas with Adjectives

In the blanks write a pair of adjectives for each sentence. Use a variety of coordinate and cumulative adjectives. Insert any necessary commas in your answers. Be prepared to explain your answers. ***(Answers will vary.)***

1. On a ***cool*** ***spring*** evening, my friend and I went to a play in the park, Shakespeare's *Much Ado About Nothing*.
2. Because we were not sure of the exact location of the park, we drove up and down ***several*** ***small*** roads before we found it.
3. Arriving somewhat late, we carried our ***borrowed*** ***lawn*** chairs to the back of the crowd and sat down.
4. Some of the ***early,*** ***enthusiastic*** spectators sat on blankets near the stage.
5. Most people had ***delicious*** ***picnic*** dinners, but my friend and I had forgotten to take anything to eat or drink.
6. The ***movable*** ***wooden*** stage consisted of a castle front, a platform, an elevated pier, and a few small boats.
7. From our position we sometimes could not hear the ***soft,*** ***mellow*** voice of the actress playing Hero.
8. Of course, we were in stitches over the ***animated,*** ***ignorant*** antics of Dogberry.
9. I was surprised by the ***beautiful*** ***double*** marriage at the end of the play.
10. The ***well-performed,*** ***entertaining*** play combined with the enjoyable atmosphere of the park made for an experience that my friend and I will never forget.

Name____________________________

Teaching Help 12c: Commas with Restrictive and Nonrestrictive Elements

Identify each italicized phrase or clause as restrictive *(R)* or nonrestrictive *(NR)*. Insert any missing commas.

NR 1. The United States Chess Federation (USCF), *a nonprofit organization*, is committed to promoting the game of chess in America.

R 2. The competitor *with the white chess pieces* moves first.

NR 3. The most powerful chess piece is the queen, *which can move in all directions and for any number of spaces.*

R 4. The trend *that prefers sudden death matches over lengthier matches* often frustrates players who have a definite advantage over their opponents but do not have sufficient time to checkmate them.

NR 5. *When he has only five minutes left*, a player may ask the director to declare the game a draw to avoid losing the match due to time constraints.

R 6. Most of the students *who won the National Chess Championship this year* are from a different school district than previous winners.

R 7. Women's world champion *Zsuzsa Polgar of Hungary* first became the champion in 1996.

R 8. Larry Christiansen earned the title of grandmaster *after winning the Malaga tournament in 1977.*

NR 9. Novice tournaments, *which involve only a minimal fee*, provide beginners with an opportunity to experience chess tournaments.

NR 10. Benjamin Franklin, *one of America's greatest philosophers*, praised the game of chess as a stimulant for the mind.

Name________________________________

Teaching Help 13: Punctuation Placement

Identify each statement as true *(T)* or false *(F)*. Then rewrite each false statement to make it correct. ***(Some answers may vary.)***

F 1. Make the possessive form of singular nouns ending in *s* and plural nouns ending in *s* or *es* by adding an apostrophe followed by *s*.

Make the possessive form of singular nouns ending in* s *by adding an apostrophe followed by* s *and plural nouns ending in* s *or* es *by adding an apostrophe.

T 2. Ellipses taking the place of the end of a sentence and the beginning of another are preceded by a period.

T 3. Periods and commas always go inside closing quotation marks.

T 4. Set off an internal appositive series with dashes.

F 5. Exclamation points and question marks precede the closing quotation mark if the entire sentence is an exclamation or question.

Exclamation points and question marks follow the closing quotation mark if the entire sentence is an exclamation or question.

F 6. While commas set off short phrases and clauses, parentheses signal less formal but important material and dashes indicate that the enclosed material is less important.

While commas set off short phrases and clauses, dashes signal less formal but important material and parentheses indicate that the enclosed material is less important.

___*F*___ 7. To set off material within a set of parentheses, use another set of parentheses.

When necessary use a set of brackets to set off material within a set of parentheses.

___*T*___ 8. In a sentence containing divisions set off by parenthetical numbers, commas or semicolons are still necessary between items in the list.

___*T*___ 9. Never enclose the title of your own essay or paper in quotation marks on the title page.

___*F*___ 10. Use a hyphen to divide a word at the end of a line according to the following guidelines: between syllables, with at least three letters and the hyphen on the first line, and with at least two letters on the second line.

Use a hyphen to divide a word at the end of a line according to the following guidelines: between syllables, with at least two letters and the hyphen on the first line, and with at least three letters on the second line.

Name ____________________

ESL Help 2B: Exercise in Positions of Adjectives

Rewrite the sentences, placing the adjectives in the correct order to modify the noun that immediately follows the adjectives. Do not forget to capitalize the first word of each sentence.

1. *(sweet, the, elderly)* teacher reached for the phone.

   The sweet elderly teacher reached for the phone.

2. She checked *(old, faded, yellow, the)* phone book for the number.

   She checked the faded old yellow phone book for the number.

3. *(yellow, the, bright)* sun was just peeping over the horizon.

   The bright yellow sun was just peeping over the horizon.

4. The teacher hoped that it was not too early to call the mother of Victoria, one of *(fifth-grade, shyest, her)* students.

   The teacher hoped that it was not too early to call the mother of Victoria, one of her shyest fifth-grade students.

5. Earlier in the week some of the other fifth graders had asked their teacher for permission to hold *(little, a, surprise)* party for Victoria's birthday.

   Earlier in the week some of the other fifth graders had asked their teacher for permission to hold a little surprise party for Victoria's birthday.

6. They wanted to bring *(fancy, chocolate, some)* cupcakes for the whole class.

   They wanted to bring some fancy chocolate cupcakes for the whole class.

7. One student even planned to serve *(pink, cold, delicious)* lemonade.

   One student even planned to serve delicious cold pink lemonade.

8. Hence, the teacher thought she should check with Victoria's mother to make sure that she had made *(no, special)* plans already.

   Hence, the teacher thought she should check with Victoria's mother to make sure that she had made no special plans already.

ESL Help 2B: Exercise in Positions of Adjectives (continued)

9. As soon as the phone was answered, the teacher immediately began to explain *(big, elaborate, the)* plans that had been made.

   As soon as the phone was answered, the teacher immediately began to explain the big elaborate plans that had been made.

10. However, it was Victoria who had answered *(the, phone, early)* call, and to this day she has kept her secret.

    However, it was Victoria who had answered the early phone call, and to this day she has kept her secret.

Name ______________________________

ESL Help 2E: Exercise in Article Usage

Choose the correct article *(a, an,* or *the)* to put in each blank. If no article is needed, put an *X* in the blank. Above each answer list the appropriate rule number from the Article Usage sheet.

When someone visits another country, he must learn to communicate with __*the* (2.1)__ inhabitants of that country. Sometimes it is possible to know __*the* (5.2)__ language spoken in that country and still have __*X* (4.1)__ problems. At other times one is able to communicate even without words. In one particular instance a couple from __*the* (1.3)__ United States went to visit __*X* (1.3)__ France. __*The* (1.1)__ Stowes had studied __*X* (5.1)__ French for only one semester. After a pleasant airplane flight, the couple arrived at __*X* (1.2)__ Charles de Gaulle Airport barely able to understand __*X* (4.1)__ traffic signs and menus. While in __*the* (2.2)__ airport, they had to pick up their luggage, decipher transportation options, and purchase the necessary tickets to travel to their hotel. Having a limited use of __*X* (1.2)__ French, they began __*X* (3.2)__ their challenge of traversing __*the* (3.3)__ maze of bus, rail, and subway lines. Getting on and off at __*the* (3.3)__ right stops, hauling luggage up and down stairs, and trying not to stare at various musicians along the way were all challenges. After riding __*the* (2.3)__ third subway train, the couple arrived at __*the* (5.2)__ metro stop closest to their hotel. They still had to make their way to street level with all their bags and then decide which way to walk to __*the* (2.2)__ hotel. Evidently they looked somewhat bedraggled because __*a* (3.1)__ kind French woman helped them. __*The* (5.2)__ door that she identified led to __*a* (3.1)__ hidden escalator. The French woman rode with them and asked in __*X* (1.2)__ halting English what hotel they wanted to go to. After they informed her, she flagged down __*a* (3.1)__ bus and told __*the* (2.1)__ driver where to take them. While trying to convey their deep gratitude, the couple hurried onto __*the* (2.2)__ bus. As its door closed, they heard their newfound friend say, "No thank, I'm __*a* (3.1)__ Christian!"

Name________________________

ESL Help 2G: Exercise in Adverb Placement

Decide whether the italicized adverbs are placed correctly. If the placement is correct, write *C* in the blank to the left. If the placement is incorrect, write *I* in the blank and then rewrite the sentence correctly. ***(Answers will vary.)***

I 1. The mountain climber lost *almost* his way in the heavy fog.

The mountain climber almost lost his way in the heavy fog.

I 2. Delphino *outside* peered at the crowd gathered at the train station.

Delphino peered outside at the crowd gathered at the train station.

C 3. Malea was *happily* working in her garden.

I 4. The father takes *usually* his daughter along when he goes jogging.

The father usually takes his daughter along when he goes jogging.

C 5. Campers will *often* exchange addresses.

C 6. Duke wagged his tail *very* energetically when we arrived.

C 7. *Yesterday* she searched for buttons to match her dress.

I 8. *Methodically* at the crime scene the police questioned all bystanders.

At the crime scene the police methodically questioned all bystanders. or
At the crime scene the police questioned all bystanders methodically.

C 9. Jana is *seldom* late for class.

I 10. The sun is always *somewhere* shining.

The sun is always shining somewhere. or Somewhere the sun is always shining.

Name ______________________

ESL Help 21: Exercise in Making Sentences Negative Using *Not*

Rewrite the following sentences to make them negative. Follow these steps:

A. If there is a word or phrase in parentheses, use it to replace something from the original sentence.

B. Add *not* to each sentence.

C. Change the form of the verb and add an auxiliary if necessary.

EXAMPLE Tyler enjoys working in the garden. (*Zachary*)
Zachary does not enjoy working in the garden.

1. Spring months are usually rainy. (*fall*)

   Fall months are not usually rainy.

2. Sometimes it rains three or four days a week.

   Sometimes it does not rain three or four days a week.

3. However, "April showers bring May flowers." (*March*)

   However, "March showers do not bring May flowers."

4. Of course, along with spring comes tornado season. (*hurricane*)

   Of course, along with spring does not come hurricane season. or Of course, hurricane season does not come along with spring.

5. The weatherman's forecast of late afternoon showers often includes tornado watches. (*morning*)

   The weatherman's forecast of morning showers does not often include tornado watches.

6. Occasionally a watch becomes a warning. (*often*)

   A watch does not often become a warning.

7. A tornado watch suggests the possibility of a tornado forming. (*certainty*)

   A tornado watch does not suggest the certainty of a tornado forming.

8. However, the spotting of an actual tornado prompts a warning. (*tornado conditions*)

   However, the spotting of tornado conditions does not prompt a warning.

9. Some tornadoes have been particularly devastating.

   Some tornadoes have not been particularly devastating.

10. Strong winds and huge hailstones often accompany tornadoes. (*small thunderstorms*)

    Small thunderstorms do not often accompany tornadoes.

Name ______________________

ESL Help 2K: Exercise in Using Prepositions

Choose the correct word for each blank from the choices in parentheses. If none of the suggested words is correct or if no preposition is needed, put an *X* in the blank.

1. Rich asked me if the chess tournament would be played ___X___ there. *(at, on)*
2. I told him that I thought it was being held ___X___ downtown somewhere. *(in, at)*
3. The tournament is supposed to be ___during___ the Memorial Day weekend. *(during, while)*
4. The games are scheduled ___at___ different times throughout the day. *(on, at, in)*
5. Rich hopes to play early ___in___ the morning. *(on, in)*
6. Everyone should be very quiet ___while___ the games are being played. *(during, while)*
7. Rich said he needed to come ___X___ here to practice before the tournament. *(at, to)*
8. Winning the tournament would be a sign ___of___ great ability. *(of, at)*
9. The winner will be announced at 5:00 P.M. ___on___ Monday. *(on, at, in)*
10. It would be wonderful if Rich brought ___X___ home the winning trophy. *(at, to)*

Name ________________________________

ESL Help 3B: Exercise in Inverted Subject and Predicate

Change each sentence to a *yes/no* question. Remember to look at the verb tense for each sentence. Then use that same tense for the question.

1. The field trip to the zoo was a successful experience.

   Was the field trip to the zoo a successful experience?

2. Everyone arrived on time for departure.

   Did everyone arrive on time for departure?

3. The students were excited about the day.

   Were the students excited about the day?

4. They sang songs during the entire bus trip.

   Did they sing songs during the entire bus trip?

5. They had been looking forward to this field trip all year.

   Had they been looking forward to this field trip all year?

Change each sentence to a *wh* question. Use the word in parentheses to form the question. Write the question and its short answer in the blank.

6. The buses arrived at the zoo around 10 A.M. (*when*)

   When did the buses arrive at the zoo? around 10 A.M.

7. Mr. Parker's group entered the zoo first. (*whose*)

   Whose group entered the zoo first? Mr. Parker's

8. The animal they liked most was the elephant. (*what*)

   What was the animal they liked most? the elephant

9. Mrs. Lewis led the most enthusiastic group. (*who*)

   Who led the most enthusiastic group? Mrs. Lewis

10. They showed their enthusiasm by cheering each time they saw a different animal. (*how*)

    How did they show their enthusiasm? by cheering each time they saw a different animal

Name ____________________

ESL Help 5B: Exercise in How to Combine Sentences

The following chart shows meaning similarities among the three main types of connecting words.

Coordinating Conjunctions	Conjunctive Adverbs	Subordinating Conjunctions
and	besides, likewise, moreover, also	—
or	otherwise	—
so	accordingly, consequently, then, therefore, thus	because, since
but, yet	however, nevertheless, still	while, whereas, although, even though

Combine the following sentences using the formulas indicated. Rewrite each sentence, adding a correct connecting word and the correct punctuation. You may leave the words in parentheses out of the sentence. ***(Answers may vary.)***

EXAMPLE Brian borrowed his father's boat. (In addition,) Charles rented some water skis.

IC, cc IC. (Formula 1): Brian borrowed his father's boat, and Charles rented some water skis.

IC; ca, IC. (Formula 5): Brian borrowed his father's boat; moreover, Charles rented some water skis.

IC. ca, IC. (Formula 4): Brian borrowed his father's boat. Moreover, Charles rented some water skis.

1. Brian is muscular. (In contrast,) Charles is very thin.

   IC, cc IC. (Formula 1): ***Brian is muscular, but Charles is very thin.***

   IC. IC, ca, IC continued. (Formula 6): ***Brian is muscular. Charles, however, is very thin.***

   IC (sc DC). (Formula 3): ***Brian is muscular while Charles is very thin.***

2. Charles practices skiing often. (As a result,) He now has been chosen for the local ski team.

   IC, cc IC. (Formula 1): ***Charles practices skiing often, so he has been chosen for the local ski team.***

   (sc DC), IC. (Formula 2): ***Because Charles practices skiing often, he now has been chosen for the local ski team.***

   IC; ca, IC. (Formula 5): ***Charles practices skiing often; therefore, he now has been chosen for the local ski team.***

Name ____________________

ESL Help 6B: Exercise in Using *Some* Correctly

Read the sentences containing the word *some*. Make each sentence negative by using *not* along with *any, anybody/anyone,* or *anything.* *(Answers may vary.)*

1. Christian attended a birthday party for someone.

   Christian did not attend a birthday party for anyone.

2. He told somebody about the party.

   He didn't tell anybody about the party.

3. Christian took someone with him to the party.

   Christian did not take anyone with him to the party.

4. While he was at the party, he ate something.

   While he was at the party, he didn't eat anything.

5. The honored guest opened some gifts.

   The honored guest didn't open any gifts.

Read the sentences containing the word *some*. Make each sentence negative by using *no, none, nobody/no one,* or *nothing.* *(Answers may vary.)*

6. Some gifts were wrapped in bright paper.

   No gifts were wrapped in bright paper.

7. Somebody arrived late to the party.

   Nobody arrived late to the party.

8. After the opening of the gifts, someone led the group in games.

   After the opening of the gifts, no one led the group in games.

9 The hostess announced something about prizes to be given.

   The hostess announced nothing about prizes to be given.

10. Some of the guests went home with multiple prizes.

    None of the guests went home with multiple prizes.

Name ______________________________

ESL Help 7F: Exercise in Active and Passive

Change one sentence or part of one sentence in each paragraph so that the new portion uses the passive voice instead of active voice. Use the principle in parentheses as a guide to know which sentence to change. Write the new sentence with passive voice in the blank.

Around 1864 a slave woman bore a son, George Washington Carver, who was probably most famous for his research with peanuts. He began life as a slave in Diamond Grove, Missouri, on a plantation owned by Moses Carver. Hence, "George Washington" gained the last name of Carver, a common practice in the days of slavery.

(The doer of the action is redundant or easy to supply.)

Around 1864 George Washington Carver, probably most famous for his research with peanuts, was born.

Carver never knew his father, who had died before Carver's birth, and his mother was a kidnap victim of slave raiders while Carver was still an infant. Being a frail child, Carver served with the household staff, probably helping with the gardening. As a result, he gained a keen interest in plants. Because no one provided a school for African Americans in Diamond Grove, the plantation owners tutored young Carver in reading and writing.

(The writer wants to be tactful about slaves not having a school.)

Because a school for African Americans in Diamond Grove was not provided, the plantation owners tutored young Carver in reading and writing.

Even though Carver lacked a formal education, he soon gained a reputation for being a "healer" of sick plants. Carver's frailty actually helped him. His not having to work in the fields allowed him time to roam the woods and learn about the local vegetation.

(The doer of the action is nonhuman.)

Carver was actually helped by his frailty.

During the next several years, Carver moved to other towns in Missouri and Kansas while trying to get an education. In 1890 he finally began Simpson College in Indianola, Iowa, and later transferred to Iowa State Agricultural College. His initial fields of study were painting and piano, but a teacher later directed him toward agriculture.

(The doer of the action is redundant or easy to supply.)

His initial fields of study were painting and piano, but he was later directed toward agriculture.

ESL Help 7F: Exercise in Active and Passive (continued)

After Carver completed both his bachelor's and master's degrees, Booker T. Washington asked him to teach at Alabama's Tuskegee Institute. As well as teaching his students to understand the basics of nature, Carver taught them to be gentle and to promote education for the common man.

(The doer of the action is a well-known person.)

After completing both his bachelor's and master's degrees, Carver was asked by Booker T. Washington to teach at Alabama's Tuskegee Institute.

In his lifetime Carver created over three hundred products from peanuts, including such items as soap, ink, and face powder. He also made numerous products from both sweet potatoes and pecans. These crops helped give the South an alternative to cotton.

(The doer of the action is nonhuman.)

Thus the South was given an alternative to cotton.

After receiving many prestigious honors, Carver died in 1943. In addition to these honors, he left a valuable legacy of work with interracial relations and the YMCA. In 1994 Iowa State posthumously awarded Carver the degree Doctor of Humane Letters, an honor he would have especially appreciated.

(The doer of the action is new information.)

The degree Doctor of Humane Letters was posthumously awarded Carver by Iowa State in 1994, an honor he would have especially appreciated.

Name ______________________

ESL Help 12C: Cumulative and Coordinate Adjectives

Adjectives that come from different meaning categories are called **cumulative adjectives** because they build on one another. They are usually placed in a specific order before the noun. (See ESL Help 2A for more information about the positions of adjectives.)

EXAMPLES My *faded old* couch looked out of place with the *new leather* chair.
The rabbit nibbled on the *leafy green* lettuce.

Sometimes speakers of English may use two descriptive adjectives from the same meaning category (e.g., two evaluative words, two condition words, etc.). When two such adjectives from the same category have similar meanings, they are usually separated with a comma. These adjectives are called **coordinate adjectives.** There is never a comma between a determiner and another adjective. Also, there is never a comma between a modifying noun and another adjective.

EXAMPLES The *energetic, enthusiastic* cleaning lady attacked the *dirty, cluttered* room.
The *frisky, playful* kitten got entangled in the lacy curtain.

Look at the adjectives in italics. If the adjectives are from the same meaning category, write *coordinate* in the blank and add a comma between the adjectives. If the adjectives are from different meaning categories, write *cumulative* in the blank.

cumulative 1. My relatives live in an *old Victorian* house in Illinois.

cumulative 2. Their *large shady* yard is very inviting.

coordinate 3. The smallness of the town fosters a *close-knit,helpful* community.

coordinate 4. Many families live all their lives in this *quaint,picturesque* town.

cumulative 5. The town has only *one neighborhood grocery* store.

coordinate 6. The *friendly,considerate* employees there always greet you by name.

cumulative 7. The *dilapidated brick* schoolhouse has been replaced by a new consolidated one.

cumulative 8. Now students come from *four small* towns to attend.

cumulative 9. The students are offered *many extracurricular* activities.

cumulative 10. The *mile-long oval* track is especially nice.

Name ____________________

Chapter 2: Using Parts of Speech

Practice A

In the first blank identify each italicized noun as count *(C)* or noncount *(N)* and in the second blank identify each italicized pronoun as demonstrative *(D)* or relative *(R).*

__C__ __D__ 1. Most people anticipate *vacations* as fun and exciting, but sometimes *that* isn't the case.

__C__ __R__ 2. Last Christmas, for example, a *couple* visited Paris, *which* is particularly famous for the Eiffel Tower.

__C__ __R__ 3. After an earlier *visit* to the Palace of Versailles, the two, *who* were enjoying their first trip abroad, wanted to close out the day at the Tower.

__N__ __R__ 4. Despite the rainy, gray day's not lending itself to panoramic *sightseeing*, they determined to ascend the famed icon, *whatever* the outcome.

__N__ __D__ 5. The time spent standing in line during a soggy *rain* didn't dampen their spirits at all, and *those* around them didn't seem to mind either.

Practice B

Identify each italicized word as adjective *(Adj)*, adverb *(Adv)*, or preposition *(Prep).*

__Adv__ __Adj__ 6. Finally, the two were standing on the Tower, peering *out* at the *ethereal* scene.

__Adj__ __Adv__ 7. The majesty of the *foggy* city lay *below*.

__Prep__ __Adj__ 8. *After* gazing for several minutes, they departed and headed for the *nearby* subway.

__Prep__ __Adv__ 9. They boarded *amidst* a crowd and settled *in* for a trip to the outskirts of Paris.

__Adv__ __Adj__ 10. It was *there* that the *unexpected* incident occurred.

Practice C

Underline each coordinating conjunction once and each subordinating conjunction twice.

11. Just as the train departed, the husband felt his pocket, realizing it was empty.

12. He had been pickpocketed while he was boarding the train.

13. At the next station, they disembarked, retraced their steps, and found a police officer to report the incident to.

14. The police officer questioned the couple in his broken English but gave them little hope of ever retrieving the money, passport, and credit card.

15. Although the spending money was a bit sparse, nothing could destroy their enjoyment of the trip.

Name ____________________

Chapter 3A: Sentences

Practice A

Identify each sentence as *declarative, interrogative, imperative,* or *exclamatory.* Place an appropriate punctuation mark at the end of each sentence.

interrogative 1. Do you know what an idiom is?

declarative 2. It is generally a group of words, such as *fly off the handle,* whose meaning cannot be derived from the literal meanings of the individual words.

declarative 3. Many idioms actually get their derivations from a similar source, like the use of nautical terms.

exclamatory 4. "I passed that history quiz *with flying colors*!"

interrogative 5. Do you think the speaker realized that when passing each other, sailing ships identify themselves by their colors or flags?

Practice B

Underline each simple subject once and each simple predicate twice.

6. All of us have experienced being *under the weather* at various times.
7. During rough weather ship passengers sometimes become seasick and go below deck for shelter from the storm and violent rocking.
8. These same passengers might not be too interested in getting *a square meal.*
9. However, most of us thoroughly enjoy having such a meal.
10. Old British warships served two very sparse meals, but the third one was larger, requiring a square tray to hold it.

Practice C

Write a sentence of the kind indicated in parentheses about the suggested idiom. ***(Answers will vary.)***

11. Toe the line *(interrogative)*

    Do you know what "toe the line" means?

12. Round robin *(exclamatory)*

    The round-robin tournament turned into a free for all!

13. Aboveboard *(imperative)*

    Make sure your actions are aboveboard.

14. Stem to stern *(imperative)*

    Clean your room from stem to stern.

15. Clean bill of health *(declarative)*

    The inspectors gave the school cafeteria a clean bill of health.

Name ____________________

Chapter 3B: Sentence Patterns

Practice A

Label the sentence patterns *S-TrV-DO, S-TrV-IO-DO,* or *S-TrV-DO-OC.*

S TrV DO
1. Most English courses include the study of literature.

S TrV IO DO
2. Teachers often assign students works by American authors, such as Twain, Hawthorne, and Melville.

S TrV DO
3. What student doesn't enjoy Huckleberry Finn's adventures?

S TrV DO OC
4. An assignment in Shakespeare might make a student nervous about the old-fashioned language.

S TrV DO OC
5. Other students call Shakespeare their favorite author.

Practice B

Label the sentence patterns *S-LV-PN, S-LV-PA,* or *S*-be-*Advl.* If the adverbial is a prepositional phrase, underline it.

S LV PA
6. A study of English grammar is surprisingly helpful.

S LV PN
7. Some students even become scholars of the language.

S LV PA S be Advl
8. The mastery of grammar and usage may seem unnecessary, but it can be of great value to a writer.

S LV PN
9. Knowing whether to say "he doesn't" or "he don't" is an important skill.

S be Advl
10. A writer's strength may be in his knowledge of the language.

Practice C

Rewrite each item as a sentence with the sentence pattern indicated in parentheses. ***(Answers may vary.)***

11. Elementary schools offer little choice in courses. (*S-LV-PA*)

    Course choices in elementary schools are scarce.

12. High schools, however, usually allow some options for a student. (*S-TrV-IO-DO*)

    High schools, however, usually allow a student some options.

13. Some subjects are not options but requirements for all students at the school. (*S-TrV-DO-OC*)

    Schools make some subjects requirements for all students.

14. A typical high school offers history, math, and science among its courses. (*S*-be-*Advl*)

    History, math, and science will be among the courses in a typical high school.

15. Schools almost always require an English class too. (*S-LV-PN*)

    English is almost always a required class too.

Name ______________________

Chapter 4A: Phrases

Practice A

Identify each italicized phrase as a verbal phrase *(V)*, a prepositional phrase *(P)*, or an appositive phrase *(A)*.

__V__ 1. The TGV *(pronounced tay jay vay)* is a high-speed train in France connecting major cities.

__V__ 2. *Living up to its reputation,* the train travels at speeds of 185 mph and faster.

__P__ 3. *Despite the speed,* the inside of the train is as quiet as a whisper.

__A__ 4. This bullet train, *another name for the TGV,* leaves approximately every half an hour from the station.

__V__ 5. In fact, at times it is faster *to take the TGV* than it is to fly.

Practice B

Identify each italicized phrase as a gerund phrase *(Ger)*, a participial phrase *(Part)*, or an infinitive phrase *(Inf)*.

__Part__ 6. *Boarding the train,* one finds storage for luggage immediately inside the door.

__Inf__ 7. A passenger must check his ticket *to see if his assignment is to the upper or lower level.*

__Part__ 8. *Once settled,* he waits quietly for the train's departure.

__Ger__ 9. *Leaving the station* is done slowly; the train gradually picks up speed once outside the city.

__Ger__ 10. In *keeping with the French culture,* no one speaks loudly, if at all.

Practice C

Identify each italicized phrase as a participial phrase *(Part)* or an absolute phrase *(Abs)*.

__Part__ 11. Bullet trains are not new, *having originated in Japan in 1964.*

__Abs__ 12. *Safety being a concern to some,* passengers should be encouraged to know these trains are extremely safe.

__Part__ 13. In fact, the Japanese Shinkansen Line has gone over one billion kilometers, *having never been derailed.*

__Abs__ 14. *The train having such a good safety record,* over three billion passengers have ridden this line.

__Part__ 15. It seems that many big cities in the United States, *characterized by snarled traffic jams,* could profit from such a train.

Name ______________________

Chapter 4B: Verbals

Practice A

Place parentheses around each participial phrase. Underline each present participle once and each past participle twice.

1. Puppets, (enjoyed by both adults and children,) have existed for centuries.
2. Seventeenth-century Holland was entertained by *Jan Klaasen en Katrijn,* (better known in other places as Punch and Judy.)
3. India employs an interesting twist to its puppets, (making the face color of the puppets reveal their character: orange is usually a woman, black is a bad person, and green is a hero.)
4. Turkey has a famous gypsy puppet, Karagoz, (characterized by a black beard and turban.)
5. However, one particular puppet, Guignol, (originating in France,) has achieved worldwide popularity and influence.

Practice B

Underline each gerund phrase and identify its function as subject *(S)*, direct object *(DO)*, predicate noun *(PN)*, object of the preposition *(OP)*, or appositive *(App)*.

__S__ 6. At first making puppets was just a sideline for Guignol's creator, Laurent Mourguet.

__PN__ 7. Mourguet, being a professional tooth puller, wanted a gimmick to attract patients. The solution was puppeteering.

__DO__ 8. One of his early successes involved creating the puppet Gnafron (from *gnaffre,* meaning shoemaker), who was dressed in a top hat and leather apron.

__App__ 9. Mourguet's avocation, designing puppets, soon became his passion.

__OP__ 10. In the process of sculpturing Guignol, Mourguet dressed him in a gold-buttoned brown jacket, red bow tie, and leather hat sporting earflaps.

Practice C

Rewrite each sentence to incorporate at least one infinitive phrase. ***(Answers may vary.)***

11. To this day no one knows why Mourguet chose the name of Guignol.

To this day no one knows why Mourguet chose to name his puppet Guignol.

12. Guignol favors the underdog, especially the poor, often to the detriment of local landlords or policemen.

Guignol seems to favor the underdog, especially the poor, often to the detriment of local landlords or policemen.

13. Guignol is a regular participant in all the shows.

Mourguet likes for Guignol to participate in all the shows.

14. Guignol is one of the participants in the *Moisson d'Avril,* a puppet festival hosted by Lyon, France, each April.

Guignol is one of the participants in the **Moisson d'Avril,** ***a puppet festival to be hosted by Lyon, France, each April.***

15. Truly Guignol has appealed to many throughout the years.

Truly Guignol has come to appeal to many throughout the years.

Name________________________________

Chapter 5A: Clauses

Practice A

Place parentheses around each noun clause and identify its function as subject *(S)*, predicate noun *(PN)*, direct object *(DO)*, indirect object *(IO)*, object of preposition *(OP)*, or appositive *(App)*.

__DO__ 1. A present-day visitor, wandering the streets of Perouges, France, might be surprised to learn (that Perouges dates back to at least the thirteenth century.)

__S__ 2. (Whether it gives a truly historic picture of an old feudal village)is not certain, but it's quite impressive to a casual tourist.

__App__ 3. The person,(whoever he or she might have been,)who configured the narrow cobblestone streets was a great architect.

__PN__ 4. A common conclusion is(that these streets would quickly destroy the suspension of cars and trucks today.)

__OP__ 5. Nevertheless, for(whoever is interested,)the streets, along with the flower boxes on windowsills and porch stoops, give a certain picturesque quaintness to the town.

Practice B

Place parentheses around each dependent clause and identify it as adjectival *(Adj)* or adverbial *(Adv)*.

__Adj__ 6. The entire town,(which is surrounded by fortress-like walls,)gives the appearance of strength.

__Adv__ 7. (When one approaches the town,)the first thing noticed is two entrances with huge gates; one pair was almost totally destroyed during a siege in 1468.

__Adv__ 8. (Although the gates were damaged in that siege,)the town did not fall.

__Adj__ 9. Artisans, many (who are continuing with the trade of their ancestors,)can be found throwing pottery, weaving cloth, or baking bread.

__Adj__ 10. The village square,(which is called *Place de Tilleul,*)is named for a lime tree.

Practice C

Identify each sentence as simple *(S)*, compound *(Cd)*, complex *(Cx)*, or compound-complex *(Cd-Cx)*.

Cx 11. One of the most interesting sights is the old feudal church, which is directly inside one of the gates.

S 12. At the front of the church is a statue of Saint George, the dragon slayer.

Cd-Cx 13. The windows, which are a part of the exterior village walls, were designed as long vertical slits; these slits allowed archers to shoot at enemies through the windows.

Cd 14. In spite of the burning candles, the interior was cold and lifeless, and a visitor would have no desire to linger there.

S 15. This village, located high on a hill just twenty-one miles from Lyon, is a great place to visit.

Name________________________________

Chapter 5B: Avoiding Sentence Errors

Practice A

Identify each group of words as a sentence *(S)* or a fragment *(F)*.

__*S*__ 1. Most high-school seniors either dread or greatly anticipate the thought of graduating.

__*F*__ 2. They as well as their parents looking forward to graduation and future opportunities.

__*S*__ 3. If a student is a Christian, he must prayerfully consider the Lord's will for his life.

__*F*__ 4. Several options like going to work, attending college, or learning a trade.

__*F*__ 5. Whereas the choice that is made will influence a person for life.

Practice B

Identify each group of words as a sentence *(S)*, a fragment *(F)*, a comma splice *(CS)*, or a fused sentence *(FS)*.

__*CS*__ 6. Many students apply to several colleges, some apply to only one.

__*F*__ 7. Whether or not they will be accepted at the college of their choice.

__*S*__ 8. Some even want their friends to attend the same college, making the decision more difficult.

__*FS*__ 9. In a few weeks they will become acclimated to college life anyway whether their friends are there isn't deemed very important.

__*S*__ 10. But everyone wants to succeed.

Practice C

Identify each group of words as a sentence *(S)*, a fragment *(F)*, a comma splice *(CS)*, or a fused sentence *(FS)*. If the item is a sentence error, rewrite the sentence correctly. ***(Answers may vary.)***

__*CS*__ 11. Seniors often wonder what lies ahead, they're apprehensive about the unknown.

Seniors often wonder what lies ahead; they're apprehensive about the unknown.

__*S*__ 12. One of their fears is whether they will pass or fail in college.

__*F*__ 13. Because not all students have the same abilities.

Some will not excel in their studies because not all students have the same abilities.

_FS_ 14. A few students even want to go to summer school they hope to graduate early.

A few students even want to go to summer school, hoping to graduate early.

_CS_ 15. Most, though, desire to leave summers free, a time for making money is often a necessity.

Most, though, desire to leave summers free because a time for making money is often a necessity.

Name ________________________

Chapter 6A: Subject-Verb Agreement

Practice A

Underline the simple subject(s) of each sentence. Then underline the correct verb from the choices in parentheses.

1. Starting around 1914, the 4-H club—referring to head, heart, hands, and health—(*is, are*) still in existence today.
2. The concern for rural education and the promotion of technologically advanced agricultural techniques (*was, were*) the reasons for creating these clubs.
3. Some of the farmers (*was, were*) slow to adopt these new methods.
4. Also at that time nearly everybody in the farming communities (*was, were*) skeptical of full-time formal schooling.
5. Involved in these 4-H clubs (*was, were*) people from both the public and private sectors.

Practice B

Underline the simple subject of each clause. Then rewrite each sentence that has a subject-verb agreement error to correct it.

6. The year 1948 brought a move to advance the 4-H club to international status, a development that is still active today.

7. Plans for a foreign exchange program involving young 4-Hers' staying with a host family was implemented.

   Plans for a foreign exchange program involving young 4-Hers' staying with a host family were implemented.

8. Approximately forty thousand youth from all over the country is involved presently in this undertaking.

   Approximately forty thousand youth from all over the country are involved presently in this undertaking.

9. One of the changes that has occurred since 1960 is that over half of those involved in 4-H clubs is from the larger cities rather than the rural areas.

   One of the changes that has occurred since 1960 is that over half of those involved in 4-H clubs are from the larger cities rather than the rural areas.

10. Each year volunteer leaders for these clubs exceeds more than two billion dollars in time and out-of-pocket expenses.

    Each year volunteer leaders for these clubs exceed more than two billion dollars in time and out-of-pocket expenses.

Practice C

Write the correct form of the italicized verb in the blank.

have 11. At least one quarter of all children in grades 1–8 *have* been involved in 4-H at some time during those eight years.

offers 12. The 4-H leadership *offer* many different projects for boys and girls to participate in.

is 13. Cooking projects or some kind of sewing *be* among the more popular choices.

is 14. Working with animals *be* another kind of project one might choose.

delights 15. Taking projects to a county or state fair *delight* many 4-H members.

Name ____________________

Chapter 6B: Pronoun-Antecedent Agreement

Practice A

Underline the correct pronoun from the choices in parentheses.

1. Undoubtedly most men decry the day that the common necktie was created for *(him, them)*.
2. Although most historians date ties to the mid-1600s, some trace *(it, them)* back as far as Chinese emperor Qin Shi Huang in 210 B.C.
3. The more readily accepted origin, however, stems from Louis XIV's admiration of the Croatian soldier, who wore soft scarves around the neck as part of *(his, their)* uniform.
4. In fact, most believe the word *cravat* (a soft necktie) gets *(its, their)* name from the word *croat*.
5. King George II of England introduced the tie to the English when *(he, they)* returned to the throne from exile.

Practice B

Underline each personal pronoun and draw an arrow from it to its antecedent.

6. Sometimes cravats were so stiff that a man had to turn his body instead of his neck in order to see.
7. Cravats could be embroidered, plaid, tasseled—as different as the men who wore them.
8. No gentleman would have considered going anywhere without a cravat around his neck.
9. The 1840s experienced the bow tie; of course, it was the hand-tied kind, not a clip-on.
10. Nearly a hundred different knots could be used for tying, with one, the four-in-hand, getting its origin from the knotted reins a coach driver might use.

Practice C

Questions 11–15: Underline the five incorrect pronouns and then write the correct pronoun above each error.

Neither Qin Shi Huang nor Louis XIV could have foreseen the long-range effects of their (*his*) use of neckties on men's fashion. These ties change its (*their*) "look" almost as often as women's dress styles change. In the '60s and '70s ties expanded to 5 inches wide in order to keep pace with the wider lapels on men's suits. To be both safe and stylish, a man can always conform his ties to the 2½ to 3½ inch width, regardless of current trends. Length of a tie might be anywhere from 52 to 58 inches, with their (*its*) tip just touching the waistband of the slacks. Of course, some men prefer bow ties. In fact, one particular college basketball coach, Jim Phelan, always wore it (*them*). During the last game of his final season at Mount St. Mary's, several other coaches also donned the bow tie. Everyone wanted to honor their (*his*) colleague Phelan. Ties, regardless of the kind, seem to have become a permanent fixture in menswear and allow every man a chance to demonstrate his individuality.

Name ____________________

Chapter 7A: Verb Tense

Practice A

Underline the complete verb and identify its tense as *present, past,* or *future; present perfect, past perfect,* or *future perfect;* or *one of these tenses in the progressive.*

present perfect 1. John Calvin, born on July 10, 1509, in Noyon, France, has become well known as one of the foremost theologians of the Reformation.

past perfect 2. A brilliant student, Calvin had been born again at the age of twenty-three.

past progressive 3. Previously a Catholic, Calvin was working for the reform of Catholicism shortly following his conversion.

past 4. His passion for reform caused him to be exiled from Paris.

future 5. Even today people will remember his *Institutes of the Christian Religion,* presenting a systematic explanation of the Protestant position.

Practice B

In the blank, write each italicized verb in the correct tense.

began 6. In 1559 Calvin *begin* a school now known as the University of Geneva.

carried 7. Students *carry* Reformation theology across Europe.

continues 8. Even today Calvin's work *continue* to influence evangelical Christianity.

preached, was 9. Calvin *preach* at the famous St. Peter's Cathedral, the oldest building in Geneva, and *be* influential in the conversion of the church to Protestantism in 1536.

are gracing, will continue 10. Calvin's original chair and his ornate pulpit, reached by a winding staircase, *be* still *grace* St. Peter's and *continue* to attract tourist in years to come.

Practice C

Underline each verb in incorrect tense and write an appropriate correction in the blank.

enjoy 11. A small chapel is to the right of the main door of St. Peter's, and visitors enjoyed seeing it.

finds 12. Written above the pulpit in this chapel one found the words *Post Tenebras Lux,* meaning "after darkness, light" or "after ignorance, understanding [of the Bible]."

Chapter 7A: Verb Tense (continued)

was built 13. About a block from the cathedral stands the Reformation Wall, which is built in 1917.

have chiseled 14. Sculptors had chiseled statues of Calvin, Bèze, Knox, and Farel, all Protestant reformers.

will find 15. One also finds the Mayflower Compact on that wall, written in both French and English.

Name ________________________________

Chapter 7B: Voice and Mood

Practice A

Identify each italicized verb as active voice *(A)* or passive voice *(P)*.

__*A*__ 1. Any snow skiing enthusiast *would recognize* the name of Mont Blanc, which is the tallest mountain in the Swiss Alps.

__*A*__ 2. This mountain boasts twelve ski areas and includes a lift that *goes* above 12,500 feet.

__*P*__ 3. Mont Blanc *has been described* as the most famous extreme ski area in the world.

__*P*__ 4. *Included* in extreme skiing *is* going off piste, skiing where no trail exists.

__*A*__ 5. Those who attempt this type of skiing *should* always *check* the avalanche bulletins and ski in groups of three or more.

Practice B

Rewrite each sentence, changing the passive-voice verbs to active voice. ***(Answers may vary.)***

6. Although the name *Chamonix* is used for the valley that is occupied by Mont Blanc, it is also used for a Swiss village.

   Although the name* Chamonix *refers to the valley that Mont Blanc occupies, it is also the name of a Swiss village.

7. The picturesque restaurants and shops become breathtaking when the backdrop of the Swiss Alps is added.

   The picturesque restaurants and shops become breathtaking when one adds the backdrop of the Swiss Alps.

8. The town is also occupied by a pristine brook, and many restaurants have been built overlooking it.

   Many restaurants overlook a pristine brook that runs through the town.

9. Colored lights are hung above the streets, and Americans are reminded of Christmastime in the United States.

   The villagers hang colored lights above the streets, and the decorations remind Americans of Christmastime in the United States.

10. Wonderful Swiss chocolate is sold in many of the picturesque shops along the brick streets.

   Many of the picturesque shops along the brick streets sell wonderful Swiss chocolate.

Practice C

Identify the mood of each italicized verb as *indicative, imperative,* or *subjunctive.*

imperative 11. If you are traveling in this area of the world, *be* careful not to overindulge in the delicious sweets.

subjunctive 12. If a traveler *would* plan carefully, he could counterbalance the food temptations with the various kinds of exercise available here.

indicative 13. Skiing, mountain biking, ice skating, and mountain climbing *are* available to the Mont Blanc tourists.

subjunctive 14. Children might wish that they *were* involved in riding summer toboggans or go-carts.

indicative 15. A visit to Chamonix and Mont Blanc *offers* a trip of a lifetime.

Name ____________________

Chapter 8A: Correct Use of Pronoun Case

Practice A

Underline the correct pronoun from the choices in parentheses.

1. C. S. Lewis was born to *(him, his)* parents, Albert and Flora Lewis, on November 29, 1898.
2. Although C. S. Lewis's full name was Clive Staples Lewis, *(he, him)* was referred to as "Jack" by most of his friends.
3. Lewis's mother died on August 23, 1908, after a battle *(she, her)* had with cancer.
4. "Jack" married Joy Davidman Gresham in December 1956, but a few years later she died after *(she, her)* own battle with cancer.
5. About three years after his wife's death, Lewis died as a result of various health problems, but *(we, us)* still read his work.

Practice B

Underline each personal pronoun and identify it as subjective *(S)*, objective *(O)*, possessive *(P)*, or independent possessive *(IP)*.

__P__ 6. Lewis made his name known through a variety of writings ranging from children's fantasy to Christian apologetics.

__S__ 7. *The Chronicles of Narnia* are possibly Lewis's best-known books, and they have captured children's imaginations for years.

__O__ 8. Lewis wrote quite a number of letters to close friends, and many of them have been published as part of Lewis's collection of writings.

__P__ 9. One of Lewis's works is known for its similarities in style to John Bunyan's *The Pilgrim's Progress.*

__IP__ 10. Several writers have written stories inspired by *The Pilgrim's Progress.* Lewis's *The Pilgrim's Regress* is the title of his.

Practice C

Insert an appropriate personal pronoun in each sentence. ***(Answers may vary.)***

his 11. *The Chronicles of Narnia* began when four children stayed with Lewis at ? home during World War II.

them 12. The children had not been exposed to many imaginative stories, so Lewis began writing one for ?.

mine 13. As Lewis wrote the *Chronicles,* he made the concept of time in Narnia's world very different from the concept of time in yours and ?.

They 14. The writing and publishing of the seven books in the series moved quickly. ? were all published between 1950 and 1956.

his 15. While writing the first few Narnia tales, Lewis thought *The Voyage of the Dawn Treader* would be ? last book of the series, but soon found he had several more to write before finishing.

Name____________________

Chapter 8B: Pronoun Usage

Practice A

Evaluate the pronoun usage and then identify each sentence as correct *(C)* or incorrect *(I)*.

__*I*__ 1. Many people who visit Charleston, South Carolina, discover numerous attractions to occupy your time.

__*C*__ 2. Much of the city itself has been historically preserved and gives tourists a sense of days gone by.

__*I*__ 3. Last summer, me and my family traveled to Charleston for a week of vacation.

__*I*__ 4. Us staying there was quite a treat because we had never vacationed along the East Coast before.

__*C*__ 5. My family and I had a lovely view of the historic section of Charleston from the window of our room in one of the local bed and breakfast inns.

Practice B

Underline the correct pronoun from the choices in parentheses.

6. Throughout the week, my brother and (*I*, *me*) each enjoyed different aspects of our visit in Charleston.
7. He enjoyed our evening boat ride around the Charleston Harbor more than (*I*, *me*).
8. I had a better time than (*he*, *him*) when we went on an afternoon shopping excursion to the Old City Market.
9. We both thoroughly enjoyed (*ourself*, *ourselves*) at one of the seafood restaurants downtown.
10. (*He and I*, *Him and me*) hope to go back to Charleston soon to see the attractions we did not have time to see last summer.

Practice C

Choose the letter that corresponds to the correct pronoun(s).

__*A*__ 11. While we shopped at the market, ? picked out souvenirs to take home to our grandparents.
A. my family and I
B. my family and me

__*B*__ 12. ? else should we buy gifts for?
A. Who
B. Whom

__*A*__ 13. We decided to buy handmade sweetgrass baskets for the rest of ? friends.
A. our
B. their

A 14. Our parents enjoyed picking out the baskets, but _?_ children were even more enthusiastic than _?_.

A. we, they

B. us, them

A 15. Before we left the market in Charleston, I decided to buy _?_ a basket as well.

A. myself

B. me

Name______________________________

Chapter 8C: *Who* and *Whom*

Practice A

Identify each sentence as correct *(C)* or incorrect *(I)*.

__*I*__ 1. Whom was the first writer of the American short story?

__C__ 2. It is difficult to determine exactly who was the first American author to write a short story.

__C__ 3. Early American magazine publishers who were willing to include fiction in their magazines exposed the American people to short fiction beginning in 1789.

__C__ 4. Washington Irving, a writer who modeled elements of the short story in his tales, preceded the authors who established the short story in its modern form.

__*I*__ 5. Nathaniel Hawthorne and Edgar Allan Poe were the writers whom established the modern form of the American short story in the 1830s and 1840s.

Practice B

Underline the correct pronoun from the choices in parentheses.

6. (*<u>Who</u>, Whom*) were Nathaniel Hawthorne and Edgar Allan Poe?
7. Nathaniel Hawthorne was the author (*<u>who</u>, whom*) brought the short story to the American people in his collection entitled *Twice-Told Tales*, published in 1837.
8. Edgar Allan Poe is the author to (*who, <u>whom</u>*) we are grateful for printing his definition of the short story in a review in *Graham's Magazine* in 1842.
9. (*Who, <u>Whom</u>*) did Hawthorne and Poe influence through their writing?
10. Robert Louis Stevenson and Rudyard Kipling, (*<u>who</u>, whom*) were both British authors, were directly affected by Hawthorne and Poe.

Practice C

Choose the letter that corresponds to the correct pronoun.

__*A*__ 11. ? is the author you like better, Hawthorne or Poe?
A. Who
B. Whom

__*A*__ 12. Hawthorne, ? was best known for his novel *The Scarlet Letter,* often used guilt as a theme in his writing.
A. who
B. whom

__*B*__ 13. Poe was the author ? we consider to be the father of the modern American short story.
A. who
B. whom

___A___ 14. _?_ were some of the well-known American writers to follow the short story form begun by Poe?

A. Who

B. Whom

___A___ 15. Ernest Hemingway, Katherine Anne Porter, and Sherwood Anderson are just a few of the writers _?_ wrote using the modern form of the short story.

A. who

B. whom

Name ____________________

Chapter 9: Pronoun Reference

Practice A

Underline each pronoun once and each clear antecedent twice. Identify the pronoun reference in each sentence as clear *(C)*, ambiguous *(A)*, or remote *(R)*.

___*C*___ 1. Although marble games are not as prevalent as they once were, most children have some game requiring marbles.

___*A*___ 2. As children, Mark often played a game of Aggravation with Todd, and he always hoped to be the winner.

___*A*___ 3. After the game Todd would ask Mark to give him another chance.

___*R*___ 4. Usually he was willing to play again.

___*C*___ 5. One old marble game that is still played is Chinese checkers.

Practice B

Underline each pronoun that demonstrates a reference error and write an appropriate correction in the blank. Avoid informal English. ***(Answers may vary.)***

___*The instruction manual*___ 6. It says to divide the marbles evenly.

___*the game*___ 7. If the game's main purpose is to shoot marbles, then practice will be needed to play it well.

___*a person*___ 8. In other games you must rely on chance, not skill, to win.

___*game*___ 9. Mousetrap is an interesting one that uses only one ball or marble.

___*a result that*___ 10. Playing the same game several times becomes boring, which is not good.

Practice C

Underline the five pronoun reference errors in the following paragraph and rewrite the paragraph correctly. ***(Answers may vary.)***

Although you would think that marbles are made from marble, most are made from glass, a much cheaper material. Other marble materials of the past have been clay, wood, stone, or even steel, which seems a little strange. As a person might expect, the earliest glass marbles were made in Venice prior to 1800, where they would blow each marble individually. Not until approximately 1920 were they made in America. The alleys (the expensive marbles) are hard to find; their scarcity means that they have become collectors' items. The expression "knuckling down" comes from a method marble experts use when shooting them.

Although a person would think that marbles are made from marble, most are made from glass, a much cheaper material. Other marble materials of the past have been clay, wood, stone, or even steel: materials that seem a little strange. As a person might expect, the earliest glass marbles were made in Venice prior to 1800, where glassblowers would blow each marble individually. Not until approximately 1920 were marbles made in America. The alleys (the expensive marbles) are hard to find; their scarcity means that they have become collectors' items. The expression "knuckling down" comes from a method marble experts use when shooting marbles.

Name ______________________

Chapter 10A: Adjective and Adverb Use

Practice A

Underline each adjective once and each adverb twice.

1. The Butchart Gardens, considered one of the world's most famous and beautiful gardens, covers fifty acres.
2. Located on Vancouver Island, it is only a few miles from Victoria.
3. The name comes from Robert Pim Butchart, who owned and operated a cement company on Tod Inlet, the present site of the gardens.
4. However, it was definitely his wife, Jennie, who decided to reclaim the dismal limestone pit after it had been depleted of useful limestone.
5. Currently, that pit has been transformed into the gorgeous Sunken Garden.

Practice B

Underline each incorrectly used adjective or adverb and write the correction in the blank.

earliest 6. The earlier garden in the entire collection is the Japanese Garden.

unique 7. Its picturesque pagodas, rustic footbridges, and whimsical statues provide a most unique experience.

any 8. Some visitors do not have no interest in leaving this garden.

almost 9. Nevertheless, most all of them eventually continue to view the other gardens on Tod Inlet.

most famous 10. One of the famousest smaller gardens is the English Rose Garden.

Practice C

Underline the correct adjective or adverb from the choices in parentheses.

11. The (*most perfect, most nearly perfect*) time to visit the Gardens is late afternoon and early evening.
12. Nighttime provides a whole new perspective for (*real, really*) good viewing.
13. The Saturday night fireworks are choreographed especially (*good, well*).
14. Not a note of music that sounds (*bad, badly*) will ever be heard at this display.
15. Visitors may go home (*some, somewhat*) fatigued, but they'll have enjoyed an experience of a lifetime.

Name ______________________

Chapter 10B: Misplaced and Dangling Modifiers

Practice A

Underline each misplaced modifier.

1. Young Brandon enjoys thoroughly hearing Grandpa ask, "Would you like to explore the nearby stream?"
2. The question has hardly been completed before the child is standing at the door impatiently ready to go.
3. Grandpa and grandchild head for the local park, wearing old tennis shoes.
4. Of course Sam, the yellow lab, begs pleadingly to also be allowed to go.
5. In this particular case three grandchildren fall into step quickly looking ahead with wonderful anticipation.

Practice B

Underline each incorrect modifier and identify it as a misplaced modifier *(M)* or a dangling modifier *(D)*.

D 6. Upon reaching the stream, chatter grows to a crescendo.

M 7. Six small feet try to precariously balance upon the midstream rocks.

D 8. Leaving caution to the wind, a huge splash hits Grandpa as Sam leaps into the water.

D 9. Everyone laughs until Sam happily shakes water upon one and all, causing a mild panic.

M 10. Trying to flee quickly causes each child to tumble into the water.

Practice C

Rewrite each sentence, correcting any misplaced or dangling modifiers. ***(Answers may vary.)***

11. Squeals of either delight or dismay follow, depending upon the child's personality.

    The squeals of delight or dismay that follow reflect each child's personality clearly.

12. Hoping to distract the children from their wet plight, a school of beautiful red minnows is pointed out by Grandpa.

    Hoping to distract the children from their wet plight, Grandpa points out a school of beautiful red minnows.

13. Fascinated by the fish, all six eyes peer into the stream's crystal depths.

    Fascinated by the fish, all three grandchildren peer into the stream's crystal depths.

Chapter 10B: Misplaced and Dangling Modifiers (continued)

14. Even adults wander by curiously wondering what has transfixed the attention of the children.

    Even adults wander curiously by, wondering what has transfixed the attention of the children.

15. While exploring at the local park, the stream proved an exciting focal point for Grandpa and the children.

    While Grandpa and the children were exploring at the local park, the stream proved an exciting focal point.

Name ____________________

Chapter 11: Capitalization

Practice A

Underline every word that demonstrates a capitalization error.

1. Nearly every child—even from other parts of the World—has owned a Piggy Bank at one time or another.
2. Many times at birth the child will receive such a bank, often silver, from Grandma or aunt Sarah or even from the Hospital where the child was born.
3. Interestingly, these Banks were not always in the shape of a pig; In fact, they probably had nothing to do with pigs.
4. The origin of the piggy bank probably comes from the middle ages when people had storage jars made from an orange clay called "Pygg."
5. Another theory (probably my Grandmother's) is that leftovers of one's change were fed to the "pig" until it was fat enough to be smashed and its money used for something special.

Practice B

Rewrite each italicized word correctly. If the word is already capitalized correctly, write *C* in the blank.

C	*C*	6. These piggy banks probably originated in *Europe* sometime during the *sixteenth century.*
C	*New Year's*	7. Even *today* in some European countries, "lucky pigs" are a part of the *new year's* celebration.
state fairs	*C*	8. Piggy banks can now be found nearly everywhere as prizes at *State Fairs*, in Hallmark *card* stores, in hospital gift shops, and in many other places.
camp	*holidays*	9. Children in *Camp* often construct piggy banks as a craft project, sometimes in conjunction with *Holidays*.
World	*C*	10. Many piggy banks are smashed to get money for such things as Walt Disney *world* or the *World* of Coca-Cola.

Practice C

Rewrite the following paragraph, correcting the ten errors in capitalization. (Multiple capitalization errors in a proper noun count as only one error.)

Piggy banks have even become Collectibles. Banks sometimes give them away to encourage a child to save. One Bank in the uk held such a promotion in 1983. For a new account of at least three Pounds, children could receive Baby Woody, the youngest in a family of five pigs. As the accounts grew, Annabel, Maxwell, lady Hillary, and Sir Nathaniel Westminster could be added to the collection. Nathaniel required an investment of one hundred pounds or more, so relatively few british children acquired him. Five years later the offer ended, only to be resurrected in 1998 when cousin Wesley came on the scene. The bank was responsible for six little pigs, quite a different scenario from the famous "three little pigs" story. anyone interested in following the continuing saga should contact the Wade Collectors club.

Piggy banks have even become collectibles. Banks sometimes give them away to encourage a child to save. One bank in the UK held such a promotion in 1983. For a new account of at least three pounds, children could receive Baby Woody, the youngest in a family of five pigs. As the accounts grew, Annabel, Maxwell, Lady Hillary, and Sir Nathaniel Westminster could be added to the collection. Nathaniel required an investment of one hundred pounds or more, so relatively few British children acquired him. Five years later the offer ended, only to be resurrected in 1998 when Cousin Wesley came on the scene. The bank was responsible for six little pigs, quite a different scenario from the famous "Three Little Pigs" story. Anyone interested in following the continuing saga should contact the Wade Collectors Club.

Name ____________________

Chapter 12A: End Marks and Other Periods

Practice A

Label the end punctuation of each sentence as correct *(C)* or incorrect *(I)*.

___I___ 1. The AMF Bowling Worldwide icon is easily recognizable today, but few people realize that bowling might be the first sport ever played!

___I___ 2. Historians wonder whether some form of bowling dates back to the ancient Egyptians of 3200 B.C.?

___C___ 3. The contents of an Egyptian pyramid included a round ball-like object and marble bars.

___I___ 4. Can you believe that German monks even partook of the sport around A.D. 300.

___C___ 5. During the time of Julius Caesar, bocce (a kind of lawn bowling) was a popular pastime for Roman soldiers and continues to be popular in Italy today.

Practice B

Insert any necessary periods.

6. By A.D. 1650 the Dutch colonists had transported bowling to America.

7. Of course, Rip Van Winkle found little men playing nine pins near Catskill, New York.

8. In 1895 the ABC (American Bowling Congress) was formed.

9. In the early 1900s Skee-Ball, similar to bowling and invented by J.D.Estes, arrived on the scene.

10. These facts would not be taught by Dr.Riebe in History 101, but they are still quite interesting to me.

Practice C

Insert any necessary end marks or other periods.

11. The earliest ten-pin bowlers used candlepins, which lost their popularity about 1850 but were reintroduced in 1881 by Justin P. White.

12. These candlepins stood about 11 in. high and narrowed on both ends.

13. Getting a strike with the 3 lb. ball was extremely difficult.

14. No one has ever scored a perfect game! or .

15. I wonder whether anyone ever will.

Name ______________________

Chapter 12B: Commas

Practice A

Identify each sentence as correctly punctuated *(C)* or incorrectly punctuated *(I)*.

__I__ 1. Any budding writer, who is studying writing techniques in school knows that writing can be a very rewarding job.

__C__ 2. One might be a technical writer, a fiction writer, or even a textbook writer.

__I__ 3. However despite one's inherent skills, writing requires much concentration and self-discipline.

__I__ 4. While being factual a newspaper reporter must write and revise his articles in order to conserve space.

__C__ 5. The supervisor of any newspaper, the editor, may work overtime to finalize an edition of the paper.

Practice B

Insert any necessary commas.

6. In addition to inherent talent,^ writers must have a practical,^ in-depth knowledge of the computer.

7. An understanding of word processing,^ which is assumed by an employer,^ is only the beginning.

8. To do any research,^ writers must be adept at accessing the Internet and also at giving official credit for quotations and other borrowings.

9. Then,^ too,^ a writer must learn specific formats of spacing,^ font size,^ and styles,^ which are often complex.

10. No,^ a career in writing is not all glamour and fame.

Practice C

Rewrite the following paragraph, inserting any necessary commas. There are ten errors.

Children believe it or not are very discerning readers. Therefore writing literature for children may seem to be an easy vocation but it is actually quite complex. The writer must first have an original idea but thinking of one can be difficult. To be successful a story usually also requires realistic characters and dialogue. Knowing how to get a story published whether it is short or book length requires an understanding of how publishing works. Most successful stories were "kid-tested" read to or by children before they were submitted to a publisher. Dedicated children's authors are involved in a true labor of love.

Children, believe it or not, are very discerning readers. Therefore, writing literature for children may seem to be an easy vocation, but it is actually quite complex. The writer must first have an original idea, but thinking of one can be difficult. To be successful, a story usually also requires realistic characters and dialogue. Knowing how to get a story published, whether it is short or book length, requires an understanding of how publishing works. Most successful stories were "kid-tested," read to or by children, before they were submitted to a publisher. Dedicated children's authors are involved in a true labor of love.

Name ____________________

Chapter 12C: Commas, Semicolons, and Colons

Practice A

Identify the use of semicolons in each sentence as correct *(C)* or incorrect *(I)*.

__*I*__ 1. Most people claim to be somewhat knowledgeable about a few kinds of cars; but everyone has at least heard of the Volkswagen.

__*I*__ 2. Regardless of one's attitude toward the VW; the car is extremely popular.

__C__ 3. In the 1930s, Adolph Hitler influenced the design and purpose of the Volkswagen; he contracted Ferdinand Porsche to make a car for the common man.

__*I*__ 4. Hitler wanted a motor mounted in the rear; a speed of sixty-two miles per hour; and a capacity of two adults and three children.

__*I*__ 5. Driving over forty miles per hour was considered fast; quite a feat for that era.

Practice B

Insert any necessary colons. If the sentence is already correct, write *C* in the blank.

____ 6. Throughout their history Volkswagens have had some unusual names:^ Beetles, Things, and Rabbits.

____ 7. In 1960 Volkswagen even produced the Volks-Liner:^ a small wooden boat using a Beetle motor.

__C__ 8. However, the boat was short-lived, with only a few actually in existence.

__C__ 9. Albert Klein claims to have driven his 1960s Beetle over one million miles, making one wonder whether he had to replace motors, tires, and brakes several times.

____ 10. A few Volkswagen owners, however, are disenchanted with their vehicles and claim:^ "I wouldn't buy another Volkswagen if it were the last car on Earth!"

Chapter 12C: Commas, Semicolons, and Colons (continued)

Practice C

Insert the ten necessary commas, semicolons, or colons in the following paragraph.

During the 1970s the Guthrie family eagerly purchased a used Volkswagen camper, which they affectionately labeled their "camp mobile." The camper included a sink, a refrigerator, a table, and beds. Even the roof lifted, so an adult could stand upright. Believing that they had acquired an economical camper, they tested it a few times close to home. Soon they decided to take it on a longer trip: a Christmas trek from South Carolina to Illinois. The family anticipated going through Knoxville, Tennessee; Lexington, Kentucky; and Indianapolis, Indiana. However, anticipation faded on I-40 in the North Carolina mountains about 1:00 A.M. when the camper decided that hauling luggage, Christmas packages, two adults, and four children was simply too much to ask. Dying on a sharp curve, the camper rolled to a stop. Mr. Guthrie managed to get it to a gas station, where the family waited several hours while he acquired another car; finally, they continued the trip. On the return trip the family had to pick up the camper and tow it back to South Carolina. Consequently, the Guthrie family decided that a Volkswagen camper was not the right vehicle for them.

Name ____________________

Chapter 13A: Quotation Marks, Ellipses, and Underlining for Italics

Practice A

Identify each sentence as correctly punctuated *(C)* or incorrectly punctuated *(I)*.

__C__ 1. Last week in music class, we studied Frances Ridley Havergal, the British hymn writer who wrote "Take My Life and Let It Be."

__I__ 2. Mr. Spaulding told us "that Havergal wrote the hymn as a result of a visit with some friends during which two of the friends were saved."

__C__ 3. Larissa asked, "Doesn't one of the lines of that song say, 'Take my silver and my gold; not a mite would I withhold'?"

__C__ 4. "Yes," answered Mr. Spaulding, "that is a line in the hymn. Miss Havergal learned a very important lesson from those exact words."

__I__ 5. Mr. Spaulding explained that Frances Havergal gave her jewelry to the "Church Missionary House" because of that line from her hymn.

Practice B

In the blank indicate whether the sentence has an error with ellipses *(E)* or underlining *(U)*. If the sentence is correct, write *C* in the blank.

__E__ 6. This text says, "Frances Havergal showed her talent...when, at the age of seven, she began writing poetry."

__U__ 7. Some of her early poetry was published in a periodical called Good Words.

__U__ 8. During her lifetime, she wrote several <u>volumes of hymns</u>, some of which were published after her death.

__C__ 9. <u>The Ministry of Song</u>, one of Miss Havergal's books of hymns, was published in 1869.

__E__ 10. "In addition to her interest in music," Mr. Spaulding concluded, "Miss Havergal also studied modern languages, Latin and um. . . . Hebrew."

Practice C

Insert any missing quotation marks or underlining. If the sentence is already correct, write *C* in the blank.

__C__ 11. In 1851 during her teenage years, Miss Havergal trusted Christ as her Savior.

______ 12. Concerning her salvation experience, she said, "I committed my soul to the Savior. . . . Earth and heaven seemed brighter from that moment; I did trust the Lord Jesus."

______ 13. Miss Havergal wrote several devotional books in the years following her salvation; one of these is entitled <u>Kept for the Master's Use</u>.

Chapter 13A: Quotation Marks, Ellipses, and Underlining for Italics (continued)

_______ 14. The title of the first chapter in Havergal's book Kept for the Master's Use is "Our Lives Kept for the Master."

___C___ 15. In this chapter, Miss Havergal emphasizes the need for each Christian to be fully consecrated to Christ.

Name ______________________

Chapter 13B: Apostrophes

Practice A

Identify each item as correctly punctuated *(C)* or incorrectly punctuated *(I)*.

__I__ 1. Charles Dickens' family background greatly influenced his writing.

__C__ 2. Dickens's father, who worked as a clerk in the Navy Pay Office, struggled financially and was eventually imprisoned for debt.

__C__ 3. The Dickenses' lives were affected in different ways. Charles worked at a blacking factory to earn money for the family while his sister Fanny continued her studies at the Royal Academy of Music.

__I__ 4. Charles's education was put on hold because his family could'nt afford for him to stop working.

__I__ 5. Fanny's and Charles's younger siblings lived with their father and mother in the prison, but Fanny and Charles didn't join them.

Practice B

Rewrite each italicized word, correcting any apostrophe errors. If the italicized word is already correct, write *C* in the blank.

__C__ 6. Eventually, his father was released from prison, and Dickens attended Wellington House Academy for a few years during the *1820s*.

__children's__ 7. Dickens spent some of his time at school making up stories and acting out scenes for the other *childrens'* enjoyment.

__lawyers'__ 8. After leaving school, he worked as a clerk in various *lawyers's* offices, but he soon turned to reporting instead.

__its__ 9. To prepare for a job as a court reporter, Dickens learned shorthand with all *it's* intricacies.

__C__ 10. After a few years in the field of court reporting, *Dickens's* career took another turn when he switched to newspaper journalism.

Practice C

Questions 11–15: Correct the five apostrophe errors in the following paragraph.

The first published stories of Dickens appeared in *Monthly Magazine.* A few years later, Dickens began writing novels with characters who resembled his acquaintances. Many of the characters' idiosyncrasies reflect the behaviors of a family member, a friend, or an employer. Dickens also regularly included scenes drawn from his memory's storehouse. For example, *David Copperfield* is a partially autobiographical account of the author's troubles as a child and a young man. It's not accurate, however, to say that every adventure in *David Copperfield* really happened in Dickens's life.

Name ______________________________

Chapter 13C: Brackets, Hyphens, Dashes, and Parentheses

Practice A

Identify each sentence as correctly punctuated *(C)* or incorrectly punctuated *(I)*.

___*I*___ 1. Sleep deprivation—a serious lack of sleep, creates several negative results.

___*C*___ 2. Individuals (often teenagers) who are sleep deprived may experience health problems as well as difficulty completing normal tasks properly.

___*I*___ 3. There are numerous reasons [some of which are valid] behind the lack of sleep experienced by so many people today.

___*I*___ 4. Parents with babies who are 0—2 months old often get little sleep because their babies do not sleep on a regular schedule.

___*C*___ 5. On the other hand, teenagers often inflict a less-than-desirable amount of sleep on themselves by choosing to stay up late at night.

Practice B

Identify the punctuation missing from each sentence. In the blank write the letter that corresponds to the correct answer. If the sentence is already correct, write *C* in the blank.

A. brackets
B. dashes
C. hyphen
D. parentheses
E. correct

___*E*___ 6. The amount of sleep necessary to function properly throughout the day varies from person to person.

___*C*___ 7. Toddlers require an average of thirteen fourteen hours of sleep each day.

___*B or D*___ 8. Some adults although they are rare may be able to cope with as little as four hours of sleep per night.

___*B or D*___ 9. Other individuals especially teenagers may need as much as ten hours of sleep to feel rested.

___*A*___ 10. A sleep expert has written, "The average recommended amount of sleep for individuals to recieve *sic* each night is eight hours."

Chapter 13C: Brackets, Hyphens, Dashes, and Parentheses (continued)

Practice C

Questions 11–15: Insert five missing hyphens, dashes, and parentheses. (Punctuation marks used as a pair count as a single error.) ***(Some answers may vary.)***

Sleep deprivation (a common problem today) has a strong effect on teenagers. Some experts believe a lack of sleep can cause school-related problems among teens. Low concentration, lack of effort, and behavior problems—each of these is a possible consequence for adolescents who receive inadequate sleep. In order to combat these problems, experts suggest that teens allow themselves about nine and one-half hours of sleep each night. This change (which some may find difficult) would greatly benefit teenagers in their school performance and fulfillment of daily tasks.

Chapter 10A: Sonnet (continued)

Questions about Sonnet 130

1. What kind of picture is Shakespeare presenting in the first twelve lines of this sonnet?

   He is describing his beloved, who does not fit the stereotype of a beautiful woman.

2. Why do you think the speaker describes the object of his love in this manner?

   He is being realistic rather than idealistic (as many sonneteers are) in his description. He is emphasizing her individuality and humanity rather than the beauty of an ideal.

3. What hints prepare the reader for the shift of thought in the couplet?

   The speaker "love[s] to hear her speak" even though music is "far more pleasing."

4. What is Shakespeare communicating about love in this sonnet?

   Love goes deeper than physical appearance. Love is not the result of a perfect or stereotypical appearance.

5. Does the resolution of the couplet satisfy you? Why or why not?

   Answers will vary.

Name________________________________

Chapter 11A: Research Report

Primary and Secondary Sources

Assume that you are writing a research report about the repercussions of Operation Desert Storm. Identify each source as a primary source *(P)* or a secondary source *(S)*.

__S__ 1. a website honoring soldiers from the Gulf War

__S__ 2. an encyclopedia entry on Desert Storm

__P__ 3. a book co-authored by someone who was an air force commander during the war

__S__ 4. a magazine article discussing the "Gulf War Syndrome"

__P__ 5. an interview with a corporal from the Gulf War

__P__ 6. a copy of a TV speech by General H. Norman Schwarzkopf

__S__ 7. a newspaper article discussing the use of nerve gas during the war

__P__ 8. a diary from a nurse involved in the Gulf War

__S__ 9. a taped radio program giving a news commentator's view of the war

__S__ 10. a historian's notes about the impact of the Gulf War on China

Chapter 13: Response to a Dramatic Scene (continued)

When quoting a source be careful not to misrepresent the meaning of the source. Quoting words out of context or leaving out key words in a quotation may change the meaning of the source and is a type of plagiarism.

INCORRECT	Ragueneau observes that Montfleury will act in the play because Cyrano wants him "to show his face on the stage for one whole month."
CORRECT	Ragueneau reminds Lignière that Cyrano "has forbidden [Montfleury] strictly / To show his face on the stage for one whole month."
INCORRECT	Cuigy describes Cyrano as a man "well skilled in all tricks."
CORRECT	Along with Cyrano's other good qualities, he is "a fellow well skilled in all tricks of fencing."

Identify the statements that faithfully represent the source.

A 1. A. Cyrano, "the choicest of earthly beings," portrays a "fantastic . . . presence" in his abilities, dress, and fighting skill.

B. Cyrano, "whimsical, wild, [and] the maddest fighter / Of all the Gascon crew . . . [acts] like an insolent cocktail."

B 2. A. With great delight Cyrano "plays a joke on" all by wearing a fake nose.

B. Cyrano's nose, "above his ruff," attracts the attention of all who see him.

Return address:

TAPE SHUT—DO NOT STAPLE

NO POSTAGE NECESSARY IF MAILED IN THE UNITED STATES

BUSINESS REPLY MAIL
FIRST-CLASS MAIL PERMIT NO. 344 GREENVILLE, SC

POSTAGE WILL BE PAID BY ADDRESSEE

BJU PRESS
TEXTBOOK DIVISION
1700 WADE HAMPTON BLVD.
GREENVILLE, SC 29609-9971

Fold here

Fold here

Working Together

Whether you have been teaching for many years or are just getting started, your comments are vital in helping us maintain our standard of excellence. In fact, most of the improvements in our materials started with good advice from consumers. So after you have put our products to the test, please give us your thoughtful comments and honest assessment.

And thanks for your valuable help!

Book Title ______________________ **Grade level** __________

Material was ☐ used in classroom. ☐ used in home school. ☐ examined only.

How did you hear about us?

____

____

____

I liked

____

____

____

I'd like it better if

____

____

____

How did our material compare with other publishers' materials?

____

____

____

Other comments?

____

____

____

(OPTIONAL)

☐ Dr. ☐ Miss ☐ Mrs. ☐ Mr. ______________________

School ______________________

Street ______________________

City __________ State ______ ZIP __________

Phone (___) ______________________

E-mail ______________________

Fold and tape. DO NOT STAPLE.
Mailing address on the other side.

BJU PRESS
Greenville, SC 29614